Pillsbury Best Cookies

COOKBOOK

Pillsbury Best Cookies

COOKBOOK

Favorite Recipes from America's Most-Trusted Kitchens

THE PILLSBURY COMPANY

Clarkson Potter/Publishers
New York

Credits

PILLSBURY PUBLICATIONS
The Pillsbury Company

Publisher: Sally Peters
Publication Manager: Diane B. Anderson
Senior Editor: Betsy Wray
Senior Food Editor: Andi Bidwell
Recipe Editor: Grace Wells
Contributing Writer: Mary Caldwell
Photography: Glenn Peterson Photography, Graham
    Brown Photography, Hedstrom/Blessing Photo,
    Tad Ware Photography
Food Stylists: Lynn Boldt, JoAnn Cherry, Sharon Harding,
    Barb Standal
Recipe Typist: Michelle Barringer

PILLSBURY PUBLICATIONS
Publisher: Sally Peters
Publication Managers: Diane B. Anderson, William Monn
Senior Editors: Jackie Sheehan, Betsy Wray
Senior Food Editor: Andi Bidwell
Test Kitchen Coordinator: Pat Peterson
Circulation Manager: Karen Goodsell
Circulation Coordinator: Rebecca Bogema
Recipe System Administrator: Bev Gustafson
Recipe Production Specialists: Mary Prokott, Nolan Vaughan
Publication Secretary: Jackie Ranney

Bake-Off is a registered trademark of The Pillsbury Company.

CLARKSON POTTER/PUBLISHERS
The Crown Publishing Group

President and Publisher: Chip Gibson
Vice President-Editorial Director: Lauren Shakely
Senior Editor: Katie Workman
Editorial Assistant: Erica Youngren
Designer: Susan DeStaebler
Executive Managing Editor: Laurie Stark
Managing Editor: Amy Boorstein
Production Manager: Jane Searle
Publicist: Wendy Schuman

Published by Clarkson Potter/Publishers,
201 East 50th Street, New York, New York 10022.
Member of the Crown Publishing Group.

Random House, Inc. New York, Toronto, London, Sydney, Auckland

http://www.randomhouse.com/

CLARKSON N. POTTER, POTTER, and colophon are trademarks of Clarkson N. Potter, Inc.

Printed in Japan

Design by Susan DeStaebler

Library of Congress Cataloging-in-Publication Data
Pillsbury, best cookies cookbook / by the Pillsbury Company.
     p.   cm.
   Includes index.
   1. Cookies.   I. Pillsbury Company.
TX772.P48   1997
641.8'654—dc21   97-1773
                                CIP

ISBN 0-609-60084-2

10 9 8 7 6 5 4 3 2 1

First Edition

*Frontispiece: Chocolate
Macadamia Cookies with
White Chocolate Chunks,
page 38; Chocolate Ginger
Zebras, page 131; Opposite:
Whole Wheat Gingerbread
Cutouts, page 178.*

Contents

Jumbo Candy Cookies, page 28

Nut-edged Lemon Cookie Slices, page 106

Rolled Cookies · 113

Tri-Cornered Cream Cheese Cookies, page 120

Bars & Brownies · 133

Holiday Cookies · 175

Chocolate Valentine Cookies, page 206

Bake-Off® Favorites · 213

Index · 250

Salted Peanut Chews, page 216

Cookie Know-How

Is there anyone in America without a memory of favorite warm-from-the-oven cookies with milk, or a grandmother's kitchen filled with the aroma of cinnamon, or the taste of chewy, chocolaty brownies made from scratch?

We hope to bring back some treasured memories, and create some new ones as well, with this collection of more than 175 of our all-time favorite cookies. You'll find cookies in an infinite variety of guises, from delicate morsels for an elegant party to chewy, nut-studded cookies that are right at home for the most casual get-togethers.

Cookie Basics

Cookies fall into several categories, including drop cookies, hand-formed cookies, refrigerator cookies, rolled cookies, plus bars and brownies. This book offers chapters on each of these, as well as a chapter with prize-winning recipes from the Pillsbury Bake-Off® Contest and another with special cookies for holidays. Each chapter provides detailed information specific to the type of cookie, but some general techniques will help you to get started.

Preheating

Always preheat the oven to be sure it's the proper temperature before you put the cookies in the oven. Allow at least 10 minutes to reach the desired heat; an oven thermometer can help you to be sure.

Measuring dry ingredients

Use plastic or metal dry measuring cups so you can level off the top. To measure flour, use the same technique we use when testing our recipes: Spoon the flour into a dry measuring cup (rather than dipping the cup into the flour), then smooth off the top with the flat side of a knife. Do not pack the flour.

Measuring liquid ingredients

Use a glass liquid measuring cup with space above the top printed measure. Check the contents at eye level for accuracy.

Softening butter

Softening margarine or butter is necessary to make sure it blends evenly with sugar and other ingredients. If you don't have time to soften it on the counter for an hour or so, heat it very **briefly** in the microwave oven on LOW power or DEFROST. (You want it to just soften, not melt.) Watch it carefully, so that it doesn't suddenly "explode" and splatter the inside of the microwave. Cover the butter with a piece of waxed paper before microwaving to minimize any potential messes. (Melted butter will produce flatter cookies.)

Greasing pans

Many cookie and bar recipes call for greasing (or greasing and flouring) the baking pan to prevent the baked goods from sticking. Use a piece of paper toweling or waxed paper to rub a thin, even layer of solid vegetable shortening over the pan. Grease the pan before the first batch only.

If the recipe requires greasing and flouring, spoon a teaspoon or so of flour into the greased pan, then tilt it from side to side as you tap the edges to distribute the flour evenly. Turn the pan over the sink and tap out any excess.

If you wish to use nonstick cooking spray instead of shortening, spray it lightly but evenly over the pan and bake as usual. To prevent spray buildup for multiple bakes, wipe off the pan with a paper towel between batches and then spray again.

Doughs with a high proportion of fat may not require greased pans; meringues and other nonfat egg white–based recipes also require ungreased pans so they can expand properly.

Chilling dough

Some recipes specify chilling the dough prior to baking for easier handling, especially for cookies that are rolled or shaped. Refrigerate other doughs, too, if they seem too sticky to work with.

Baking cookies

Place the cookie sheet on a rack set in the center of the oven, leaving space on all sides for even circulation

Equivalent Measures and Weights

Dash = less than $1/8$ teaspoon

3 teaspoons = 1 tablespoon

2 tablespoons = $1/8$ cup or 1 fluid ounce

4 tablespoons = $1/4$ cup

$5 1/3$ tablespoons = $1/3$ cup

8 tablespoons = $1/2$ cup

12 tablespoons = $3/4$ cup

16 tablespoons = 1 cup

1 cup = 8 fluid ounces

2 cups = 1 pint or 16 fluid ounces

4 cups = 1 quart

4 quarts = 1 gallon

16 ounces = 1 pound

of air. It's best to bake just one sheet at a time. If you must do two at once, swap shelves and turn trays around about halfway through baking time.

Testing for doneness

Most recipes specify a range of cooking times, to compensate for variations in ovens, ingredients, size of the cookies, etc. Check at the minimum time, looking for cookies that are firmly set or browned according to recipe directions. When you touch them lightly with your finger, almost no imprint will remain.

Cooling sheets

To prevent the cookie dough from spreading out too rapidly, always begin with a cool baking sheet. Do not put the next batch of dough onto a sheet until it has cooled. This is easiest if you have two or three baking sheets to work with.

Cooling cookies

Let cookies remain on the tray for a minute or two to firm up for easier handling, then use a spatula to transfer individual cookies from baking sheets to a wire rack to cool.

To cool bar cookies and brownies, set the entire pan on a wire rack for better air circulation.

Storing soft cookies

Store soft cookies in a tightly closed container, layered between waxed paper to prevent sticking (or in a single layer if frosted or filled). Good choices: plastic containers or cookie tins with tight-fitting lids and self-sealing plastic bags. **Store different kinds of cookies in separate containers.**

Storing crisp cookies

A container with a looser-fitting cover, such as a cookie jar or glass casserole dish with a lid, is best unless the weather is very humid, in which case crisp cookies will do better in a container with a tight lid. To revive crisp cookies that have gone soft, reheat them on a baking tray in a 300°F. oven for 3 to 5 minutes; cool on a rack.

Freezing

To freeze unfrosted baked cookies, package them in containers with tight-fitting lids and freeze them for up to twelve months. Freeze frosted cookies uncovered on a baking sheet, then package the frozen cookies between layers of waxed paper in a rigid container, tightly covered, for up to two months.

Thawing

Thaw soft-textured cookies in the container at room temperature or zap them briefly in the microwave oven. For crisp-textured cookies, remove them from the container before thawing.

Basic Equipment

While molds, presses and fancy gizmos are available for elaborate cookies, basic cookie baking requires very little special equipment.

Cookie sheets

You'll want to have several so you can bake one tray while you're preparing another, and a third is cooling. Cookie sheets are available in four basic styles:

Shiny. Shiny, silver-colored aluminum cookie sheets without sides are best. The shiny metal reflects heat, so the cookies will not burn as quickly.

Double layer. Cookie sheets with an insulating "cushion of air" between two sheets of metal are designed to enhance circulation of hot air around the cookies. The sheets are more expensive and cookies do not brown as much on the bottom, which can make doneness harder to judge. In addition, cooking time increases slightly.

Black surface. Cookies bake faster on dark, nonreflective surfaces, which absorb heat, so you must watch more closely to prevent the bottoms from burning.

Nonstick. While many cookies have enough butter that the sheet does not require greasing anyway, nonstick pans are still convenient for easier cleanup.

Baking pans for bar cookies

Always use the size specified in the recipe, or your results may be less than perfect. As for baking sheets, shiny aluminum is best. If you use a nonstick pan, be aware that cutting the bars may mar the nonstick finish.

Chocolate Chip Yogurt Cookies, page 34

Wooden spoons

They're traditional and also more effective (and quieter) than metal kitchen spoons for creaming butter and blending doughs properly.

Hand mixers or standing mixers

These are convenient for mixing large quantities of dough. Creaming butter by itself may be easier by hand with a wooden spoon, since the butter tends to get stuck in the beaters if it's not mixed with sugar or another ingredient. As soon as all the ingredients are uniformly blended, stop mixing.

Measuring spoons
Use a properly calibrated set for accurate measurement; do not rely on ordinary silverware or estimates.

Wire cooling racks
They're essential for cooling cookies and pans of bars or brownies.

Liquid and dry measuring cups
Yes, you do need both. See "Measuring Dry Ingredients" and "Measuring Liquid Ingredients," page 8 .

Pancake turner or metal spatula
These are efficient for transferring cookies from baking trays to cooling racks.

Starlight Mint Surprise Cookies, page 243

Ingredients

Flour

Most cookie recipes call for all-purpose flour. Either bleached or unbleached may be used. Do not substitute bread flour, which has a higher gluten content that may make tough cookies, or cake flour, which is softer and more delicate.

Most basic cookie recipes will also yield good results made with part or all whole wheat flour. A cookie made with whole wheat flour will contain about four times the fiber of one made with white flour and will also be somewhat browner (unless it's chocolate!), with a slightly heartier texture and nuttier flavor.

Butter and butter substitutes

Butter or another fat provides tenderness and moisture to cookies. Butter offers more flavor, but the recipes in this book will all yield excellent results made with either regular butter or regular margarine.

Whipped margarines or butters incorporate air for a lighter-textured, easier-to-spread topping. Use these by weight rather than volume for accurate results.

Low-fat spreads contain a higher proportion of water and air, making baked results less predictable. For the best finished product, follow the recipes as written. If you wish to experiment with lower-fat cooking, make gradual modifications to the recipe and see how you like the results. The finished cookie will probably be less crisp, more cakelike, with a slightly tougher texture, smoother top and less browned exterior. You may enjoy the lower-fat cookie better if you modify an unfamiliar recipe rather than a tried-and-true family favorite that may be disappointing in an altered form.

Vegetable oil does not allow the proper incorporation of air as the dough is beaten and should not be substituted.

Baking powder and baking soda

Either or both of these are used as leaveners for many cookies. Baking soda is used to help neutralize acidic ingredients. Baking powder and soda are not interchangeable.

Eggs

The recipes in this book have been tested using large eggs. If you use a different size, you will alter the recipe's ingredient proportions and results may differ.

Sweeteners

Sugar listed in a recipe simply means white, granulated sugar. It adds sweetness, tenderness and moisture to recipes and aids in browning. Measure it in a dry measuring cup, leveled off at the top.

Emergency Substitutions

Ingredient	Substitute
Baking powder, 1 teaspoon	$1/4$ teaspoon baking soda plus $1/2$ teaspoon cream of tartar
Buttermilk, 1 cup	1 tablespoon vinegar or lemon juice plus enough milk to make 1 cup
Sour cream, 1 cup	1 cup plain yogurt
Honey, 1 cup	$1 1/4$ cups sugar plus $1/4$ cup water or another liquid such as milk or fruit juice
Yogurt (plain), 1 cup	1 cup sour cream
Semi-sweet chocolate, 1 ounce	1 ounce unsweetened chocolate plus 1 tablespoon sugar **or** 3 tablespoons semi-sweet chocolate chips
Unsweetened chocolate, 1 ounce	3 tablespoons unsweetened cocoa plus 1 tablespoon shortening or margarine

Brown sugar is a mixture of granulated sugar and molasses and contributes moistness, color and flavor to recipes. The dark version has a more pronounced flavor than the lighter version. Pack brown sugar firmly into a dry measuring cup.

Powdered sugar, also known as confectioners' sugar, is made from granulated sugar that has been ground extra fine, with a tiny bit of cornstarch added to prevent clumping. Because it dissolves more readily than granulated sugar, powdered sugar is most often used in icings and as a final sprinkle, though some recipes use it in the cookie dough itself. Sift it before using to get rid of any lumps.

Honey, like sugar, adds moistness and sweetness, but it contributes a distinct flavor, too.

Molasses, a by-product of sugar refining, is a thick, sweet liquid available in light and dark varieties. The bitterness of a third type, blackstrap molasses, makes it unsuitable for baking. Light and dark molasses can be substituted for each other; dark molasses has a heavier flavor and is a little less sweet.

Corn syrup is a thick, sweet liquid that comes in light and dark varieties. It's widely used as a sweetener in commercial products, and once in a while in cookie recipes, too. The dark one has a slightly stronger flavor, but either can be used.

Altitude Adjustments

Tried-and-true baking recipes may yield less than perfect results when mixed and baked at high altitudes (over 3,500 feet above sea level). As the altitude increases, air pressure decreases, altering the way leavening agents, sweeteners and liquids interact.

Bread and cakes are most sensitive to altitude, but cookie recipes may react, too. All the recipes in this book have been tested at high altitude and include specific changes for high-altitude bakers, or indicate that the recipes need no adjustments. If you have trouble with a particular cookie recipe that doesn't specify altitude adjustments, try adding 2 to 4 tablespoons flour or reducing the sugar by 3 tablespoons per cup.

Shaping Cookies

Intricate cookie cutters are fun, but time-consuming to use. Here are some ideas for quicker ways to shape rolled dough:

- Cut across the entire surface of the dough in two directions to create rectangles, squares or diamonds; cut across diamonds or squares to make triangles. Use a knife for straight edges or a pastry wheel for ruffled borders.

- Use the rim of a drinking glass dipped in flour to cut circles. Use your imagination to find everyday kitchen objects to stamp a design in the top. Gently press dough with the bottom of a cut-glass sugar bowl, for example, or a meat mallet.
- Crimp the edges with a fork dipped in sugar.

Mailing Cookies

A "care package" of homemade goodies guarantees instant popularity in the dorm or barracks and is equally welcomed by friends and family of any age. Here are tips for mailing:

- Choose moist, firm-textured cookies for mailing that will remain fresh and intact during transport. Good choices usually include drop cookies, unfrosted bars, fudgy brownies or other sturdy cookies. Delicate, intricately shaped specialties are best reserved for personal delivery.
- Pack the cookies into a firm-sided cardboard, metal or plastic container lined with plastic wrap or foil for extra protection and to keep cookies from absorbing cardboard odors. Insulate the sides of the container with a "wall" of crumpled waxed paper. Layer the cookies between layers of waxed paper or wrap them in pairs, flat sides together.

- For extra protection, place the container into a larger box padded on all sides with crumpled paper or packing material. Wrap securely, mark it "perishable" and send it the speediest way possible, whether first-class mail or private carrier.

Kids in the Kitchen

With a little patience, imagination and common sense, baking with children can be a wonderful experience. Kids enjoy the "grown-up" task of real cooking, especially with the delicious end results. Along the way, they gain valuable hands-on experience with abstract math skills such as counting, measuring and sequencing, as well as practical cooking skills. Now is the time to instill good life-long kitchen habits.

- Wash everyone's hands thoroughly before beginning, and again if children pick up toys, etc. while waiting for the next step.
- Tie back long hair and roll up sleeves. Cover clothes with a clean apron.
- Keep peace in the kitchen by giving each child a "job." One child can stir dry ingredients while another mixes liquids, or all can take turns adding ingredients to the mixing bowl. Keep very young children busy with their own bowl and spoon and perhaps a little uncooked oatmeal—even if their contribution is not really destined for the main recipe.
- For a project involving several children, seat all the bakers around the table and pass the mixing bowl from child to child, allowing each one a chance to add the next ingredient or to have the next turn stirring.
- If the dough contains raw eggs, discontinue the old-fashioned fun ritual of licking the spoon at the end, to avoid the slim but genuine possibility of becoming sick from salmonella bacteria.
- Keep the project manageable. Choose a simple recipe with only a few ingredients for more immediate gratification.
- Consider the attention span of the junior cooks and divide the task into a project for more than one day, if necessary. Mix the dough today and cook one or two sheets; freeze remaining dough in small batches for quick slice-and-bake or rolled-and-cut treats another day.
- Give each child a tray of cookies to decorate. Muffin tins can neatly hold a variety of decorative toppings—sprinkles, cinnamon red-hots, raisins, chocolate chips, etc.
- To save yourself work in years to come, emphasize that the job is not complete until the kitchen is clean again!

Cookie Troubleshooting Guide

For best results, measure all ingredients accurately and mix according to recipe directions. If you run into problems, consult this chart.

Problem: Sticky, unworkable cookie dough.

Possible Solution: Chill the dough until it's firm enough to handle, usually about an hour. If it's still too sticky, work in additional flour, a tablespoon at a time, until the texture improves.

Problem: Crumbly cookie dough.

Possible Solution: Work in an additional tablespoon or two of milk (or another liquid from the recipe) or softened butter.

Problem: Cookies run together on the baking sheet.

Possible Solution: Space the dough for subsequent batches farther apart. Make sure the baking sheet is cool before placing the dough on it. A dough made with all butter also may cause the cookies to run together; use part butter, part shortening.

Problem: Overly flat, thin cookies.

Possible Solution: Make sure to begin with a cool baking sheet to prevent premature melting of the dough. Do not overgrease the baking sheet. Don't melt the butter or margarine for the recipe if the directions call for softened butter or margarine.

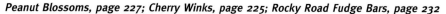

Peanut Blossoms, page 227; Cherry Winks, page 225; Rocky Road Fudge Bars, page 232

Problem: Tough rolled cookies.
Possible Solution: Handle the dough gently, use as little flour as possible on the rolling pin and work surface and don't reroll scraps more than twice.

Problem: Baked cookies stick to the pan.
Possible Solution: Return the pan to the oven for about 30 seconds to rewarm and loosen the cookies. For the next batch, lightly regrease the baking sheets, or start over with a clean sheet without stuck-on cookie crumbs.

Problem: Cookies break when removed from the pan.
Possible Solution: Let cookies cool and firm up for an additional minute or two before attempting to remove them from the pan. Handle them delicately. Use a pancake turner with a wide, thin metal blade to get under the cookie easily and support it fully.

Problem: Burned cookie bottoms.
Possible Solution: Use a silver-colored rather than dark-colored baking sheet, and watch cooking times carefully. Bake one sheet at a time, on the center shelf of the oven, and rotate the sheet halfway through the baking time.

Problem: Soft cookies.
Possible Solution: Increase the baking time slightly.

Problem: Unevenly baked cookies.
Possible Solution: Size and space the cookie dough uniformly. Do not use a pan with sides, which reflect heat back down on the cookies around the edge of the pan. Bake only one sheet at a time, in the center of the oven, and rotate the baking sheet halfway through the baking time because some ovens may be hotter in the back than the front. If you bake two sheets at a time, exchange the top sheet with the bottom sheet halfway through baking, and rotate the sheets halfway.

How Long Will It Take?

To help you plan your kitchen stint, each recipe indicates "Prep Time." This includes the amount of time necessary to mix the ingredients and bake all of the dough. If the recipe requires additional unattended time (such as chilling dough, baking brownies or bars that don't need attention until the end of the cooking time or lengthy cooling before frosting), we also specify a "Ready In" time.

About the Tips and Flags

Sprinkled throughout this book, you will find helpful hints accompanying each recipe. The information falls into the following categories:

Recipe Fact

imparts a bit of culinary background.

About (Ingredient)

shares a nugget of information about a component of the recipe.

Kitchen Tip

explains the best way to prepare certain ingredients or carry out special techniques.

Ingredient Substitution

gives good alternatives in case your pantry lacks a specific ingredient.

Recipe Variation

outlines an easy way to transform the recipe at hand into a new version.

Make It Special

offers easy ideas for embellishing or serving.

Storage Tip

suggests how best to keep dough or baked goods fresh.

Bake-Off® Trivia

gives you a look at some of the people and recipes from Pillsbury's famous cooking contest.

Holiday Note

tells how the recipe fits into the celebration of a particular culture or recommends easy ways to make special occasions more festive.

In addition, these special "flags" help categorize recipes at a glance:

Editor's Favorite flags our staff's very favorite treats.
Kid Pleaser features popular flavors with children.
Chocoholic's Choice are our most chocolaty selections.

Drop C

Drop Cookie

recipes usually specify "drop dough by rounded teaspoonfuls"; for larger cookies, tablespoons may be specified. In either case, it's easy to get into the rhythm: Scoop a spoonful of dough with one spoon, then push it off of the spoon and onto the baking sheet with a second spoon or a narrow rubber scraper. Keep the dough uniformly sized so the cookies will bake evenly, and spaced as directed in the recipe to prevent the cookies from running all over the pan and creating one giant cookie. As an alternative to ordinary spoons, try shaping the dough with a miniature ice-cream scoop fitted with a lever-release bar.

Cranberry and Vanilla Chip Cookies

Prep Time: 1 hour 15 minutes

½ cup margarine or butter, softened
1⅓ cups sugar
½ cup refrigerated or frozen fat-free egg product, thawed, or 2 eggs
1 teaspoon imitation butter flavor

1¾ cups all-purpose flour
1 cup old-fashioned rolled oats
1½ teaspoons baking soda
½ teaspoon salt
1 cup sweetened dried cranberries
⅔ cup white vanilla chips

1. Heat oven to 350°F. Spray cookie sheets with non-stick cooking spray. In large bowl, combine margarine and sugar; beat until light and fluffy. Add egg product and butter flavor; mix well. Add flour, oats, baking soda and salt; mix well. Stir in cranberries and vanilla chips. Drop dough by tablespoonfuls 2 inches apart onto sprayed cookie sheets.

2. Bake at 350°F. for 9 to 11 minutes or until edges are golden brown. Cool 1 minute; remove from cookie sheets. Cool on wire racks 15 minutes or until completely cooled.

Yield: 4 dozen cookies
High Altitude (Above 3,500 Feet): Decrease sugar to 1¼ cups; increase flour to 2 cups. Bake at 350°F. for 10 to 12 minutes.

Nutrition Information Per Serving
Serving Size: 1 Cookie. Calories 90 • Calories from Fat 25 • Total Fat 3 g
Saturated Fat 1 g • Cholesterol 1 mg • Sodium 85 mg • Dietary Fiber 1 g
Dietary Exchanges: 1 Fruit, ½ Fat OR 1 Carbohydrate, ½ Fat

About Dried Cranberries

Dried sweetened cranberries are a relative newcomer to the market. They resemble reddish raisins and can be used in the same ways as raisins. Unsweetened dried cranberries also are available; they're slightly more tart.

About Egg Substitute

Fat-free egg product is actually real egg whites with a bit of coloring and flavoring to compensate for the lack of a yolk. It's available frozen or in the dairy section of the supermarket.

Ingredient Substitution

Substitute raisins, currants or chopped dried apricots for the dried cranberries.

Frosted Cashew Cookies

Prep Time: 1 hour 15 minutes

Cookies

1 cup firmly packed brown sugar
½ cup butter, softened
½ teaspoon vanilla
1 egg
2 cups all-purpose flour
¾ teaspoon baking powder
¾ teaspoon baking soda
⅓ cup sour cream
¾ cup coarsely chopped salted cashews

Frosting

½ cup butter (do not use margarine)
2 cups powdered sugar
3 tablespoons half-and-half or milk
½ teaspoon vanilla

1. Heat oven to 375°F. Lightly grease cookie sheets. In large bowl, combine brown sugar and ½ cup butter; beat until light and fluffy. Add ½ teaspoon vanilla and egg; blend well. Add flour, baking powder, baking soda and sour cream; mix well. Stir in cashews. Drop dough by rounded teaspoonfuls 2 inches apart onto greased cookie sheets.

2. Bake at 375°F. for 8 to 10 minutes or until golden brown. Immediately remove from cookie sheets. Cool 15 minutes or until completely cooled.

3. Meanwhile, heat ½ cup butter in medium saucepan over medium heat until light golden brown. Remove from heat. Stir in powdered sugar, half-and-half and ½ teaspoon vanilla; beat until smooth. Frost cooled cookies.

Yield: 4 dozen cookies
High Altitude (Above 3,500 Feet): No change.

Nutrition Information Per Serving

Serving Size: 1 Cookie. Calories 110 • Calories from Fat 45 • Total Fat 5 g
Saturated Fat 3 g • Cholesterol 15 mg • Sodium 85 mg • Dietary Fiber 0 g
Dietary Exchanges: 1 Fruit, 1 Fat OR 1 Carbohydrate, 1 Fat

Brown Sugar Shortbread Puffs

Prep Time: 1 hour

1 cup firmly packed brown
   sugar
1¼ cups butter, softened

1 teaspoon vanilla
1 egg yolk
2¼ cups all-purpose flour

1. Heat oven to 350°F. In large bowl, combine brown sugar and butter; beat until light and fluffy. Add vanilla and egg yolk; blend well. Add flour; stir until mixture forms a smooth dough. Drop dough by rounded teaspoonfuls 2 inches apart onto ungreased cookie sheets.
2. Bake at 350°F. for 10 to 15 minutes or until light golden brown and set.

Yield: 4 dozen cookies
High Altitude (Above 3,500 Feet): No change.

Nutrition Information Per Serving

Serving Size: 1 Cookie. Calories 80 • Calories from Fat 45 • Total Fat 5 g
Saturated Fat 3 g • Cholesterol 15 mg • Sodium 50 mg • Dietary Fiber 0 g
Dietary Exchanges: ½ Starch, 1 Fat OR ½ Carbohydrate, 1 Fat

About Brown Sugar

Though many people believe brown sugar is a more "natural" product than white sugar, it is actually granulated white sugar that has been mixed with molasses.

Kitchen Tip

Softening margarine or butter is necessary to make sure it blends evenly with sugar and other ingredients. If you don't have time to soften it on the counter for an hour or so, heat it very **briefly** in the microwave oven on LOW power or DEFROST. (You want it to just soften, not melt.) Watch it carefully, so that it doesn't suddenly "explode" and splatter the inside of the microwave. (Melted butter will produce flatter cookies.)

Make It Special

Dress up these simple cookies with a drizzle of icing made from 1 cup of sifted powdered sugar mixed with 3 to 5 teaspoons of milk or hot water and a few drops of vanilla extract.

Chocolate Chip Cookies

Prep Time: 35 minutes

¾ cup firmly packed brown
    sugar
½ cup sugar
½ cup margarine or butter,
    softened
½ cup shortening
1½ teaspoons vanilla
1 egg

1¾ cups all-purpose flour
1 teaspoon baking soda
½ teaspoon salt
1 (6-oz.) pkg. (1 cup) semi-
    sweet chocolate chips
½ cup chopped nuts or shelled
    sunflower seeds, if desired

1. Heat oven to 375°F. In large bowl, combine brown sugar, sugar, margarine and shortening; beat until light and fluffy. Add vanilla and egg; blend well. Add flour, baking soda and salt; mix well. Stir in chocolate chips and nuts. Drop dough by rounded teaspoonfuls 2 inches apart onto ungreased cookie sheets.
2. Bake at 375°F. for 8 to 10 minutes or until light golden brown. Cool 1 minute; remove from cookie sheets.

Yield: 3 dozen cookies
High Altitude (Above 3,500 Feet): No change.

Nutrition Information Per Serving

Serving Size: 1 Cookie. Calories 130 • Calories from Fat 70 • Total Fat 8 g
Saturated Fat 2 g • Cholesterol 6 mg • Sodium 95 mg • Dietary Fiber 1 g
Dietary Exchanges: 1 Fruit, 1½ Fat OR 1 Carbohydrate, 1½ Fat

Variations

Chocolate Chunk Cookies: Prepare dough as directed in recipe, substituting 8 oz. coarsely chopped semi-sweet chocolate for chocolate chips. Drop dough by tablespoonfuls 3 inches apart onto ungreased cookie sheets. Bake at 375°F. for 9 to 12 minutes or until light golden brown. Immediately remove from cookie sheets.

Yield: 3 dozen cookies

Recipe Fact

It seems hard to believe that chocolate chip cookies, the most popular cookies in America, didn't come over on the **Mayflower**. In fact, they have gained their popularity in a relatively short time, since Ruth Wakeman first made them at her Toll House Inn in 1930. The recipe came about accidentally when the innkeeper ran out of nuts for a favorite recipe and, on a whim, substituted chocolate chunks.

About Sunflower Seeds

Sunflower seeds, which are consumed in movie theaters in Spain the way Americans munch on popcorn, add crunch and nutty flavor to these cookies. For baking, purchase the seeds unsalted and out of the shell.

Kitchen Tip

A 6-ounce package of chocolate chips yields approximately 1 cup; a 12-ounce package, 2 cups.

Jumbo Candy Cookies, page 28

Jumbo Candy Cookies: Prepare dough as directed in recipe, omitting ½ cup sugar, 1 cup semi-sweet chocolate chips and ½ cup chopped nuts. Increase vanilla to 2 teaspoons. Stir 1 cup candy-coated chocolate pieces and ½ cup shelled sunflower seeds into dough. Refrigerate if necessary for easier handling. Shape dough into 2-inch balls. Place 4 inches apart on ungreased cookie sheets. Press an additional ½ cup candy-coated chocolate pieces into balls to decorate tops of cookies. Bake at 350°F. for 15 to 20 minutes or until light golden brown. Cool 2 minutes; remove from cookie sheets.

Yield: 14 cookies

Chocolate Chip Cookie Bars: Prepare dough as directed in recipe. Spread in ungreased 13 × 9-inch pan. Bake at 375°F. for 15 to 25 minutes or until light golden brown. Cool completely. Cut into bars.

Yield: 36 bars

Chocolate Chocolate Chip Cookies: Prepare dough as directed in recipe, doubling margarine or butter to 1 cup, omitting shortening and decreasing vanilla to 1 teaspoon. Add ¼ cup unsweetened cocoa with flour. Drop dough by teaspoonfuls 2 inches apart onto ungreased cookie sheets. Bake at 375°F. for 7 to 11 minutes or until set. Cool 1 minute; remove from cookie sheets.

Yield: 4 dozen cookies

Fresh Orange Cookies

Prep Time: 1 hour 15 minutes

Cookies
1½ cups sugar
1 cup margarine or butter,
  softened
1 cup sour cream
2 eggs
4 cups all-purpose flour
1 teaspoon baking powder
1 teaspoon baking soda
½ teaspoon salt
⅔ cup orange juice

3 tablespoons grated orange
  peel

Frosting
¼ cup margarine or butter,
  melted
2 cups powdered sugar
1 tablespoon grated orange
  peel
2 to 3 tablespoons orange juice

1. Heat oven to 375°F. In large bowl, combine sugar and 1 cup margarine; beat until light and fluffy. Add sour cream and eggs; blend well. Add all remaining cookie ingredients; mix well. Drop dough by rounded teaspoonfuls onto ungreased cookie sheets.
2. Bake at 375°F. for 8 to 11 minutes or until edges are light golden brown. Immediately remove from cookie sheets.
3. Meanwhile, in small bowl, combine all frosting ingredients, adding enough orange juice for desired spreading consistency. Frost warm cookies.

Yield: 6 dozen cookies
High Altitude (Above 3,500 Feet): No change.

Nutrition Information Per Serving
Serving Size: 1 Cookie. Calories 90 • Calories from Fat 35 • Total Fat 4 g
Saturated Fat 1 g • Cholesterol 5 mg • Sodium 80 mg • Dietary Fiber 0 g
Dietary Exchanges: 1 Fruit, ½ Fat OR 1 Carbohydrate, ½ Fat

Kitchen Tip

To grate orange peel, use a fine-hole grater or a special tool called a citrus zester. Or peel off thin strips with a sharp vegetable peeler or paring knife and cut the strips into thin slivers. In any case, use only the colored outer portion of the rind, not the bitter white inner part of the rind.

Kitchen Tip

For a shiny glaze that melts into the cookies, spread on the frosting while the cookies are still warm. For more distinctive icing, frost the cookies after they have cooled. In either case, be sure to let the icing set before stacking cookies on top of each other.

Recipe Variation

To make Fresh Lemon Cookies, substitute lemon juice and lemon peel for the orange.

Cherry Poppy Seed Twinks

About Poppy Seeds

The tiny black seeds of the poppy plant add a slight nutty nuance to these cookies. Like other seeds, poppy seeds have a high oil content and are best purchased in small quantities so you can use them up before they spoil. Store them in a cool, dry, dark place (or the freezer). White poppy seeds, favored in Indian cooking, have a similar flavor but are more perishable.

Recipe Variation

Substitute strawberry, apricot, peach or blackberry preserves for the cherry, or use an assortment.

1 cup powdered sugar
1 cup margarine or butter, softened
1 teaspoon vanilla
1 egg

2 cups all-purpose flour
2 tablespoons poppy seed
$\frac{1}{2}$ teaspoon salt
$\frac{1}{2}$ cup cherry preserves

1. Heat oven to 300°F. In large bowl, combine powdered sugar and margarine; beat until light and fluffy. Add vanilla and egg; blend well. Add flour, poppy seed and salt; mix well. Drop dough by rounded teaspoonfuls 1 inch apart onto ungreased cookie sheets.

2. With thumb or handle of wooden spoon, make imprint in center of each cookie. Fill each with about $\frac{1}{2}$ teaspoon preserves.

3. Bake at 300°F. for 20 to 25 minutes or until edges are light golden brown. Immediately remove from cookie sheets.

Yield: 30 cookies
High Altitude (Above 3,500 Feet): No change.

Nutrition Information Per Serving
Serving Size: 1 Cookie. Calories 120 • Calories from Fat 60 • Total Fat 7 g
Saturated Fat 1 g • Cholesterol 5 mg • Sodium 110 mg • Dietary Fiber 0 g
Dietary Exchanges: 1 Fruit, 1½ Fat OR 1 Carbohydrate, 1½ Fat

Cherry Poppy Seed Twinks

Caramel Frosted Banana Drops

Prep Time: 1 hour 15 minutes

Cookies

1 cup firmly packed brown sugar
1 cup margarine or butter, softened
$\frac{1}{2}$ cup (1 large) mashed banana
2 teaspoons vanilla
$2\frac{1}{3}$ cups all-purpose flour
$\frac{1}{4}$ teaspoon salt
$\frac{3}{4}$ cup chopped walnuts or pecans

Frosting

$\frac{3}{4}$ cup firmly packed brown sugar
$\frac{1}{4}$ cup margarine or butter, softened
$1\frac{1}{4}$ cups powdered sugar
$\frac{1}{2}$ teaspoon vanilla
1 to 3 tablespoons milk

1. Heat oven to 350°F. In large bowl, combine 1 cup brown sugar and 1 cup margarine; beat until light and fluffy. Add banana and 2 teaspoons vanilla; blend well. Add flour and salt; mix well. Stir in walnuts. Drop dough by rounded teaspoonfuls 2 inches apart onto ungreased cookie sheets.

2. Bake at 350°F. for 9 to 14 minutes or until light golden brown. Immediately remove from cookie sheets. Cool 15 minutes or until completely cooled.

3. Meanwhile, in small saucepan, combine $\frac{3}{4}$ cup brown sugar and $\frac{1}{4}$ cup margarine. Cook over medium heat until sugar is dissolved, stirring constantly. Cool slightly. Stir in powdered sugar, $\frac{1}{2}$ teaspoon vanilla and enough milk for desired spreading consistency. Frost cooled cookies.

Yield: 5 dozen cookies
High Altitude (Above 3,500 Feet): In cookies, decrease brown sugar to $\frac{3}{4}$ cup; increase flour to $2\frac{2}{3}$ cups. Bake as directed above.

Nutrition Information Per Serving

Serving Size: 1 Cookie. Calories 100 • Calories from Fat 45 • Total Fat 5 g
Saturated Fat 1 g • Cholesterol 0 mg • Sodium 55 mg • Dietary Fiber 0 g
Dietary Exchanges: 1 Fruit, 1 Fat OR 1 Carbohydrate, 1 Fat

Cocoa-Mallow Cookie-wiches

Prep Time: 1 hour 15 minutes

Cookies

1 cup sugar
½ cup margarine or butter,
　softened
1 teaspoon vanilla
1 egg
1 cup milk
2 cups all-purpose flour
½ cup unsweetened cocoa
1½ teaspoons baking soda
½ teaspoon baking powder

½ teaspoon salt

Filling

2 cups powdered sugar
1 cup marshmallow creme
¼ cup margarine or butter,
　softened
¼ cup shortening
3 to 4 teaspoons milk
　1 teaspoon vanilla

About Vanilla

Pure vanilla extract is made from vanilla "beans" (which are really the pods of an orchid plant) and alcohol. For best flavor, look for bottles labeled "pure vanilla extract" rather than artificially flavored imitations.

Recipe Variation

Mix ⅓ cup chopped peanuts into the filling.

1. Heat oven to 375°F. Grease cookie sheets. In large bowl, combine sugar and ½ cup margarine; beat until light and fluffy. Add 1 teaspoon vanilla and egg; blend well. Stir in 1 cup milk. Add remaining cookie ingredients; mix well. Drop dough by rounded teaspoonfuls 2 inches apart onto greased cookie sheets.

2. Bake at 375°F. for 7 to 9 minutes or until edges appear set. Cool 1 minute; remove from cookie sheets. Cool 15 minutes or until completely cooled.

3. Meanwhile, in large bowl, combine all filling ingredients; beat 2 minutes or until light and fluffy. To make sandwich cookies, spread filling between 2 cooled cookies, placing flat sides together. Repeat with remaining frosting and cookies. Store in tightly covered container.

Yield: 30 sandwich cookies
High Altitude (Above 3,500 Feet): No change.

Nutrition Information Per Serving
Serving Size: 1 Cookie. Calories 170 • Calories from Fat 60 • Total Fat 7 g
Saturated Fat 2 g • Cholesterol 10 mg • Sodium 170 mg • Dietary Fiber 1 g
Dietary Exchanges: ½ Starch, 1 Fruit, 1½ Fat OR 1½ Carbohydrate, 1½ Fat

Chocolate Chip Yogurt Cookies

Prep Time: 45 minutes

¹/₂ cup sugar
¹/₂ cup firmly packed brown sugar
¹/₄ cup margarine or butter, softened
¹/₄ cup shortening
¹/₂ cup nonfat plain yogurt

1¹/₂ teaspoons vanilla
1³/₄ cups all-purpose flour
¹/₂ teaspoon baking soda
¹/₂ teaspoon salt
¹/₂ cup miniature chocolate chips or carob chips

1. Heat oven to 375°F. In large bowl, combine sugar, brown sugar, margarine and shortening; beat until light and fluffy. Add yogurt and vanilla; blend well. Stir in flour, baking soda and salt; mix well. Stir in chocolate chips. Drop dough by rounded teaspoonfuls 2 inches apart onto ungreased cookie sheets.
2. Bake at 375°F. for 8 to 12 minutes or until light golden brown. Cool 1 minute; remove from cookie sheets.

Yield: 3 dozen cookies
High Altitude (Above 3,500 Feet): Decrease sugar to ¹/₃ cup; decrease brown sugar to ¹/₃ cup. Bake as directed above.

Nutrition Information Per Serving

Serving Size: 1 Cookie. Calories 80 • Calories from Fat 25 • Total Fat 3 g
Saturated Fat 1 g • Cholesterol 0 mg • Sodium 65 mg • Dietary Fiber 0 g
Dietary Exchanges: 1 Fruit, ¹/₂ Fat OR 1 Carbohydrate, ¹/₂ Fat

Chocolate Chip Yogurt Cookies

Chocolate Raisin Smile Cookies

Prep Time: 1 hour 30 minutes

Cookies
1½ cups sugar
1 cup firmly packed brown sugar
1½ cups margarine or butter, softened
2 teaspoons vanilla
3 eggs
3 cups all-purpose flour
1 cup unsweetened cocoa
1 teaspoon baking soda
¼ teaspoon salt
2 cups raisins

Frosting
1 cup powdered sugar
1 drop red food color
2 drops yellow food color
2 to 4 teaspoons milk

1. Heat oven to 350°F. In large bowl, combine sugar, brown sugar and margarine; beat until light and fluffy. Add vanilla and eggs; blend well. Add flour, cocoa, baking soda and salt; mix well. Stir in raisins. Drop dough by rounded tablespoonfuls 2 inches apart onto ungreased cookie sheets.

2. Bake at 350°F. for 10 to 14 minutes or until set. Cool 1 minute; remove from cookie sheets.

3. In medium bowl, combine all frosting ingredients, adding enough milk for desired decorating consistency. Using decorating bag, decorating bottle, plastic bag or small spoon, make smiling faces on cookies.

Yield: 5 dozen cookies
High Altitude (Above 3,500 Feet): Decrease sugar to 1¼ cups; decrease brown sugar to ¾ cup. Increase flour to 3½ cups. Bake as directed above.

Nutrition Information Per Serving
Serving Size: 1 Cookie. Calories 130 • Calories from Fat 45 • Total Fat 5 g
Saturated Fat 1 g • Cholesterol 10 mg • Sodium 90 mg • Dietary Fiber 1 g
Dietary Exchanges: 1½ Fruit, 1 Fat OR 1½ Carbohydrate, 1 Fat

Variation

Giant Smile Cookies: Prepare cookie dough as directed in recipe. For each cookie, use ¼ cup of dough; place 3 inches apart on ungreased cookie sheets. Bake at 350°F. for 10 to 14 minutes or until set. Cool 1 minute; remove from cookie sheets. Prepare frosting and decorate cookies as directed in recipe.

Yield: 2½ dozen cookies

Coconut Macaroons

Prep Time: 30 minutes

2 egg whites
⅓ cup sugar
2 tablespoons all-purpose flour

Dash salt
¼ teaspoon almond extract
2 cups coconut

1. Heat oven to 325°F. Grease and lightly flour cookie sheet. In medium bowl, beat egg whites until frothy. Add sugar, flour, salt and almond extract; blend well. Stir in coconut. Drop dough by tablespoonfuls 2 inches apart onto greased and floured cookie sheet.
2. Bake at 325°F. for 13 to 17 minutes or until set and light golden brown. Immediately remove from cookie sheet.

Yield: 12 cookies
High Altitude (Above 3,500 Feet): No change.

Recipe Fact

Coconut macaroons, a delicious variation of the classic almond macaroon cookie, gain chewy texture from the lightly beaten egg whites and shredded coconut.

Make It Special

Top each cookie with two or three toasted slivered almonds before baking.

Nutrition Information Per Serving

Serving Size: 1 Cookie. Calories 90 • Calories from Fat 35 • Total Fat 4 g
Saturated Fat 4 g • Cholesterol 0 mg • Sodium 50 mg • Dietary Fiber 1 g
Dietary Exchanges: ½ Starch, 1 Fat OR ½ Carbohydrate, 1 Fat

Chocolate Macadamia Cookies with White Chocolate Chunks; Chocolate Ginger Zebras, page 131

Chocolate Macadamia Cookies with White Chocolate Chunks

Prep Time: 45 minutes

$3/4$ cup firmly packed brown sugar
$1/2$ cup sugar
1 cup margarine or butter, softened
1 teaspoon almond extract
1 egg
2 cups all-purpose flour
$1/4$ cup unsweetened cocoa

1 teaspoon baking soda
$1/2$ teaspoon salt
6 oz. white chocolate baking bar, cut into $1/2$-inch chunks, or 1 cup white vanilla chips*
1 ($3^1/2$-oz.) jar macadamia nuts, coarsely chopped

1. Heat oven to 375°F. In large bowl, combine brown sugar, sugar and margarine; beat until light and fluffy. Add almond extract and egg; blend well. Add flour, cocoa, baking soda and salt; mix well. Stir in white chocolate chunks and nuts. Drop dough by rounded tablespoonfuls 2 inches apart onto ungreased cookie sheets.
2. Bake at 375°F. for 8 to 12 minutes or until set. Cool 1 minute; remove from cookie sheets.

Yield: 3 dozen cookies
High Altitude (Above 3,500 Feet): Increase flour to 2 cups plus 3 tablespoons.
Bake as directed above.

*Tip: If baking bar is difficult to cut, place in microwave-safe bowl and microwave on MEDIUM for 10 seconds.

Nutrition Information Per Serving
Serving Size: 1 Cookie. Calories 150 • Calories from Fat 80 • Total Fat 9 g
Saturated Fat 2 g • Cholesterol 5 mg • Sodium 125 mg • Dietary Fiber 1 g
Dietary Exchanges: 1 Fruit, 2 Fat OR 1 Carbohydrate, 2 Fat

Coconut Macadamia Jumbos

Prep Time: 45 minutes

1 cup firmly packed brown
   sugar
$^3/_4$ cup sugar
1 cup margarine or butter,
   softened
$1^1/_2$ teaspoons vanilla
2 eggs

3 cups all-purpose flour
1 teaspoon baking soda
$^1/_4$ teaspoon salt
1 cup coconut
1 ($3^1/_2$-oz.) jar macadamia nuts,
   coarsely chopped

1. Heat oven to 350°F. In large bowl, combine brown sugar, sugar and margarine; beat until light and fluffy. Add vanilla and eggs; blend well. Add flour, baking soda and salt; mix well. Stir in coconut and macadamia nuts. Drop dough by rounded tablespoonfuls 2 inches apart onto ungreased cookie sheets.

2. Bake at 350°F. for 10 to 12 minutes or until golden brown. Cool 1 minute; remove from cookie sheets.

Yield: 3 dozen cookies
High Altitude (Above 3,500 Feet): Decrease brown sugar to $^3/_4$ cup. Bake as directed above.

Nutrition Information Per Serving
Serving Size: 1 Cookie. Calories 160 • Calories from Fat 70 • Total Fat 8 g
Saturated Fat 2 g • Cholesterol 10 mg • Sodium 110 mg • Dietary Fiber 1 g
Dietary Exchanges: $1^1/_2$ Fruit, $1^1/_2$ Fat OR $1^1/_2$ Carbohydrate, $1^1/_2$ Fat

---

About Coconut

The coconut, the seed of the coconut palm tree, yields many edible products, including coconut oil, coconut juice and coconut meat, which is often shredded or flaked for use in cooking. In this recipe, use the lightly sweetened shredded or flaked coconut sold in plastic bags in the baking aisle of the supermarket.

Kitchen Tip

For chewy cookies, bake these until just light golden brown. For crisper cookies, bake them a minute or two longer.

Cranberry Cookies

Prep Time: 45 minutes

½ cup sugar
½ cup firmly packed brown
  sugar
¼ cup margarine or butter,
  softened
2 tablespoons milk
1 tablespoon lemon juice
½ teaspoon vanilla
1 egg

1½ cups all-purpose flour
½ teaspoon baking powder
¼ teaspoon baking soda
¼ teaspoon salt
1 cup fresh or frozen
  cranberries, coarsely
  chopped
½ cup chopped nuts

1. Heat oven to 375°F. Grease cookie sheets. In large bowl, combine sugar, brown sugar and margarine; beat until light and fluffy. Add milk, lemon juice, vanilla and egg; blend well. Add flour, baking powder, baking soda and salt; mix well. Stir in cranberries and nuts. Drop dough by rounded teaspoonfuls 2 inches apart onto greased cookie sheets.

2. Bake at 375°F. for 8 to 12 minutes or until edges are light golden brown. Immediately remove from cookie sheets.

Yield: 3 dozen cookies
High Altitude (Above 3,500 Feet): Increase flour to 2 cups. Bake as directed above.

Nutrition Information Per Serving

Serving Size: 1 Cookie. Calories 70 • Calories from Fat 25 • Total Fat 3 g
Saturated Fat 0 g • Cholesterol 5 mg • Sodium 50 mg • Dietary Fiber 0 g
Dietary Exchanges: ½ Starch, ½ Fat OR ½ Carbohydrate, ½ Fat

About Cranberries

Fresh cranberries, grown in bogs and harvested in autumn, make their appearance in the market sometime in late fall and can usually be found until mid-winter. Remove any tiny stems, then rinse and drain the berries before using. Discard any mushy berries. Frozen cranberries are available in the frozen fruit section.

Kitchen Tip

Stock up on fresh cranberries early in the season before supplies are depleted in the market. Pick off any stems, then freeze the cranberries in a single layer on a baking sheet. Transfer the frozen berries to a heavy freezer bag or plastic container.

Oatmeal Carrot Cookies

Prep Time: 45 minutes

1 cup all-purpose flour
1 cup quick-cooking rolled oats
1 teaspoon baking powder
¼ teaspoon baking soda
½ cup margarine or butter, softened

½ cup honey
1 teaspoon vanilla
1 egg
½ cup chopped nuts
½ cup shredded carrot

1. Heat oven to 350°F. Grease cookie sheets. In large bowl, combine all ingredients except nuts and carrot; beat at low speed until well blended. Stir in nuts and carrot. Drop dough by rounded teaspoonfuls 2 inches apart onto greased cookie sheets.

2. Bake at 350°F. for 8 to 12 minutes or until edges are light golden brown. Immediately remove from cookie sheets.

Yield: 3 dozen cookies
High Altitude (Above 3,500 Feet): No change.

Nutrition Information Per Serving

Serving Size: 1 Cookie. Calories 80 • Calories from Fat 35 • Total Fat 4 g
Saturated Fat 1 g • Cholesterol 5 mg • Sodium 55 mg • Dietary Fiber 0 g
Dietary Exchanges: ½ Fruit, 1 Fat OR ½ Carbohydrate, 1 Fat

Recipe Variation

Add ½ cup raisins or chopped dried apricots to the batter.

Storage Tip

Layer these soft, chewy cookies between sheets of waxed paper and store them in a tightly covered container.

Oatmeal Carrot Cookies; Cranberry Cookies, page 41

Oatmeal Coconut Fun Chippers

Kitchen Tip

Choose old-fashioned rolled oats for cookies with a moister, coarser texture; use quick-cooking oats for a smoother cookie.

Recipe Variation

To make these Fun Chippers into Deluxe Jumbly Chippers, use ½ cup chocolate chips, ½ cup raisins and ½ cup chopped nuts in place of the candy-coated chocolate baking bits.

1½ cups firmly packed brown sugar
1 cup margarine or butter, softened
1 tablespoon milk
1 tablespoon vanilla
2 eggs
2¼ cups all-purpose flour
2 teaspoons baking powder
1 teaspoon baking soda
½ teaspoon salt
2 cups rolled oats
1 cup coconut
1 (12-oz.) pkg. miniature candy-coated chocolate baking bits or 1½ cups semi-sweet chocolate chips

1. Heat oven to 375°F. In large bowl, combine brown sugar and margarine; beat until light and fluffy. Add milk, vanilla and eggs; blend well. Add flour, baking powder, baking soda and salt; mix well. Stir in oats, coconut and baking bits. Drop dough by rounded tablespoonfuls 2 inches apart onto ungreased cookie sheets.

2. Bake at 375°F. for 9 to 13 minutes or until light golden brown. Cool 1 minute; remove from cookie sheets.

Yield: 4 dozen cookies
High Altitude (Above 3,500 Feet): Decrease brown sugar to 1¼ cups; increase flour to 2½ cups. Bake as directed above.

Nutrition Information Per Serving

Serving Size: 1 Cookie. Calories 140 • Calories from Fat 60 • Total Fat 7 g
Saturated Fat 2 g • Cholesterol 10 mg • Sodium 125 mg • Dietary Fiber 1 g
Dietary Exchanges: 1 Starch, 1½ Fat OR 1 Carbohydrate, 1½ Fat

Oatmeal Raisin Cookies

Prep Time: 45 minutes

¾ cup sugar
¼ cup firmly packed brown
    sugar
½ cup margarine or butter,
    softened
½ teaspoon vanilla
1 egg
¾ cup all-purpose flour

½ teaspoon baking soda
½ teaspoon cinnamon
¼ teaspoon salt
1½ cups quick-cooking rolled
    oats
½ cup raisins
½ cup chopped nuts

1. Heat oven to 375°F. Grease cookie sheets. In large bowl, combine sugar, brown sugar and margarine; beat until light and fluffy. Add vanilla and egg; blend well. Add flour, baking soda, cinnamon and salt; mix well. Stir in oats, raisins and nuts. Drop dough by rounded teaspoonfuls 2 inches apart onto greased cookie sheets.

2. Bake at 375°F. for 7 to 10 minutes or until edges are light golden brown. Cool 1 minute; remove from cookie sheets.

Yield: 3½ dozen cookies
High Altitude (Above 3,500 Feet): Increase flour to 1 cup. Bake as directed above.

Nutrition Information Per Serving
Serving Size: 1 Cookie. Calories 70 • Calories from Fat 25 • Total Fat 3 g
Saturated Fat 1 g • Cholesterol 5 mg • Sodium 55 mg • Dietary Fiber 0 g
Dietary Exchanges: ½ Starch, ½ Fat OR ½ Carbohydrate, ½ Fat

About Cinnamon

Cinnamon is ground from the bark of a tree native to Sri Lanka. Cassia, a similar, though stronger-flavored ingredient, is often sold as cinnamon.

Kitchen Tip

To plump up raisins that have become a bit dried out, soak them in hot water for about 10 minutes. Rinse with cool water, squeeze dry and toss with a little flour from the recipe before adding them to the dough.

Ingredient Substitution

For a chewier cookie, substitute old-fashioned rolled oats for the quick-cooking variety.

Orange Cappuccino Drops

Prep Time: 1 hour

Recipe Fact

These cookies take their inspiration from Italian cappuccino—strong espresso coffee topped with foamy steamed milk.

About Powdered Sugar

Powdered sugar, also known as confectioners' sugar, is made from ordinary granulated white sugar that has been processed until it is very fine. A tiny bit of cornstarch is added to prevent clumping.

Recipe Variation

Use ½ teaspoon vanilla extract in the frosting instead of grated orange peel.

Cookies
1 cup firmly packed brown sugar
½ cup margarine or butter, softened
⅔ cup sour cream
½ cup strong coffee*
3 oz. unsweetened chocolate, melted, cooled
1 teaspoon vanilla
1 egg

2 cups all-purpose flour
½ teaspoon baking soda

Frosting
2 cups powdered sugar
2 tablespoons margarine or butter, melted
1½ teaspoons grated orange peel
2 to 3 tablespoons milk

1. Heat oven to 375°F. In large bowl, combine brown sugar and ½ cup margarine; beat until light and fluffy. Add sour cream, coffee, chocolate, vanilla and egg; blend well. Add flour and baking soda; mix well. (Cookie dough will be very soft.) Drop dough by teaspoonfuls 2 inches apart onto ungreased cookie sheets.

2. Bake at 375°F. for 5 to 7 minutes or until set. Immediately remove from cookie sheets. Cool 15 minutes or until completely cooled.

3. Meanwhile, in small bowl, combine all frosting ingredients, adding enough milk for desired spreading consistency. Frost cooled cookies.

Yield: 5 dozen cookies
High Altitude (Above 3,500 Feet): No change.

*Tip: Two teaspoons instant coffee granules or crystals dissolved in ½ cup hot water can be substituted for strong coffee.

Nutrition Information Per Serving
Serving Size: 1 Cookie. Calories 70 • Calories from Fat 25 • Total Fat 3 g
Saturated Fat 1 g • Cholesterol 5 mg • Sodium 40 mg • Dietary Fiber 0 g
Dietary Exchanges: 1 Starch, ½ Fat OR 1 Carbohydrate, ½ Fat

Orange Cappuccino Drops

Honey Nut Chews

Prep Time: 1 hour 15 minutes

About Oatmeal

Oatmeal is commonly found in three varieties in the supermarket: old-fashioned (or rolled oats), quick-cooking and instant. Old-fashioned oatmeal, which has a coarser, chewier texture, and quick-cooking are best for baking.

Kitchen Tip

Honey keeps indefinitely on the pantry shelf. If it crystallizes, place the jar into a pan of hot water until it liquefies again.

$\frac{1}{2}$ **cup firmly packed brown sugar**
1 cup margarine or butter, softened
$\frac{1}{2}$ **cup honey**
2 tablespoons milk
1 tablespoon molasses
1 egg

$2\frac{1}{2}$ **cups all-purpose flour**
$\frac{1}{2}$ **teaspoon salt**
$1\frac{1}{2}$ **cups rolled oats**
1 cup coconut
1 cup raisins
$\frac{1}{2}$ **cup chopped nuts**

1. Heat oven to 350°F. Lightly grease cookie sheets. In large bowl, combine brown sugar, margarine, honey, milk, molasses and egg; blend well. Add flour and salt; mix well. Stir in remaining ingredients. Drop dough by rounded teaspoonfuls 2 inches apart onto greased cookie sheets.
2. Bake at 350°F. for 12 to 14 minutes or until light golden brown. Immediately remove from cookie sheets.

Yield: 5 dozen cookies
High Altitude (Above 3,500 Feet): No change.

Nutrition Information Per Serving

Serving Size: 1 Cookie. Calories 90 • Calories from Fat 35 • Total Fat 4 g
Saturated Fat 1 g • Cholesterol 4 mg • Sodium 55 mg • Dietary Fiber 1 g
Dietary Exchanges: $\frac{1}{2}$ Starch, 1 Fat OR $\frac{1}{2}$ Carbohydrate, 1 Fat

Honey-roasted Peanut Cookies

Prep Time: 2 hours

Cookies

1½ cups firmly packed brown sugar
¾ cup sugar
1½ cups margarine or butter, softened
1½ cups peanut butter
½ cup honey
1½ teaspoons vanilla
3 eggs
3¾ cups all purpose flour

1½ teaspoons baking soda
1 teaspoon salt

Glaze

⅓ cup creamy peanut butter
3 tablespoons honey
¼ cup hot water
1¼ to 1½ cups powdered sugar
1 cup chopped honey-roasted peanuts

1. Heat oven to 350°F. In large bowl, combine brown sugar, sugar and margarine; beat until light and fluffy. Add 1½ cups peanut butter, ½ cup honey, vanilla and eggs; blend well. Add flour, baking soda and salt; mix well. Drop dough by rounded teaspoonfuls 2 inches apart onto ungreased cookie sheets. With fork dipped in flour, flatten slightly in crisscross pattern.

2. Bake at 350°F. for 9 to 12 minutes or until golden brown. Remove from cookie sheets. Cool 15 minutes or until completely cooled.

3. Meanwhile, in medium bowl, combine ⅓ cup peanut butter, 3 tablespoons honey and hot water; blend well. Stir in enough powdered sugar for desired drizzling consistency. Drizzle glaze over cooled cookies. Sprinkle ½ teaspoon peanuts over each cookie. Let stand until set.

Yield: 8 dozen cookies
High Altitude (Above 3,500 Feet): No change.

Nutrition Information Per Serving

Serving Size: 1 Cookie. Calories 120 • Calories from Fat 50 • Total Fat 6 g
Saturated Fat 1 g • Cholesterol 5 mg • Sodium 110 mg • Dietary Fiber 1 g
Dietary Exchanges: 1 Starch, 1 Fat OR 1 Carbohydrate, 1 Fat

Recipe Fact

Peanut butter cookies traditionally sport a cross-hatch surface design made with a fork prior to baking.

About Hot Water

In recipes that specify hot water, it's best to begin as you would for the best-tasting coffee or tea, with fresh cold tap water (or bottled water) to eliminate the chance of impurities sometimes found in water that has been languishing for hours in the water heater. Heat the water in the microwave or a teakettle rather than relying on hot tap water.

Recipe Variation

Drizzle the cookies with chocolate icing instead of the peanut butter. Or, instead of using chopped nuts, sprinkle the tops with miniature candy-coated peanut butter chips.

Pumpkin Cookies with Penuche Frosting

Prep Time: 1 hour

Cookies

½ cup sugar

½ cup firmly packed brown sugar

1 cup margarine or butter, softened

1 cup canned pumpkin

1 teaspoon vanilla

1 egg

2 cups all-purpose flour

1 teaspoon baking powder

1 teaspoon baking soda

1 teaspoon cinnamon

¼ teaspoon salt

¾ cup chopped nuts

Frosting

3 tablespoons margarine or butter

½ cup firmly packed brown sugar

¼ cup milk

1½ to 2 cups powdered sugar

1. Heat oven to 350°F. In large bowl, combine sugar, ½ cup brown sugar and 1 cup margarine; beat until light and fluffy. Add pumpkin, vanilla and egg; blend well. Add flour, baking powder, baking soda, cinnamon and salt; mix well. Stir in nuts. Drop dough by rounded teaspoonfuls 2 inches apart onto ungreased cookie sheets.

2. Bake at 350°F. for 10 to 12 minutes or until light golden brown around edges. Immediately remove from cookie sheets. Cool 15 minutes or until completely cooled.

3. Meanwhile, in medium saucepan, combine 3 tablespoons margarine and ½ cup brown sugar; bring to a boil. Cook over medium heat for 1 minute or until slightly thickened, stirring constantly. Cool 10 minutes. Add milk; beat until smooth. Beat in enough powdered sugar for desired spreading consistency. Frost cooled cookies.

Yield: 5 dozen cookies
High Altitude (Above 3,500 Feet): No change.

Nutrition Information Per Serving

Serving Size: 1 Cookie. Calories 100 • Calories from Fat 45 • Total Fat 5 g
Saturated Fat 1 g • Cholesterol 4 mg • Sodium 85 mg • Dietary Fiber 0 g
Dietary Exchanges: 1 Fruit, 1 Fat OR 1 Carbohydrate, 1 Fat

About Penuche

Penuche (puh-NOO-chee) is a brown sugar fudge-like candy. The name is derived from the Mexican word for "raw sugar" or "brown sugar."

About Canned Pumpkin

Canned pumpkin appears in the market in two forms: the plain cooked, pureed vegetable, and a variation labeled "pumpkin pie filling," which contains sweeteners and spices. Choose the plain version for these nut-spiked cookies.

Kitchen Tip

For easy shaping of these spice cookies, try manipulating the dough using a small ice cream scoop with a release bar.

Make It Special

Sprinkle minced nuts on top of the penuche frosting before it sets.

Pumpkin Cookies with Penuche Frosting

Granola Apple Cookies

Prep Time: 55 minutes

About Granola

Granola, a purchased or homemade cereal and snack, varies widely but usually includes oatmeal, brown sugar or honey and a range of extra ingredients, such as wheat germ, nuts, raisins or other dried fruit. Although it is associated with "healthy" cooking, read labels of packaged granolas carefully, as they are often high in calories and fat.

Kitchen Tip

To extract the most juice from a lemon, roll it with your hand on the counter, or microwave it for 20 to 40 seconds before cutting and squeezing.

Storage Tip

Make sure the icing has set before storing these glazed cookies. Then layer the cookies between sheets of waxed paper in a tightly covered container.

Cookies

1½ cups firmly packed brown sugar
½ cup margarine or butter, softened
¼ cup milk
1 tablespoon lemon juice
1 teaspoon grated lemon peel
1 egg
1½ cups all-purpose flour
1 cup whole wheat flour
1 teaspoon baking soda
1 teaspoon cinnamon or nutmeg
¼ teaspoon salt
1½ cups finely chopped apples
1 cup granola

Glaze

¾ cup powdered sugar
2 to 3 teaspoons lemon juice

1. Heat oven to 375°F. In large bowl, combine brown sugar and margarine; beat until light and fluffy. Add milk, 1 tablespoon lemon juice, lemon peel and egg; blend well. Add all-purpose flour, whole wheat flour, baking soda, cinnamon and salt; mix well. Stir in apples and granola. Drop dough by heaping teaspoonfuls 2 inches apart onto ungreased cookie sheets.
2. Bake at 375°F. for 9 to 13 minutes or until light golden brown. Immediately remove from cookie sheets. Cool 15 minutes or until completely cooled.
3. Meanwhile, in small bowl, combine glaze ingredients, adding enough lemon juice for desired drizzling consistency. Drizzle over cooled cookies.

Yield: 3 dozen cookies
High Altitude (Above 3,500 Feet): Decrease brown sugar to 1 cup. Bake as directed above.

Nutrition Information Per Serving

Serving Size: 1 Cookie. Calories 130 • Calories from Fat 35 • Total Fat 4 g
Saturated Fat 1 g • Cholesterol 5 mg • Sodium 85 mg • Dietary Fiber 1 g
Dietary Exchanges: 1½ Fruit, 1 Fat OR 1½ Carbohydrate, 1 Fat

Peanut and Candy Jumbles

Prep Time: 35 minutes

1 cup firmly packed brown
   sugar
½ cup margarine or butter,
   softened
½ cup creamy peanut butter
1 tablespoon vanilla
1 egg

1 cup all-purpose flour
½ cup whole wheat flour
1 teaspoon baking soda
¾ cup salted peanuts
¾ cup candy-coated chocolate
   pieces

1. Heat oven to 375°F. In large bowl, combine brown sugar, margarine and peanut butter; beat until light and fluffy. Add vanilla and egg; blend well. Add all-purpose flour, whole wheat flour and baking soda; mix well. Stir in peanuts and candy-coated chocolate pieces. Drop dough by rounded tablespoonfuls 2 inches apart onto ungreased cookie sheets.

2. Bake at 375°F. for 6 to 10 minutes or until light golden brown. Immediately remove from cookie sheets.

Yield: 3 dozen cookies

High Altitude (Above 3,500 Feet): Decrease brown sugar to ¾ cup. Bake as directed above.

Nutrition Information Per Serving

Serving Size: 1 Cookie. Calories 130 • Calories from Fat 60 • Total Fat 7 g
Saturated Fat 2 g • Cholesterol 5 mg • Sodium 105 mg • Dietary Fiber 1 g
Dietary Exchanges: 1 Fruit, 1½ Fat OR 1 Carbohydrate, 1½ Fat

About Peanut Butter

At its most basic, peanut butter consists of nothing more than ground peanuts, sometimes with just a bit of salt added. Commercial brands usually contain a bit of sweetener, vegetable oils for homogenization and salt.

Ingredient Substitution

You can substitute chunky peanut butter for the smooth, and chocolate chips for the candy-coated chocolate pieces.

Saucepan Mocha Fudgies

editor's favorite • chocoholic's choice

Prep Time: 1 hour

Kitchen Tip

To streamline preparation, mix these soft chocolate cookies in the same bowl you use to melt the chocolate and the butter: In a large, microwave-safe mixing bowl, partially melt the chocolate on LOW power. Stir, add the butter and finish melting on low power. Mix the remaining ingredients in the same bowl.

Ingredient Substitution

Use instant espresso powder in place of regular instant granules for a stronger coffee flavor.

Cookies

½ cup butter
2 oz. unsweetened chocolate
1 teaspoon instant coffee granules or crystals
1 cup firmly packed brown sugar
1 egg
2 cups all-purpose flour
1 teaspoon baking powder
¼ teaspoon salt
½ cup milk
½ cup chopped nuts

Frosting

½ teaspoon instant coffee granules or crystals
2 teaspoons hot water
2 cups powdered sugar
¼ cup unsweetened cocoa
2 tablespoons butter
2 to 4 tablespoons milk

1. Heat oven to 350°F. Grease cookie sheets. In medium saucepan, combine ½ cup butter, chocolate and 1 teaspoon coffee granules; cook over low heat until melted, stirring constantly. Remove from heat; cool 5 minutes. Stir in brown sugar and egg; blend well.

2. In medium bowl, combine flour, baking powder and salt. Stir flour mixture into chocolate mixture alternately with milk, beginning and ending with flour mixture; mix well. Stir in nuts. Let stand 5 minutes.

3. Drop dough by rounded teaspoonfuls onto greased cookie sheets. Bake at 350°F. for 7 to 9 minutes or until set. Immediately remove from cookie sheets; cool.

4. Meanwhile, in small bowl, dissolve ½ teaspoon coffee granules in hot water. Add remaining frosting ingredients; beat until smooth, adding enough milk for desired spreading consistency. Frost cooled cookies.

Yield: 4 dozen cookies
High Altitude (Above 3,500 Feet): No change.

Nutrition Information Per Serving

Serving Size: 1 Cookie. Calories 100 • Calories from Fat 35 • Total Fat 4 g
Saturated Fat 2 g • Cholesterol 10 mg • Sodium 50 mg • Dietary Fiber 1 g
Dietary Exchanges: 1 Starch, ½ Fat OR 1 Carbohydrate, ½ Fat

Toffee Crisps

Prep Time: 1 hour 15 minutes

1 cup sugar
1/2 cup firmly packed brown sugar
1/2 cup margarine or butter, softened
1 teaspoon vanilla
2 eggs

2 1/4 cups all-purpose flour
1 teaspoon baking powder
1/2 teaspoon baking soda
1/2 teaspoon salt
1 cup almond brickle baking chips

1. Heat oven to 375°F. Spray cookie sheets with nonstick cooking spray. In large bowl, combine sugar, brown sugar and margarine; beat until light and fluffy. Add vanilla and eggs; blend well. Add flour, baking powder, baking soda and salt; mix well. Stir in chips. Drop dough by rounded teaspoonfuls 2 inches apart onto sprayed cookie sheets.
2. Bake at 375°F. for 8 to 12 minutes or until light golden brown. Immediately remove from cookie sheets.

Yield: 6 dozen cookies
High Altitude (Above 3,500 Feet): No change.

Nutrition Information Per Serving

Serving Size: 1 Cookie. Calories 60 • Calories from Fat 20 • Total Fat 2 g
Saturated Fat 1 g • Cholesterol 10 mg • Sodium 50 mg • Dietary Fiber 0 g
Dietary Exchanges: 1/2 Starch, 1/2 Fat OR 1/2 Carbohydrate, 1/2 Fat

About Almond Brickle Baking Chips

Almond brickle baking chips—small bits of English toffee—offer a convenient way to add toffee flavor to cookies and other baked goods.

About Baking Soda

Baking soda helps raise the dough while neutralizing acidic ingredients, including the obvious ones such as citrus or vinegar, as well as chocolate, brown sugar and other not so apparent items.

Supreme Chocolate Mint Chip Cookies

Prep Time: 1 hour

Kitchen Tip

To cool the frosting quickly, place the saucepan on ice in a large bowl. If the glaze becomes too thick, reheat it slightly until it attains spreading consistency.

Ingredient Substitution

To make these cookies more intensely minty, use peppermint extract instead of vanilla in the frosting.

Make It Special

Before the frosting cools, decorate the cookies with chocolate chips or crushed peppermint candy.

Cookies
4 cups all-purpose flour
1 cup unsweetened cocoa
1 teaspoon baking soda
$\frac{1}{2}$ teaspoon salt
$1\frac{1}{2}$ cups sugar
1 cup firmly packed brown sugar
$1\frac{1}{2}$ cups margarine or butter, softened

3 eggs
1 (10-oz.) pkg. mint-flavored chocolate chips

Glaze
2 cups sugar
$\frac{1}{2}$ cup unsweetened cocoa
$\frac{1}{2}$ cup margarine or butter
$\frac{1}{2}$ cup milk
1 teaspoon vanilla

1. Heat oven to 350°F. Lightly grease cookie sheets. In large bowl, combine flour, 1 cup cocoa, baking soda and salt. In another large bowl, combine $1\frac{1}{2}$ cups sugar, brown sugar and $1\frac{1}{2}$ cups margarine; beat until light and fluffy. Add eggs; blend well. Add flour mixture; mix well. Stir in chips. Drop dough by tablespoonfuls 3 inches apart onto greased cookie sheets; flatten slightly.

2. Bake at 350°F. for 8 to 10 minutes or until set. Cool 1 minute; remove from cookie sheets. Cool 15 minutes or until completely cooled.

3. Meanwhile, in medium saucepan, combine all frosting ingredients except vanilla. Bring to a boil; boil 1 minute. Remove from heat; stir in vanilla. Cool 5 to 10 minutes or until slightly cooled. Beat until smooth and of spreading consistency. Glaze cooled cookies. Let stand until set.

Yield: 6 dozen cookies
High Altitude (Above 3,500 Feet): Increase flour to 4 cups plus 2 tablespoons.
Bake as directed above.

Supreme Chocolate Mint Chip Cookies;
Honey-roasted Peanut Cookies, page 49

Nutrition Information Per Serving
Serving Size: 1 Cookie. Calories 160 • Calories from Fat 60 • Total Fat 7 g
Saturated Fat 2 g • Cholesterol 10 mg • Sodium 95 mg • Dietary Fiber 1 g
Dietary Exchanges: $\frac{1}{2}$ Starch, 1 Fruit, $1\frac{1}{2}$ Fat OR $1\frac{1}{2}$ Carbohydrate, $1\frac{1}{2}$ Fat

Ranger Crispies

Prep Time: 1 hour 30 minutes

About Shortening

Shortening is a solid fat made from vegetable oils. In cookie recipes, it contributes to a softer-textured and more cakelike product.

Recipe Variation

Stir 1 cup of miniature chocolate chips with the cereal into the batter.

1 cup sugar
1 cup firmly packed brown
   sugar
½ cup margarine or butter,
   softened
⅓ cup shortening
1 teaspoon vanilla

2 eggs
2¼ cups all-purpose flour
1 teaspoon baking powder
1 teaspoon baking soda
1 teaspoon salt
3 cups crisp rice cereal

1. Heat oven to 375°F. Lightly grease cookie sheets. In large bowl, combine sugar, brown sugar, margarine and shortening; beat until light and fluffy. Add vanilla and eggs; blend well. Add flour, baking powder, baking soda and salt; mix well. Stir in cereal. Drop dough by rounded teaspoonfuls 2 inches apart onto greased cookie sheets.
2. Bake at 375°F. for 8 to 12 minutes or until golden brown. Cool 1 minute; remove from cookie sheets.

Yield: 5 dozen cookies
High Altitude (Above 3,500 Feet): Decrease baking powder and baking soda to ½ teaspoon each. Bake as directed above.

Nutrition Information Per Serving
Serving Size: 1 Cookie. Calories 80 • Calories from Fat 25 • Total Fat 3 g
Saturated Fat 1 g • Cholesterol 5 mg • Sodium 105 mg • Dietary Fiber 0 g
Dietary Exchanges: 1 Fruit, ½ Fat OR 1 Carbohydrate, ½ Fat

Whole Wheat Zucchini Cookies

Prep Time: 1 hour 15 minutes

3/4 cup sugar
3/4 cup firmly packed brown sugar
1 cup margarine or butter, softened
1 teaspoon grated lemon peel
1 teaspoon vanilla
2 eggs
2 1/2 cups whole wheat flour

1 teaspoon baking soda
1 teaspoon cinnamon
1/2 teaspoon salt
2 cups quick-cooking rolled oats
2 cups shredded zucchini, drained
1 (12-oz.) pkg. (2 cups) miniature chocolate chips

1. Heat oven to 350°F. Lightly grease cookie sheets. In large bowl, combine sugar, brown sugar and margarine; beat until light and fluffy. Add lemon peel, vanilla and eggs; blend well. Add flour, baking soda, cinnamon and salt; mix well. Stir in remaining ingredients. Drop dough by rounded teaspoonfuls onto greased cookie sheets.
2. Bake at 350°F. for 9 to 13 minutes or until golden brown. Immediately remove from cookie sheets. Cool 15 minutes or until completely cooled.

Yield: 5 dozen cookies
High Altitude (Above 3,500 Feet): No change.

Nutrition Information Per Serving
Serving Size: 1 Cookie. Calories 110 • Calories from Fat 45 • Total Fat 5 g
Saturated Fat 2 g • Cholesterol 5 mg • Sodium 80 mg • Dietary Fiber 1 g
Dietary Exchanges: 1 Fruit, 1 Fat OR 1 Carbohydrate, 1 Fat

About Zucchini

Zucchini, a cousin of the cucumber and the pumpkin, grows prolifically, sometimes sprouting from finger size to baseball-bat dimension seemingly overnight. While this green vegetable is most often used in savory dishes, it can also add moisture and flavor to sweet recipes for cookies, cakes, muffins and quick breads.

Kitchen Tip

Zucchini contains a lot of moisture. To avoid making the batter watery, drain the shredded squash by pressing it down in a colander or sieve set in the sink or over a bowl before mixing it with other ingredients.

Hand-Fo

Some of the world's most beloved cookies—biscotti, shortbread, peanut butter cookies—are made from doughs that are molded or formed by hand in some fashion. The resulting treats may be round, wedge-shaped or slanted, with tops that are plain, sprinkled with sugar or embossed with a design . . . irresistible, every last one!

rmed Cookies

Hand-Formed Cookies, like rolled cookies, usually do

best with chilled dough. A batch of hand-formed cookies may or may not be quicker to make than rolled cookies, depending on whether the dough bakes in a large portion that's quickly divided after baking (as for biscotti or shortbread), or if the recipe calls for shaping small, individual bits of dough before baking.

In any case, handle the dough gently and as little as possible to keep the cookies tender. A little flour on your hands and the work surface can prevent sticking, but if you find yourself repeatedly having to sprinkle on more flour, it might be best to chill the dough a bit longer.

Previous page: Chocolate Orange Blossoms, page 63; Snickerdoodles, page 64

Chocolate Orange Blossoms

Prep Time: 1 hour (Ready in 2 hours)

½ cup sugar
½ cup firmly packed brown
    sugar
¼ cup unsweetened cocoa
½ cup shortening
½ cup margarine or butter,
    softened
1 tablespoon grated orange
    peel

1 teaspoon vanilla
1 egg
1¾ cups all-purpose flour
1 teaspoon baking soda
½ teaspoon salt
Sugar
48 milk chocolate candy
    kisses, unwrapped

Kitchen Tip

If the cookies cool before you have had a chance to place the chocolate candy kiss into the center, "glue" a kiss to each cookie with a dab of chocolate or vanilla icing.

Recipe Variation

Instead of topping the cookies with chocolate kisses, pipe a stylized flower of chocolate, vanilla or orange icing onto each.

1. In large bowl, combine ½ cup sugar, brown sugar, cocoa, shortening and margarine; beat until light and fluffy. Add orange peel, vanilla and egg; blend well. Add flour, baking soda and salt. Cover with plastic wrap; refrigerate 1 hour for easier handling.
2. Heat oven to 375°F. Shape dough into 1-inch balls; roll in sugar. Place 2 inches apart on ungreased cookie sheets.
3. Bake at 375°F. for 10 to 12 minutes or until set. Immediately top each cookie with a candy kiss, pressing down firmly so cookie cracks around edges. Remove from cookie sheets.

Yield: 4 dozen cookies
High Altitude (Above 3,500 Feet): No change.

Nutrition Information Per Serving
Serving Size: 1 Cookie. Calories 110 • Calories from Fat 50 • Total Fat 6 g
Saturated Fat 2 g • Cholesterol 5 mg • Sodium 75 mg • Dietary Fiber 0 g
Dietary Exchanges: 1 Fruit, 1 Fat OR 1 Carbohydrate, 1 Fat

Snickerdoodles

Recipe Fact

The whimsical name of this favorite cookie, which originated in New England, is a nineteenth-century nonsense word for a quickly made confection.

Recipe Variation

To make Whole Wheat Snickerdoodles, substitute 1 cup whole wheat flour for 1 cup of the all-purpose flour.

Make It Special

For fancier cookies, combine minced nuts with the cinnamon and sugar.

1½ cups sugar
½ cup margarine or butter, softened
1 teaspoon vanilla
2 eggs
2¾ cups all-purpose flour

1 teaspoon cream of tartar
½ teaspoon baking soda
¼ teaspoon salt
2 tablespoons sugar
2 teaspoons cinnamon

1. Heat oven to 400°F. In large bowl, combine 1½ cups sugar and margarine; beat until light and fluffy. Add vanilla and eggs; blend well. Add flour, cream of tartar, baking soda and salt; mix well.

2. In small bowl, combine 2 tablespoons sugar and cinnamon. Shape dough into 1-inch balls; roll in sugar-cinnamon mixture. Place 2 inches apart on ungreased cookie sheets.

3. Bake at 400°F. for 8 to 10 minutes or until set. Immediately remove from cookie sheets.

Yield: 4 dozen cookies
High Altitude (Above 3,500 Feet): No change.

Nutrition Information Per Serving

Serving Size: 1 Cookie. Calories 70 • Calories from Fat 20 • Total Fat 2 g
Saturated Fat 0 g • Cholesterol 9 mg • Sodium 50 mg • Dietary Fiber 0 g
Dietary Exchanges: ½ Starch, ½ Fat OR ½ Carbohydrate, ½ Fat

Variation

Chocolate Snickerdoodles: Prepare dough as directed in recipe, substituting ½ cup unsweetened cocoa for ½ cup of the flour. Bake at 400°F. for 6 to 9 minutes or until set. Immediately remove from cookie sheets.

Yield: 4 dozen cookies

Anise Honey Bites

Prep Time: 1 hour

$\frac{1}{2}$ cup sugar
$\frac{1}{2}$ cup honey
1 egg
1$\frac{3}{4}$ to 2$\frac{1}{4}$ cups all-purpose
flour

1$\frac{1}{2}$ teaspoons anise seed
1 teaspoon baking soda
$\frac{1}{8}$ teaspoon salt
2 tablespoons powdered sugar

1. Heat oven to 350°F. Grease cookie sheets. In large bowl, combine sugar, honey and egg; blend well. Add remaining ingredients except powdered sugar, stirring in enough flour to form a soft dough; mix well. With floured hands, shape dough into 1-inch balls. Place 2 inches apart on greased cookie sheets.

2. Bake at 350°F. for 4 to 8 minutes or until bottoms of cookies are light golden brown. Immediately remove from cookie sheets. Cool 15 minutes or until completely cooled. Sprinkle with powdered sugar.

Yield: 3$\frac{1}{2}$ dozen cookies

High Altitude (Above 3,500 Feet): Increase flour to 2 to 2$\frac{1}{2}$ cups. Bake as directed above.

Nutrition Information Per Serving
Serving Size: 1 Cookie. Calories 50 • Calories from Fat 0 • Total Fat 0 g
Saturated Fat 0 g • Cholesterol 5 mg • Sodium 40 mg • Dietary Fiber 0 g
Dietary Exchanges: 1 Fruit OR 1 Carbohydrate

About Anise Seed

Anise seed, native to the Middle East, imparts a licorice flavor to sweet and savory dishes.

Recipe Variation

To make Swedish Honey Bites, substitute crushed coriander seed or crushed cardamom seed, two traditionally Scandinavian spices, for the anise seed.

Cardamom Shortbread Wedges

Recipe Fact

Shortbread, the national cookie of Scotland, is a rich, crumbly textured treat with a high butter content. Traditional shapes include wedges, as in this recipe, and narrow rectangles.

About Cardamom

A fragrant spice, cardamom can be purchased in seed pods, as whole seeds or ground. It is popular in Europe, Africa, Asia and the Middle East for uses as diverse as coffee flavoring, aphrodisiac, breath freshener and seasoning for sweet and savory dishes.

Ingredient Substitution

If your pantry lacks cardamom, substitute 1 teaspoon ground cinnamon.

Prep Time: 40 minutes (Ready in 1 hour 10 minutes)

Cookies
1/3 cup sugar
1 cup butter, softened
2 1/2 cups all-purpose flour
1 to 3 teaspoons cardamom
1 teaspoon vanilla
1/4 teaspoon almond extract

Glaze
1 cup powdered sugar
1/4 teaspoon vanilla
1/8 teaspoon almond extract
1 to 3 tablespoons milk

1. Heat oven to 350°F. Line two 9-inch pie pans with foil so foil extends over sides of pans; spray foil with nonstick cooking spray. In large bowl, combine sugar and butter; beat until light and fluffy. Add all remaining cookie ingredients; mix well. Dough will be crumbly. Divide dough in half; press in bottom of lined pans.

2. Bake at 350°F. for 18 to 22 minutes or until light golden brown. Cool in pans 10 minutes. Remove cookies from pans by lifting foil. While warm, cut each shortbread into 16 wedges. Cool 15 minutes or until completely cooled.

3. In small bowl, combine all glaze ingredients, adding enough milk for desired drizzling consistency. Drizzle over cooled cookies. Carefully remove from foil. Store in loosely covered container.

Yield: 32 cookies
High Altitude (Above 3,500 Feet): No change.

Nutrition Information Per Serving
Serving Size: 1 Cookie. Calories 110 • Calories from Fat 50 • Total Fat 6 g
Saturated Fat 4 g • Cholesterol 15 mg • Sodium 60 mg • Dietary Fiber 0 g
Dietary Exchanges: 1 Fruit, 1 Fat OR 1 Carbohydrate, 1 Fat

Cardamom Shortbread Wedges

Grandma's Thumbprints

Prep Time: 1 hour 30 minutes

Cookies

½ cup firmly packed brown sugar

1 cup margarine or butter, softened

2 eggs, separated

2 cups all-purpose flour

⅛ teaspoon salt

1½ cups finely chopped pecans

Frosting

2 cups powdered sugar

⅛ teaspoon salt

3 tablespoons margarine or butter, softened

½ teaspoon vanilla

Food color

1 to 2 tablespoons milk

1. Heat oven to 325°F. Lightly grease cookie sheets. In large bowl, combine brown sugar and 1 cup margarine; beat until light and fluffy. Add egg yolks; blend well. Add flour and ⅛ teaspoon salt; mix well.

2. In small bowl, slightly beat egg whites. Shape dough into ¾-inch balls. Dip in egg whites; roll in pecans. Place 2 inches apart on greased cookie sheets. With thumb or handle of wooden spoon, make indentation in center of each cookie.

3. Bake at 325°F. for 12 to 15 minutes or until edges are light golden brown. Cool 1 minute; remove from cookie sheets.

4. In small bowl, combine all frosting ingredients, adding enough milk for desired spooning consistency; blend until smooth. Spoon or pipe frosting into center of each cookie.

Yield: 5½ dozen cookies
High Altitude (Above 3,500 Feet): No change.

Nutrition Information Per Serving

Serving Size: 1 Cookie. Calories 80 • Calories from Fat 45 • Total Fat 5 g
Saturated Fat 1 g • Cholesterol 6 mg • Sodium 50 mg • Dietary Fiber 0 g
Dietary Exchanges: ½ Starch, 1 Fat OR ½ Carbohydrate, 1 Fat

Chocolate Cherry Cordial Cookies

Prep Time: 1 hour 30 minutes

Cookies

½ cup semi-sweet chocolate chips
½ cup firmly packed brown sugar
¼ cup butter, softened
1 egg
1 cup all-purpose flour
½ teaspoon baking powder

1 (16-oz.) jar maraschino cherries, well drained, reserving 2 to 3 teaspoons liquid

Frosting

½ cup semi-sweet chocolate chips
2 teaspoons oil
Reserved 2 to 3 teaspoons maraschino cherry liquid
¼ cup chopped almonds

1. Heat oven to 350°F. Melt ½ cup chocolate chips in small saucepan over low heat, stirring constantly.
2. In a small bowl, combine brown sugar and ¼ cup butter; beat until fluffy. Add egg and melted chocolate chips; mix well. Add flour and baking powder; mix well. Cover with plastic wrap; refrigerate 10 to 15 minutes for easier handling.
3. Wrap 1 teaspoon dough evenly around each cherry to completely cover. Place 1 inch apart on ungreased cookie sheets. Bake at 350°F. for 10 to 14 minutes or until set. Remove from cookie sheets; cool completely.
4. In small saucepan, melt ½ cup chocolate chips and 2 teaspoons oil over low heat until smooth, stirring constantly. Add enough reserved maraschino cherry liquid for desired dipping consistency; beat until smooth. Dip tops of cooled cookies in frosting; sprinkle with almonds.

Yield: 4 dozen cookies
High Altitude (Above 3,500 Feet): Increase flour to 1¼ cups. Bake as directed above.

Nutrition Information Per Serving
Serving Size: 1 Cookie. Calories 60 • Calories from Fat 25 • Total Fat 3 g
Saturated Fat 1 g • Cholesterol 5 mg • Sodium 20 mg • Dietary Fiber 0 g
Dietary Exchanges: ½ Starch, 1 Fat OR ½ Carbohydrate, ½ Fat

chocoholic's choice

About Maraschino Cherries

Maraschino cherries, the crowning touch to hot fudge sundaes and Shirley Temple cocktails, were originally the preserved version of a small wild cherry grown in Dalmatia (on the Adriatic coast of what is now Croatia). The jar on your supermarket shelf nowadays almost certainly contains processed cultivated cherries.

Center Stage Hazelnut Cookies

Prep Time: 1 hour 15 minutes (Ready in 3 hours 15 minutes)

1 cup sugar
1 cup powdered sugar
1 cup margarine or butter,
  softened
1 cup oil
2 teaspoons grated orange
  peel
1 teaspoon vanilla
2 eggs
4¼ cups all-purpose flour

1 teaspoon baking soda
1 teaspoon cream of tartar
1 teaspoon salt
½ teaspoon nutmeg or mace
1 cup chopped hazelnuts
  (filberts)
Sugar
Hazelnut halves or pieces of
  candied cherries for
  garnish, if desired

1. In large bowl, combine sugar, powdered sugar, margarine, oil, orange peel, vanilla and eggs; beat until well blended. Add flour, baking soda, cream of tartar, salt and nutmeg; mix well. Stir in hazelnuts. Cover with plastic wrap; refrigerate at least 2 hours or overnight for easier handling.

2. Heat oven to 375°F. Shape dough into 1-inch balls; roll in sugar. Place 2 inches apart on ungreased cookie sheets. Flatten each with bottom of glass dipped in sugar; top with hazelnut half.

3. Bake at 375°F. for 7 to 10 minutes or until set. Cool 1 minute; remove from cookie sheets.

Yield: 8 dozen cookies
High Altitude (Above 3,500 Feet): No change.

Nutrition Information Per Serving
Serving Size: 1 Cookie. Calories 90 • Calories from Fat 50 • Total Fat 6 g
Saturated Fat 1 g • Cholesterol 4 mg • Sodium 60 mg • Dietary Fiber 0 g
Dietary Exchanges: ½ Starch, 1 Fat OR ½ Carbohydrate, 1 Fat

About Hazelnuts

Hazelnuts, also known as filberts, are small, round, brown nuts that resemble fat, capless acorns.

Kitchen Tip

To bring out the nutty flavor, toast the hazelnuts on a baking sheet in the oven at 300°F. (or on a tray in a toaster oven) for about 10 minutes, stirring once or twice, or until the nuts are fragrant and begin to turn golden brown.

Center Stage Hazelnut Cookies

Chocolate and Vanilla Chip Biscotti

Prep Time: 50 minutes (Ready in 1 hour 30 minutes)

2½ cups all-purpose flour
⅓ cup unsweetened cocoa
3 teaspoons baking powder
½ cup sugar
½ cup firmly packed brown sugar

¼ cup margarine or butter, softened
3 eggs
1 cup white vanilla chips

1. Heat oven to 350°F. Spray 1 large or 2 small cookie sheets with nonstick cooking spray. In medium bowl, combine flour, cocoa and baking powder; mix well. In large bowl, combine sugar, brown sugar and margarine; beat until well blended. Add eggs; beat well. Add flour mixture; mix well. Stir in vanilla chips.

2. With sprayed hands, shape dough into three 7-inch rolls. Place rolls 3 inches apart on sprayed cookie sheet; flatten each to 7 × 3-inch rectangle.

3. Bake at 350°F. for 22 to 28 minutes or until set and light golden brown. Remove from cookie sheet; place on wire racks. Cool 5 minutes. With serrated knife, cut rectangles into ½-inch slices. Arrange slices, cut side up, on ungreased cookie sheet.

4. Bake at 350°F. for 6 to 8 minutes or until top surface is slightly dry. Turn cookies over; bake an additional 6 to 8 minutes or until top surface is slightly dry. Remove from cookie sheets; cool 15 minutes or until completely cooled. Store in tightly covered container.

Yield: 4 dozen cookies
High Altitude (Above 3,500 Feet): No change.

Nutrition Information Per Serving
Serving Size: 1 Cookie. Calories 70 • Calories from Fat 20 • Total Fat 2 g
Saturated Fat 1 g • Cholesterol 15 mg • Sodium 50 mg • Dietary Fiber 0 g
Dietary Exchanges: 1 Starch OR 1 Carbohydrate

Fruit and Nut Biscotti

Prep Time: 45 minutes (Ready in 1 hour 15 minutes)

½ cup sugar
¼ cup margarine or butter,
    softened
1 teaspoon grated lemon peel
2 tablespoons lemon juice
½ teaspoon vanilla
2 eggs

1¾ cups all-purpose flour
1 teaspoon baking powder
½ teaspoon baking soda
½ teaspoon cinnamon
½ cup finely chopped pecans
½ cup chopped assorted dried
    fruit

1. Heat oven to 350°F. Lightly grease cookie sheet. In large bowl, combine sugar and margarine; beat until light and fluffy. Add lemon peel, lemon juice, vanilla and eggs; blend well. In medium bowl, combine flour, baking powder, baking soda and cinnamon; mix well. Add to sugar mixture; mix well. Stir in pecans and dried fruit.
2. On lightly floured surface, gently knead dough 5 or 6 times. Shape dough into two 10-inch rolls. Place rolls 4 inches apart on greased cookie sheet; flatten each to 2-inch width.
3. Bake at 350°F. for 25 to 30 minutes or until set and golden brown. Remove from cookie sheet; place on wire racks. Cool 10 minutes. With serrated knife, cut rolls diagonally into ½-inch slices. Arrange slices, cut side down, on same cookie sheet.
4. Bake at 350°F. for 8 to 10 minutes or until bottoms are crisp. Turn cookies over; bake an additional 5 to 6 minutes or until crisp. Remove from cookie sheet; cool 15 minutes or until completely cooled. Store in tightly covered container.

Yield: 3 dozen cookies
High Altitude (Above 3,500 Feet): Increase flour to 2 cups. Bake as directed above.

Ingredient Substitution

Chopped walnuts or almonds can stand in for the pecans.

Recipe Variation

To make Chocolate-Nut Biscotti, substitute mini chocolate chips for the dried fruit and eliminate the lemon peel and juice.

Make It Special

Dip the ends of the biscotti in white chocolate.

Nutrition Information Per Serving
Serving Size: 1 Cookie. Calories 60 • Calories from Fat 25 • Total Fat 3 g
Saturated Fat 0 g • Cholesterol 12 mg • Sodium 50 mg • Dietary Fiber 0 g
Dietary Exchanges: ½ Starch, ½ Fat OR ½ Carbohydrate, ½ Fat

Cherry Chocolate Biscotti

Prep Time: 40 minutes (Ready in 1 hour 10 minutes)

Kitchen Tip

Use a demitasse spoon or baby spoon to drizzle the melted chocolate on the cookies in a delicate stream.

Kitchen Tip

Let the icing set before transferring the cookies to a storage container.

Recipe Variation

Use ½ cup chopped dates instead of the candied cherries.

¾ cup sugar
½ cup margarine or butter, softened
2 teaspoons almond extract
3 eggs
3 cups all-purpose flour
2 teaspoons baking powder
½ cup chopped candied cherries

½ cup miniature chocolate chips
3 tablespoons chocolate chips, melted, if desired
3 tablespoons white vanilla chips, melted, if desired

1. Heat oven to 350°F. Lightly grease cookie sheet. In large bowl, combine sugar and margarine; beat until well blended. Add almond extract and eggs; blend well. Add flour and baking powder; mix well. Stir in cherries and chocolate chips. Shape dough into two 10-inch rolls. Place rolls 5 inches apart on greased cookie sheet; flatten each to 3-inch width.
2. Bake at 350°F. for 20 to 25 minutes or until set and light golden brown. Remove from cookie sheet; place on wire racks. Cool 10 minutes. With serrated knife, cut rolls diagonally into ½-inch slices. Arrange slices, cut side down, on ungreased cookie sheets.
3. Bake at 350°F. for 8 to 10 minutes or until bottoms begin to brown. Turn cookies over; bake an additional 5 minutes or until browned and crisp. Remove from cookie sheets; cool 15 minutes or until completely cooled.
4. Drizzle cookies with melted chocolate and vanilla chips. Store in tightly covered container.

Yield: 3 dozen cookies
High Altitude (Above 3,500 Feet): No change.

Nutrition Information Per Serving
Serving Size: 1 Cookie. Calories 110 • Calories from Fat 35 • Total Fat 4 g
Saturated Fat 1 g • Cholesterol 20 mg • Sodium 70 mg • Dietary Fiber 0 g
Dietary Exchanges: 1 Fruit, 1 Fat OR 1 Carbohydrate, 1 Fat

Cherry Chocolate Biscotti

Almond Anise Biscotti

Prep Time: 1 hour (Ready in 1 hour 30 minutes)

½ cup sugar
½ cup firmly packed brown
  sugar
¼ cup margarine or butter,
  softened

1 tablespoon anise seed
3 eggs
3 cups all-purpose flour
3 teaspoons baking powder
½ cup chopped almonds

1. Heat oven to 350°F. Lightly grease cookie sheet. In large bowl, combine sugar, brown sugar and margarine; beat until well blended. Add anise seed and eggs; blend well. Add flour and baking powder; mix well. Stir in almonds. Shape dough into two 10-inch rolls. Place rolls 4 inches apart on greased cookie sheet; flatten each to 2-inch width.

2. Bake at 350°F. for 20 to 30 minutes or until golden brown. Remove from cookie sheet; place on wire racks. Cool 15 minutes or until completely cooled. With serrated knife, cut rolls diagonally into ½-inch slices. Arrange slices, cut side down, on ungreased cookie sheets.

3. Bake at 350°F. for 6 to 10 minutes or until bottoms begin to brown. Turn cookies over; bake an additional 3 to 5 minutes or until browned and crisp. Remove from cookie sheet; cool 15 minutes or until completely cooled. Store in tightly covered container.

Yield: 40 cookies
High Altitude (Above 3,500 Feet): No change.

> ## Nutrition Information Per Serving
> Serving Size: 1 Cookie. Calories 80 • Calories from Fat 20 • Total Fat 2 g
> Saturated Fat 0 g • Cholesterol 16 mg • Sodium 40 mg • Dietary Fiber 0 g
> Dietary Exchanges: 1 Starch OR 1 Carbohydrate

Recipe Fact

Biscotti cookies (literally "twice cooked," just like the German **zwieback**) are first baked in a log shape, which is then cut into diagonal slices that are baked further until dry and crisp. In their native Italy, biscotti are traditionally dunked into espresso or **vin santo** (sweet wine).

Kitchen Tip

Use a serrated knife when cutting the baked logs to minimize crumbling.

Ingredient Substitution

Hazelnuts, a traditional biscotti ingredient, can stand in for the almonds.

Low-fat Molasses Cookies

Prep Time: 1 hour 15 minutes (Ready in 3 hours 15 minutes)

5 oz. (¾ cup) pitted prunes
⅓ cup hot water
1 cup sugar
¼ cup molasses
1 egg
2¼ cups all-purpose flour

2 teaspoons baking soda
1 teaspoon cinnamon
1 teaspoon ginger
½ teaspoon cloves
¼ teaspoon salt
¼ cup sugar

1. In blender container or food processor bowl with metal blade, combine prunes and hot water. Cover; process 2 to 3 minutes or until pureed. In large bowl, combine prune mixture, 1 cup sugar, molasses and egg; blend well. Add flour, baking soda, cinnamon, ginger, cloves and salt; mix well. Cover with plastic wrap; refrigerate 2 to 3 hours for easier handling.

2. Heat oven to 350°F. Shape dough into 1-inch balls; roll in ¼ cup sugar. Place 2 inches apart on ungreased cookie sheets.

3. Bake at 350°F. for 8 to 12 minutes or until set. Cool 1 minute; remove from cookie sheets.

Yield: 5 dozen cookies
High Altitude (Above 3,500 Feet): Decrease sugar in cookie dough to ¾ cup. Bake as directed above.

Nutrition Information Per Serving
Serving Size: 1 Cookie. Calories 45 • Calories from Fat 0 • Total Fat 0 g
Saturated Fat 0 g • Cholesterol 4 mg • Sodium 50 mg • Dietary Fiber 0 g
Dietary Exchanges: ½ Starch OR ½ Carbohydrate

Recipe Fact

Indulge without guilt. In this recipe, prune puree replaces all the fat, with delicious results. The cookies will soften when stored.

About Prunes

Perhaps the prune deserves a new name— doesn't "dried sweet plums" sound more appealing than "prunes"? Whatever the name, as the plums dry, moisture evaporates, intensifying the natural sweetness of the fruit. Prune puree is a boon to the health-conscious cook, as it can substitute in many recipes for butter and eggs, thus slashing the recipe's fat content.

Chocolate Chip Orange Shortbread

Prep Time: 40 minutes (Ready in 1 hour 40 minutes)

Cookies
1 cup powdered sugar
1 cup butter, softened
1 tablespoon grated orange
   peel
1¾ cups all-purpose flour
¼ cup cornstarch

¾ cup miniature chocolate
   chips

Glaze
½ cup miniature chocolate
   chips
1 teaspoon shortening

1. Heat oven to 325°F. In large bowl, combine powdered sugar and butter; beat until light and fluffy. Add orange peel; blend well. Add flour and cornstarch; mix well. Stir in ¾ cup chocolate chips.

2. Divide dough into 4 parts; shape each into ball. On ungreased cookie sheets, press or roll each ball of dough into a 6-inch round, ¼ inch thick. With knife, score each round into 8 wedges; leave wedges in place.* Prick each wedge 3 times with fork.

3. Bake at 325°F. for 17 to 27 minutes or until edges are light golden brown. Cool 5 minutes. Prick again with fork; cut into wedges. Remove from cookie sheets. Cool 15 minutes or until completely cooled.

4. In small saucepan over low heat, melt ½ cup chocolate chips and shortening, stirring constantly. Dip rounded end of cooled shortbread wedges in melted chocolate; place on waxed paper or wire rack. Let stand until set.

Yield: 32 cookies
High Altitude (Above 3,500 Feet): No change.

*Tip: For smaller cookies, score each round of dough into 12 wedges.

Nutrition Information Per Serving
Serving Size: 1 Cookie. Calories 130 • Calories from Fat 70 • Total Fat 8 g
Saturated Fat 5 g • Cholesterol 16 mg • Sodium 60 mg • Dietary Fiber 1 g
Dietary Exchanges: 1 Fruit, 1½ Fat OR 1 Carbohydrate, 1½ Fat

Recipe Fact

Shortbread bakers often notch the edge of the shortbread round to signify the sun's rays, and prick the top of the dough with a fork before baking.

Recipe Fact

While traditional shortbread recipes call for granulated sugar, this version uses powdered sugar for a finer texture.

Recipe Variation

Make a simple icing of powdered sugar, orange juice and grated orange peel instead of the melted chocolate for dipping the wedges.

Chocolate Chip Orange Shortbread

Lemon Poppy Seed Shortbread

Recipe Fact

Shortbread, like other cookies with a high butter content, does not require greased baking sheets.

Kitchen Tip

To prevent the powdered sugar from clumping while it's being sprinkled onto the cookies, use a small sifter or rub it through a tea strainer with a teaspoon.

Make It Special

For a decorative top, place a paper doily on top of the baked shortbread round and sprinkle over it with the powdered sugar. Carefully lift off the doily to reveal the lacy pattern on the shortbread.

Prep Time: 45 minutes (Ready in 1 hour 10 minutes)

½ cup powdered sugar
¾ cup butter, softened
1 tablespoon poppy seed
1 tablespoon grated lemon peel

1½ cups all-purpose flour
1 teaspoon powdered sugar

1. Heat oven to 325°F. In large bowl, combine ½ cup powdered sugar and butter; beat until light and fluffy. Add poppy seed and lemon peel; blend well. Add flour; mix well.

2. Divide dough into 3 parts; shape each into ball. On ungreased cookie sheets, press or roll each ball of dough into a 5½-inch round. With knife, cut each round into 8 wedges; leave wedges in place. Prick dough several times with fork.

3. Bake at 325°F. for 17 to 22 minutes or until edges are light golden brown. Cool 5 minutes; remove from cookie sheets. Cool 15 minutes or until completely cooled. Break or cut into wedges. Sprinkle with 1 teaspoon powdered sugar.

Yield: 24 cookies
High Altitude (Above 3,500 Feet): Increase flour to 1¾ cups. Bake as directed above.

Nutrition Information Per Serving
Serving Size: 1 Cookie. Calories 90 • Calories from Fat 50 • Total Fat 6 g
Saturated Fat 4 g • Cholesterol 16 mg • Sodium 60 mg • Dietary Fiber 0 g
Dietary Exchanges: ½ Starch, 1 Fat OR ½ Carbohydrate, 1 Fat

Lemon Tea Cookies

Prep Time: 1 hour (Ready in 1 hour 30 minutes)

Cookies
1²⁄₃ cups all-purpose flour
¹⁄₃ cup powdered sugar
1 cup margarine or butter, softened
1 teaspoon vanilla

Filling
1 egg, beaten
²⁄₃ cup sugar

2 to 3 teaspoons grated lemon peel
1 teaspoon cornstarch
¹⁄₄ teaspoon salt
3 tablespoons lemon juice
1 tablespoon margarine or butter
1 to 2 tablespoons powdered sugar or coconut

1. In medium bowl, combine all cookie ingredients; blend well. Cover with plastic wrap; refrigerate 30 minutes for easier handling.

2. Heat oven to 350°F. Shape dough into 1-inch balls. Place 2 inches apart on ungreased cookie sheets. With thumb or handle of wooden spoon, make indentation in center of each cookie.

3. Bake at 350°F. for 8 to 10 minutes or until light golden brown. Immediately remove from cookie sheets. Cool 15 minutes or until completely cooled.

4. Meanwhile, in medium saucepan, combine all filling ingredients except powdered sugar. Cook over low heat until smooth and thickened, stirring constantly. Cool 10 minutes or until slightly cooled. Spoon ¹⁄₄ teaspoon filling into center of each cooled cookie. Sprinkle with 1 to 2 tablespoons powdered sugar.

Yield: 3 dozen cookies
High Altitude (Above 3,500 Feet): No change.

Nutrition Information Per Serving
Serving Size: 1 Cookie. Calories 90 • Calories from Fat 50 • Total Fat 6 g
Saturated Fat 1 g • Cholesterol 6 mg • Sodium 80 mg • Dietary Fiber 0 g
Dietary Exchanges: ¹⁄₂ Starch, 1 Fat OR ¹⁄₂ Carbohydrate, 1 Fat.

Kitchen Tip
To bring out the flavor of the coconut, toast it in a dry frying pan over medium heat or on a tray in the toaster oven until the shreds become golden brown and fragrant.

Kitchen Tip
To keep the lemon filling mixture from curdling, make sure to keep the saucepan over low heat and stir constantly.

Recipe Variation
For Orange Tea Cookies, use orange juice and grated orange in place of the lemon.

Ginger Snaps

Prep Time: 1 hour 15 minutes (Ready in 2 hours 15 minutes)

Recipe Fact

Ginger snaps—crackly topped cookies so named for the crisp texture of the classic version—are, surprisingly, a secret ingredient in many recipes for the German stew sauerbraten.

About Cloves

Unlike most other spices, cloves are not seeds but actually dried flower buds. The pungent flavoring (use it in small amounts) often works hand in hand with cinnamon and nutmeg.

1 cup sugar
$3/4$ cup margarine or butter, softened
$1/4$ cup molasses
1 egg
$2^1/4$ cups all-purpose flour
2 teaspoons baking soda

1 teaspoon cinnamon
$1/2$ teaspoon salt
$1/2$ teaspoon ginger
$1/2$ teaspoon cloves
$1/4$ teaspoon nutmeg
$1/4$ cup sugar

1. In large bowl, combine 1 cup sugar, margarine, molasses and egg; beat until light and fluffy. Add flour, baking soda, cinnamon, salt, ginger, cloves and nutmeg; mix well. Cover with plastic wrap; refrigerate 1 hour for easier handling.

2. Heat oven to 350°F. Shape dough into 1-inch balls; roll in $1/4$ cup sugar. Place 2 inches apart on ungreased cookie sheets.

3. Bake at 350°F. for 8 to 12 minutes or until set. (Cookies will puff up, then flatten during baking.) Cool 1 minute; remove from cookie sheets.

Yield: 5 dozen cookies
High Altitude (Above 3,500 Feet): Decrease baking soda to 1½ teaspoons.
Bake as directed above.

Nutrition Information Per Serving
Serving Size: 1 Cookie. Calories 60 • Calories from Fat 20 • Total Fat 2 g
Saturated Fat 1 g • Cholesterol 4 mg • Sodium 85 mg • Dietary Fiber 0 g
Dietary Exchanges: ½ Starch, ½ Fat OR ½ Carbohydrate, ½ Fat

Ginger Snaps; Crisp Chocolate Snaps, page 84

Crisp Chocolate Snaps

Prep Time: 1 hour 15 minutes (Ready in 2 hours 15 minutes)

Recipe Fact

The red food coloring in this recipe is used to give the cookies the deep red-brown color of a traditional devil's food cake. Omit it, if you wish.

About Baking Chocolate

Most unsweetened baking chocolate comes in a box of eight individually wrapped 1-ounce blocks.

2 cups sugar
1 cup firmly packed brown sugar
1½ cups margarine or butter, softened
6 oz. unsweetened chocolate, melted, cooled
2 teaspoons vanilla

½ teaspoon red food color, if desired
3 eggs
4 cups all-purpose flour
2 teaspoons baking soda
1 teaspoon salt
¼ cup sugar

1. In large bowl, combine 2 cups sugar, brown sugar and margarine; beat until light and fluffy. Add chocolate, vanilla, food color and eggs; blend well. Add flour, baking soda and salt; mix well. Cover with plastic wrap; refrigerate 1 to 2 hours for easier handling.

2. Heat oven to 350°F. Lightly grease cookie sheets. Shape dough into 1½-inch balls; roll in ¼ cup sugar. Place 3 inches apart on greased cookie sheets.

3. Bake at 350°F. for 8 to 12 minutes or until set. (Cookies will puff up, then flatten during baking.) Cool 1 minute; remove from cookie sheets.

Yield: 6 dozen cookies
High Altitude (Above 3,500 Feet): No change.

Nutrition Information Per Serving
Serving Size: 1 Cookie. Calories 110 • Calories from Fat 45 • Total Fat 5 g
Saturated Fat 1 g • Cholesterol 9 mg • Sodium 110 mg • Dietary Fiber 1 g
Dietary Exchanges: 1 Fruit, 1 Fat OR 1 Carbohydrate, 1 Fat

Melt-away Butter Fingers

Prep Time: 45 minutes

2 cups all-purpose flour
½ cup powdered sugar
⅛ teaspoon salt
1 cup butter

1 cup finely chopped walnuts
1 teaspoon vanilla
¼ cup powdered sugar

1. Heat oven to 400°F. In large bowl, combine flour, ½ cup powdered sugar and salt; mix well. With pastry blender or fork, cut in butter until mixture resembles coarse crumbs. Add walnuts and vanilla; mix with hands to form a smooth dough. Using about 1 tablespoon dough for each, shape into 2½-inch finger-shaped cookies. Place on ungreased cookie sheets.
2. Bake at 400°F. for 5 to 7 minutes or until set and light golden brown. Cool 1 minute; remove from cookie sheets. Cool slightly. Carefully roll in ¼ cup powdered sugar.

Yield: 3½ dozen cookies
High Altitude (Above 3,500 Feet): No change.

Nutrition Information Per Serving

Serving Size: 1 Cookie. Calories 90 • Calories from Fat 50 • Total Fat 6 g
Saturated Fat 3 g • Cholesterol 12 mg • Sodium 50 mg • Dietary Fiber 0 g
Dietary Exchanges: ½ Starch, 1 Fat OR ½ Carbohydrate, 1 Fat

Kitchen Tip

These cookies are very delicate when they emerge from the oven. Handle them gingerly when you roll them in the powdered sugar, then let them cool thoroughly before serving.

Kitchen Tip

When chopping the walnuts for this recipe, grind them as finely as possible, using on and off pulses of the blender or food processor to keep them from turning to paste.

Ingredient Substitution

Use almonds instead of the chopped walnuts.

Variation

Chocolate Chip Butterballs: Prepare dough as directed in recipe, substituting 1 cup miniature semi-sweet chocolate chips for walnuts. Shape into 1-inch balls. Place 1 inch apart on ungreased cookie sheets. Bake at 325°F. for 14 to 17 minutes or until set but not brown. DO NOT OVERBAKE. Immediately remove from cookie sheets. Cool slightly. Carefully roll in ¼ cup powdered sugar.

Yield: 3½ dozen cookies

Oatmeal and Candy Cookie Pops

Make It Special

For a kids' party, decorate the pops with faces made of candy corn or gumdrops before baking. Or use frosting in a pastry bag to pipe out alphabet letters or designs such as hearts or stars.

Prep Time: 1 hour 15 minutes (Ready in 2 hours 15 minutes)

³/₄ cup sugar
³/₄ cup firmly packed brown sugar
³/₄ cup margarine or butter, softened
1 teaspoon vanilla
2 eggs
1¹/₂ cups all-purpose flour

1 teaspoon baking soda
¹/₂ teaspoon salt
2 cups quick-cooking rolled oats
1 cup candy-coated chocolate pieces
20 flat wooden sticks with round ends

1. In large bowl, combine sugar, brown sugar and margarine; beat until light and fluffy. Add vanilla and eggs; blend well. Add flour, baking soda and salt; mix well. Stir in oats and chocolate pieces. Cover with plastic wrap; refrigerate at least 1 hour for easier handling.

2. Heat oven to 350°F. Lightly grease cookie sheets. Shape dough into 2-inch balls; insert wooden stick into each ball. Place 4 cookie pops on each greased cookie sheet; flatten dough to ¹/₄-inch thickness. If desired, press additional candy-coated chocolate pieces into top of each cookie.

3. Bake at 350°F. for 8 to 12 minutes or until light golden brown. Cool 2 minutes; remove from cookie sheets.

Yield: 20 cookie pops
High Altitude (Above 3,500 Feet): Increase flour to 2 cups. Bake as directed above.

Nutrition Information Per Serving
Serving Size: 1 Cookie. Calories 240 • Calories from Fat 90 • Total Fat 10 g
Saturated Fat 3 g • Cholesterol 23 mg • Sodium 210 mg • Dietary Fiber 1 g
Dietary Exchanges: 1 Starch, 1 Fruit, 2 Fat OR 2 Carbohydrate, 2 Fat

Maple Date Cookies

Prep Time: 1 hour 15 minutes (Ready in 2 hours)

1 cup firmly packed brown
    sugar
¾ cup margarine or butter,
    softened
½ teaspoon vanilla
½ teaspoon maple extract
1 egg

1½ cups all-purpose flour
¾ teaspoon baking powder
¾ teaspoon baking soda
¼ teaspoon salt
1 cup finely chopped dates
½ cup chopped walnuts or
    pecans

1. In large bowl, combine brown sugar and margarine; beat until light and fluffy. Add vanilla, maple extract and egg; blend well. Add flour, baking powder, baking soda and salt; mix well. Stir in dates and walnuts. Cover with plastic wrap; refrigerate 30 minutes for easier handling.
2. Heat oven to 350°F. Shape dough into 1-inch balls. Place 2 inches apart on ungreased cookie sheets.
3. Bake at 350°F. for 9 to 12 minutes or until light golden brown. Cool 1 minute; remove from cookie sheets.

Yield: 5 dozen cookies
High Altitude (Above 3,500 Feet): Increase flour to 2 cups. Bake as directed above.

Nutrition Information Per Serving

Serving Size: 1 Cookie. Calories 60 • Calories from Fat 25 • Total Fat 3 g
Saturated Fat 1 g • Cholesterol 4 mg • Sodium 60 mg • Dietary Fiber 0 g
Dietary Exchanges: ½ Starch, ½ Fat OR ½ Carbohydrate, ½ Fat

About Maple

Long before the Pilgrims arrived in New England, Native Americans tapped maple trees to extract the thin, sweet sap, which was then boiled down to make syrup. Maple flavoring has a particular affinity for dates and nuts.

Recipe Variation

For rum date cookies, substitute ½ teaspoon of rum extract for the maple flavoring.

Peanut Butter Cookies

Prep Time: 45 minutes

$\frac{1}{2}$ cup sugar
$\frac{1}{2}$ cup firmly packed brown sugar
$\frac{1}{2}$ cup margarine or butter, softened
$\frac{1}{2}$ cup peanut butter

1 teaspoon vanilla
1 egg
$1\frac{1}{4}$ cups all-purpose flour
1 teaspoon baking soda
$\frac{1}{2}$ teaspoon salt
4 teaspoons sugar

1. Heat oven to 375°F. In large bowl, combine $\frac{1}{2}$ cup sugar, brown sugar and margarine; beat until light and fluffy. Add peanut butter, vanilla and egg; blend well. Add flour, baking soda and salt; mix well. Shape dough into 1-inch balls. Place 2 inches apart on ungreased cookie sheets. With fork dipped in sugar, flatten balls in criss-cross pattern.
2. Bake at 375°F. for 6 to 9 minutes or until set and golden brown. Immediately remove from cookie sheets.

Yield: 4 dozen cookies
High Altitude (Above 3,500 Feet): Increase flour to $1\frac{1}{2}$ cups. Bake as directed above.

Nutrition Information Per Serving
Serving Size: 1 Cookie. Calories 60 • Calories from Fat 25 • Total Fat 3 g
Saturated Fat 1 g • Cholesterol 4 mg • Sodium 85 mg • Dietary Fiber 0 g
Dietary Exchanges: $\frac{1}{2}$ Starch, $\frac{1}{2}$ Fat OR $\frac{1}{2}$ Carbohydrate, $\frac{1}{2}$ Fat

Variations

Chocolate Chip Peanut Butter Cookies: Prepare dough as directed in recipe. Stir in 1 (6-oz.) pkg. (1 cup) semi-sweet chocolate chips.

Yield: $4\frac{1}{2}$ dozen cookies

Chocolate Peanut Butter Crunch Bars: Prepare dough as directed in recipe, omitting 4 teaspoons sugar. Stir in $\frac{1}{2}$ cup crisp rice cereal. Press dough in ungreased $15 \times 10 \times 1$-inch baking pan. Bake at 350°F. for 12 to 17 minutes or until golden brown. Cool 15 minutes. In medium saucepan over low heat, melt 1 (6-oz.) pkg. (1 cup) semi-sweet chocolate chips and ½ cup peanut butter. Stir in 1½ cups crisp rice cereal. Spoon mixture evenly over slightly cooled bars; spread gently. Cool completely. Cut into bars.

Yield: 48 bars

Giant Peanut Butter Candy Cookies:

Prepare dough as directed in recipe, omitting 4 teaspoons sugar. Stir in 1 cup candy-coated chocolate pieces. Using ¼ cup dough per cookie, place cookies 4 inches apart on ungreased cookie sheets. Flatten to 4-inch diameter. Bake at 350°F. for 8 to 12 minutes or until golden brown. Cool 1 minute; remove from cookie sheets.

Yield: 14 cookies

Nutty Peanut Butter Cookies:

Prepare dough as directed in recipe. Stir in 1 cup chopped peanuts.

Yield: 4½ dozen cookies

Peanut Butter Cookies with variations

Oatmeal Peanut Butter Cookies: Prepare dough as directed in recipe, decreasing flour to ¾ cup and adding ¾ cup rolled oats. Cover dough with plastic wrap; refrigerate 2 hours for easier handling. Shape and flatten balls as directed. Bake at 375°F. for 6 to 10 minutes or until golden brown. Immediately remove from cookie sheets.

Yield: 4 dozen cookies

Peanut Blossoms: Prepare dough and shape into balls as directed in recipe. Increase 4 teaspoons sugar to ¼ cup; roll balls in sugar. Place 1 inch apart on ungreased cookie sheets. Bake as directed. Immediately top each cookie with a milk chocolate candy kiss, pressing down firmly so cookie cracks around edge. Remove from cookie sheets.

Yield: 3½ dozen cookies

Peanut Butter and Jelly Thumbprints: Prepare dough and shape into balls as directed in recipe. Increase 4 teaspoons sugar to ¼ cup; roll balls in sugar. Place 1 inch apart on ungreased cookie sheets. With thumb or handle of wooden spoon, make deep indentation in center of each cookie. Bake as directed; cool completely. Spoon ½ teaspoon jelly, jam or preserves into center of each cookie.

Yield: 4 dozen cookies

Peanut Butter Brickle Cookies: Prepare dough as directed in recipe. Stir in 1 cup peanut butter chips and ⅔ cup almond brickle baking chips.

Yield: 5 dozen cookies

Peanut Butter Raisin Cookie Pops: Prepare dough as directed in recipe. Stir in 1 cup chocolate-covered raisins. Shape dough into 1½-inch balls. Place 4 cookies on each ungreased cookie sheet. With fork dipped in sugar, flatten balls in crisscross pattern. Insert wooden stick into each cookie. Bake at 350°F. for 7 to 12 minutes or until golden brown. Cool 1 minute; remove from cookie sheets.

Yield: 22 cookie pops

Triple Chocolate Strip Cookies

Prep Time: 1 hour 30 minutes

editor's favorite • chocoholic's choice

Cookies
2 cups all-purpose flour
$\frac{1}{2}$ cup unsweetened cocoa
$\frac{1}{2}$ teaspoon baking soda
$\frac{1}{4}$ teaspoon salt
$\frac{3}{4}$ cup sugar
$\frac{1}{2}$ cup firmly packed brown sugar
$\frac{3}{4}$ cup butter, softened
2 eggs
1 (12-oz.) pkg. (2 cups) semi-sweet chocolate chips

White Chocolate Glaze
2 oz. white chocolate baking bar or vanilla-flavored candy coating

Dark Chocolate Glaze
2 oz. semi-sweet chocolate, cut into pieces
$\frac{1}{2}$ teaspoon butter

Recipe Fact

Like traditional biscotti, these cookies bake in a log; unlike their Italian cousins, however, they do not require a second baking after they are cut into strips.

Make It Special

Sprinkle the icing with miniature semi-sweet chocolate chips or multi-colored sprinkles.

1. Heat oven to 350°F. Lightly grease 2 cookie sheets. In medium bowl, combine flour, cocoa, baking soda and salt; mix well. In large bowl, combine sugar, brown sugar and $\frac{3}{4}$ cup butter; beat until light and fluffy. Add eggs; blend well. Stir in flour mixture; mix well. Stir in chocolate chips. Divide dough into 4 equal parts; shape each into 12-inch roll. Place 2 rolls 2 inches apart on each greased cookie sheet.

2. Bake at 350°F. for 14 to 18 minutes or until toothpick inserted in center of each roll comes out almost clean. Remove from cookie sheets; cool.

3. In small saucepan over low heat, melt baking bar. Drizzle over 2 rolls. In same saucepan, melt semi-sweet chocolate and $\frac{1}{2}$ teaspoon butter. Drizzle over remaining 2 rolls. Cut rolls into 1-inch strips.

Yield: 4 dozen cookies
High Altitude (Above 3,500 Feet): No change.

Nutrition Information Per Serving
Serving Size: 1 Cookie. Calories 120 • Calories from Fat 50 • Total Fat 6 g
Saturated Fat 4 g • Cholesterol 15 mg • Sodium 60 mg • Dietary Fiber 1 g
Dietary Exchanges: 1 Starch, 1 Fat OR 1 Carbohydrate, 1 Fat

Refriger

ator Cookies

Refrigerator cookies offer ready-to-slice convenience with homemade flavor. The cookie dough is mixed in advance and chilled, then sliced as needed for baking. This offers a perfect solution for days when there's not enough time to complete the entire operation—you can mix one day and bake the next.

Refrigerator Cookie dough is made ahead and refrigerated until it's ready to be used. Mold it into 2-inch logs and wrap them in plastic wrap or waxed paper. Twist the ends of the wrap tightly to secure each log. Depending on the softness of the dough, shaping and wrapping may be easier if you chill the dough for an hour or so in the mixing bowl first to prevent the dough from sticking to the wrapper. You can refrigerate the rolls for up to two weeks. For longer storage, pop the rolls into a labeled self-sealing freezer bag and freeze for up to six weeks.

At baking time, unwrap the roll and slice it with a thin, sharp knife, rotating the roll after every couple of slices to keep it from flattening.

Storing the dough also offers an advantage if you should—but just can't—resist overindulging in oven-fresh cookies. Bake and enjoy a few cookies every day, rather than facing the temptation of dozens at once. Save energy by using the toaster oven tray to bake a mini-batch.

Previous page: Shortbread Triangles, page 97; Pinwheel Date Cookies, page 95

Pinwheel Date Cookies

Prep Time: 1 hour (Ready in 4 hours)

Cookies

1 cup firmly packed brown
    sugar
$\frac{1}{2}$ cup margarine or butter,
    softened
1 egg
$1\frac{1}{2}$ cups all-purpose flour
$1\frac{1}{2}$ teaspoons baking powder

$\frac{1}{4}$ teaspoon salt

Filling

$\frac{3}{4}$ cup finely chopped dates
$\frac{1}{4}$ cup sugar
$\frac{1}{3}$ cup water
2 tablespoons finely chopped
    nuts

1. In large bowl, combine brown sugar, margarine and egg; beat until light and fluffy. Add flour, baking powder and salt; mix at low speed until dough forms. Cover with plastic wrap; refrigerate 1 hour for easier handling.

2. Meanwhile, in small saucepan, combine dates, sugar and water. Bring to a boil. Reduce heat to low; cover and simmer 5 minutes or until thick. Stir in nuts. Cool 15 minutes.

3. On lightly floured surface, roll dough into 16 × 8 inch rectangle. Carefully spread with date filling. Starting with 16-inch side, roll up jelly-roll fashion; cut in half to form two 8-inch rolls. Wrap each roll in plastic wrap; refrigerate 2 hours or until firm.

4. Heat oven to 375°F. Cut dough into $\frac{1}{4}$-inch slices. Place slices 2 inches apart on ungreased cookie sheets.

5. Bake at 375°F. for 6 to 9 minutes or until light golden brown. Immediately remove from cookie sheets.

Yield: 5 dozen cookies
High Altitude (Above 3,500 Feet): Increase flour to $1\frac{1}{2}$ cups plus 2 tablespoons.
Bake as directed above.

Nutrition Information Per Serving

Serving Size: 1 Cookie. Calories 60 • Calories from Fat 20 • Total Fat 2 g
Saturated Fat 0 g • Cholesterol 4 mg • Sodium 40 mg • Dietary Fiber 0 g
Dietary Exchanges: $\frac{1}{2}$ Starch, $\frac{1}{2}$ Fat OR $\frac{1}{2}$ Carbohydrate, $\frac{1}{2}$ Fat

Ingredient Substitution

You may use raisins or dried apricots in place of the dates.

Recipe Variation

To make Orange-Spice Pinwheel Date Cookies, add $\frac{1}{2}$ teaspoon of grated orange peel and 1 teaspoon cinnamon to the cookie dough.

Basic Refrigerator Cookies

Prep Time: 1 hour (Ready in 3 hours)

3/4 cup sugar
3/4 cup firmly packed brown sugar
1 cup margarine or butter, softened
1 1/2 teaspoons vanilla

2 eggs
3 cups all-purpose flour
1 1/2 teaspoons baking powder
3/4 teaspoon salt
1 cup finely chopped nuts

1. In large bowl, combine sugar, brown sugar, margarine, vanilla and eggs; beat well. Add flour, baking powder and salt; blend well. Stir in nuts. Divide dough into 3 equal parts. Shape each into roll 1½ inches in diameter. Wrap each roll in plastic wrap; refrigerate 2 hours or until firm.

2. Heat oven to 425°F. Cut dough into ¼-inch slices. Place slices 1 inch apart on ungreased cookie sheets.

3. Bake at 425°F. for 5 to 7 minutes or until light golden brown. Immediately remove from cookie sheets.

Yield: 7½ dozen cookies
High Altitude (Above 3,500 Feet): Add 3 tablespoons milk to sugar mixture. Bake as directed above.

Nutrition Information Per Serving
Serving Size: 1 Cookie. Calories 60 • Calories from Fat 25 • Total Fat 3 g
Saturated Fat 0 g • Cholesterol 5 mg • Sodium 50 mg • Dietary Fiber 0 g
Dietary Exchanges: ½ Starch, ½ Fat OR ½ Carbohydrate, ½ Fat

Variations

Orange Refrigerator Cookies: Prepare dough as directed in recipe, adding 1 tablespoon grated orange peel with flour.

Yield: 7½ dozen cookies

Lemon Refrigerator Cookies: Prepare dough as directed in recipe, adding 1 tablespoon grated lemon peel with flour.

Yield: 7½ dozen cookies

Spice Refrigerator Cookies: Prepare dough as directed in recipe, adding 1 teaspoon cinnamon, ½ teaspoon nutmeg and ¼ to ½ teaspoon cloves with flour.

Yield: 7½ dozen cookies

Coconut Refrigerator Cookies: Prepare dough as directed in recipe, adding 1 cup coconut with nuts.

Yield: 7½ dozen cookies

Shortbread Triangles

Prep Time: 1 hour (Ready in 3 hours)

1 cup powdered sugar	**2 cups all-purpose flour**
1 cup butter, softened	**½ cup cornstarch**
1 egg yolk	

1. In large bowl, combine powdered sugar and butter; beat until light and fluffy. Add egg yolk; blend well. Add flour and cornstarch; mix well.

2. Divide dough in half; shape each half into roll 12 inches long. Wrap in plastic wrap. Press sides of roll with palm of hand to make 3 even sides, forming triangular shape. Press roll against countertop to smooth and flatten sides. Refrigerate 2 hours or until firm.

3. Heat oven to 350°F. Cut dough into ¼-inch slices. Place slices on ungreased cookie sheets. If desired, sprinkle lightly with sugar.

4. Bake at 350°F. for 8 to 13 minutes or until set and light golden brown. Prick tops of cookies with fork; remove from cookie sheets.

Yield: 4 dozen cookies
High Altitude (Above 3,500 Feet): No change.

Nutrition Information Per Serving

Serving Size: 1 Cookie. Calories 70 • Calories from Fat 35 • Total Fat 4 g
Saturated Fat 2 g • Cholesterol 15 mg • Sodium 40 mg • Dietary Fiber 0 g
Dietary Exchanges: ½ Fruit, 1 Fat OR ½ Carbohydrate, 1 Fat

Recipe Fact

One traditional method of making shortbread cookies is to press the dough into a decoratively carved, shallow earthenware mold, then cut the round into wedges after baking. In this updated version, you skip to the finish by shaping the dough into a three-sided log, chilling and slicing into individual triangles.

Make It Special

Outline the triangle shape with piped chocolate icing after the cookies have cooled.

Butterscotch Freeze 'n Slice Cookies

Recipe Fact

The term "butterscotch" loosely covers a wide range of sweets made with butter and a dark sweetener such as brown sugar, molasses or dark corn syrup. The term runs the gamut from hard candy to intensely sweet ice cream sauce and blond "brownies."

Kitchen Tip

Use a sharp, thin-bladed knife to slice the dough rolls.

Prep Time: 1 hour 15 minutes (Ready in 3 hours 15 minutes)

1 cup sugar
1 cup firmly packed brown sugar
1½ cups margarine or butter, softened
3 eggs

4½ cups all-purpose flour
2 teaspoons baking powder
1 teaspoon baking soda
1 teaspoon cinnamon
½ teaspoon salt

1. Line two 8 × 4-inch loaf pans with foil, allowing foil to extend above sides of pans. In large bowl, combine sugar, brown sugar and margarine; beat until light and fluffy. Add eggs; blend well. Add flour, baking powder, baking soda, cinnamon and salt; mix well. Press half of dough into each foil-lined pan.* Fold foil over dough to seal; freeze 2 to 3 hours or until well chilled.

2. Heat oven to 350°F. Lightly grease cookie sheets. Unfold foil; lift dough from pans. Remove foil; cut dough into ¼-inch slices. Place slices 2 inches apart on greased cookie sheets.

3. Bake at 350°F. for 8 to 12 minutes or until light golden brown. Cool 1 minute; remove from cookie sheets.

Yield: 5 dozen cookies
High Altitude (Above 3,500 Feet): Decrease granulated sugar to ¾ cup.
Bake as directed above.

*Tip: Pans can be omitted; shape dough into two 8 × 4 × 2-inch rectangles. Wrap tightly in foil; freeze. Bake as directed above.

Nutrition Information Per Serving

Serving Size: 1 Cookie. Calories 90 • Calories from Fat 25 • Total Fat 3 g
Saturated Fat 1 g • Cholesterol 11 mg • Sodium 80 mg • Dietary Fiber 0 g
Dietary Exchanges: 1 Fruit, ½ Fat OR 1 Carbohydrate, ½ Fat

Butterscotch Freeze 'n Slice Cookies

Peppermint Swirl Refrigerator Cookies

Prep Time: 1 hour 30 minutes (Ready in 10 hours 30 minutes)

1 cup sugar
1 cup margarine or butter, softened
2 tablespoons milk
1 teaspoon vanilla
1 egg

3 cups all-purpose flour
$\frac{1}{2}$ teaspoon baking soda
$\frac{1}{4}$ teaspoon salt
$\frac{1}{2}$ teaspoon peppermint extract
4 to 5 drops red food color
$\frac{1}{4}$ cup pink decorator sugar

1. In large bowl, combine sugar, margarine, milk, vanilla and egg; beat until light and fluffy. In medium bowl, combine flour, baking soda and salt; mix well. Add flour mixture to sugar mixture; blend well.

2. Place half of dough in plastic bag or wrap in plastic wrap. To remaining half of dough, add peppermint extract and red food color; mix well. Place in plastic bag or wrap. Refrigerate both portions of dough 1 hour.

3. Divide each portion of dough in half. Place 1 part white dough between 2 pieces of plastic wrap; roll into 10 × 8-inch rectangle. Repeat with 1 part pink dough. Remove top sheets of plastic wrap from white and pink dough. Place pink dough over white dough; remove plastic wrap from pink dough. Trim edges, if desired. Starting at 10-inch edge, roll up dough jelly-roll fashion, removing plastic wrap from bottom as dough is rolled. Repeat with remaining dough to form second roll.

4. Place 2 tablespoons of the pink sugar on separate sheet of plastic wrap. Roll 1 roll of dough in pink sugar, pressing gently into dough. Repeat with second roll. Wrap rolls in plastic wrap; refrigerate 8 hours or until firm.

5. Heat oven to 375°F. Cut dough into $\frac{1}{8}$-inch slices. Place slices 1 inch apart on ungreased cookie sheets.

Recipe Variation

For Orange Swirl Refrigerator Cookies, substitute orange extract and red and yellow food color for the peppermint flavoring and pink color.

Make It Special

To make heart-shaped cookies, omit rolling the dough in the pink sugar and instead gently mold the log into a heart shape after rolling the pink and white doughs together; cut into slices to make individual Valentine Cookies.

6. Bake at 375°F. for 5 to 7 minutes or until light golden brown. Cool 1 minute; remove from cookie sheets.

Yield: 10 dozen cookies
High Altitude (Above 3,500 Feet): No change.

Nutrition Information Per Serving
Serving Size: 1 Cookie. Calories 35 • Calories from Fat 20 • Total Fat 2 g
Saturated Fat 0 g • Cholesterol 2 mg • Sodium 30 mg • Dietary Fiber 0 g
Dietary Exchanges: ½ Fat

Chocolate-Nut Wafers

Prep Time: 1 hour (Ready in 4 hours)

1 cup sugar
¾ cup margarine or butter, softened
2 oz. unsweetened chocolate, melted
1 teaspoon vanilla

1 egg
2¼ cups all-purpose flour
¼ teaspoon salt
¼ teaspoon baking soda
¼ teaspoon cinnamon
½ cup chopped nuts

1. In large bowl, combine sugar, margarine, chocolate, vanilla and egg; blend well. Add all remaining ingredients; blend well. Divide dough in half. Shape each half into roll 2 inches in diameter. Wrap each roll in plastic wrap; refrigerate 3 hours or until firm.
2. Heat oven to 400°F. Cut dough into ¼-inch slices. Place 2 inches apart on ungreased cookie sheets.
3. Bake at 400°F. for 6 to 8 minutes or until set. DO NOT OVERBAKE. Immediately remove from cookie sheets.

Yield: 6 dozen cookies
High Altitude (Above 3,500 Feet): No change.

Nutrition Information Per Serving
Serving Size: 1 Cookie. Calories 50 • Calories from Fat 25 • Total Fat 3 g
Saturated Fat 1 g • Cholesterol 3 mg • Sodium 35 mg • Dietary Fiber 0 g
Dietary Exchanges: ½ Fruit, ½ Fat OR ½ Carbohydrate, ½ Fat

Kitchen Tip

Cool the chocolate slightly before adding to the other ingredients.

Make It Special

Press a nut half (of the same variety used in the dough) into the top of each cookie before baking.

Cranberry and Orange Pinwheels

Prep Time: 1 hour (Ready in 4 hours)

editor's favorite

Filling
1 tablespoon cornstarch
¾ cup whole berry cranberry
   sauce
¼ cup orange marmalade

Cookies
¾ cup firmly packed brown
   sugar

½ cup margarine or butter,
   softened
1 egg
1¾ cups all-purpose flour
1 teaspoon baking powder
1 teaspoon grated orange peel
¼ teaspoon salt
¼ teaspoon allspice

1. In small saucepan, combine all filling ingredients. Bring to a boil over medium heat, stirring constantly. Refrigerate 1 hour or until thoroughly chilled.

2. Meanwhile, in large bowl, combine brown sugar, margarine and egg; beat until light and fluffy. Add all remaining cookie ingredients; mix well. Cover with plastic wrap; refrigerate 1 hour for easier handling.

3. On lightly floured surface, roll dough into 16 × 8-inch rectangle. Spoon and spread cooled filling evenly over dough to within ½ inch of edges. Starting with 16-inch side, roll up jelly-roll fashion; cut in half to form two 8-inch rolls. Wrap each roll in plastic wrap or waxed paper; freeze 2 hours or until firm.

4. Heat oven to 375°F. Generously grease cookie sheets. Using sharp knife, cut dough into ½-inch slices. Place slices 2 inches apart on greased cookie sheets.

5. Bake at 375°F. for 9 to 13 minutes or until light golden brown. Immediately remove from cookie sheets.

Yield: 3 dozen cookies
High Altitude (Above 3,500 Feet): Increase flour to 2 cups. Bake as directed above.

Nutrition Information Per Serving
Serving Size: 1 Cookie. Calories 80 • Calories from Fat 25 • Total Fat 3 g
Saturated Fat 1 g • Cholesterol 5 mg • Sodium 65 mg • Dietary Fiber 0 g
Dietary Exchanges: 1 Fruit, ½ Fat OR 1 Carbohydrate, ½ Fat

About Orange Marmalade

Orange marmalade is made with the flesh and rind of bitter oranges, the most famous of which hail from Seville, Spain.

Kitchen Tip

To keep the cookies uniformly round, give the roll of dough a quarter turn after every three or four slices.

Storage Tip

This dough can be prepared, shaped, wrapped in plastic and refrigerated for two weeks before slicing and baking. Or freeze it for up to six weeks.

Cranberry and Orange Pinwheels;
Granola Apple Cookies, page 52

About Nutmeg

Nutmeg, widely grown in the Caribbean, yields two spices: Mace comes from the delicate, lacy outer covering; nutmeg, from the inner nut.

Kitchen Tip

For freshest nutmeg flavor, purchase the spice whole. Just before using, grind it with a fine-hole grater or a miniature grater specially designed for nutmeg.

Crisp and Chewy Molasses Cookies

Prep Time: 45 minutes (Ready in 6 hours 45 minutes)

³/₄ cup sugar	1¹/₂ teaspoons baking soda
¹/₂ cup margarine or butter, softened	¹/₂ teaspoon cinnamon
¹/₂ cup molasses	¹/₄ teaspoon cloves
1 egg	¹/₄ teaspoon nutmeg
2 cups all-purpose flour	¹/₄ teaspoon ginger

1. In large bowl, combine sugar and margarine; beat until light and fluffy. Add molasses and egg; blend well. Add all remaining ingredients; mix well. Cover with plastic wrap; refrigerate 30 minutes for easier handling.
2. On waxed paper, shape dough into roll 9 inches long. Wrap roll in waxed paper or plastic wrap; refrigerate 6 hours or until firm.
3. Heat oven to 375°F. Cut dough into ¹/₂-inch slices; cut each slice into quarters. Place slices 2 inches apart on ungreased cookie sheets.
4. Bake at 375°F. for 6 to 10 minutes or until set. Immediately remove from cookie sheets.

Yield: 6 dozen cookies
High Altitude (Above 3,500 Feet): Decrease sugar to ¹/₂ cup; decrease molasses to ¹/₄ cup. Bake as directed above.

Nutrition Information Per Serving
Serving Size: 1 Cookie. Calories 35 • Calories from Fat 10 • Total Fat 1 g
Saturated Fat 0 g • Cholesterol 3 mg • Sodium 45 mg • Dietary Fiber 0 g
Dietary Exchanges: ¹/₂ Starch OR ¹/₂ Carbohydrate

Oatmeal Refrigerator Cookies

Prep Time: 1 hour 15 minutes (Ready in 3 hours 15 minutes)

1 cup sugar

1 cup firmly packed brown sugar

1 cup margarine or butter, softened

2 eggs

2 cups all-purpose flour

1 teaspoon baking powder

1 teaspoon baking soda

1 teaspoon salt

2 cups quick-cooking rolled oats

1 cup coconut

½ to 1 cup chopped nuts

1. In large bowl, combine sugar, brown sugar, margarine and eggs; beat well. Add flour, baking powder, baking soda and salt; mix well. Stir in oats, coconut and nuts. Divide dough in half. Shape each half into roll 2 inches in diameter; wrap in plastic wrap. Refrigerate 2 hours or until firm.

2. Heat oven to 375°F. Cut dough into ¼-inch slices. Place slices 2 inches apart on ungreased cookie sheets.

3. Bake at 375°F. for 8 to 11 minutes or until golden brown. Immediately remove from cookie sheets.

Yield: 6 dozen cookies
High Altitude (Above 3,500 Feet): No change.

Nutrition Information Per Serving

Serving Size: 1 Cookie. Calories 80 • Calories from Fat 35 • Total Fat 4 g
Saturated Fat 1 g • Cholesterol 5 mg • Sodium 90 mg • Dietary Fiber 0 g
Dietary Exchanges: ½ Fruit, 1 Fat OR ½ Carbohydrate, 1 Fat

Ingredient Substitution

Use chocolate chips or candy-coated chocolate pieces instead of the nuts.

Nut-edged Lemon Cookie Slices

Take advantage of your food processor's muscle to grate lemon peel for this recipe. Remove the thin, colored layer of the lemon rind with a sharp vegetable peeler or paring knife. Process the strips with the recipe's ½ cup sugar until finely grated.

Make It Special

Decorate the baked cookies with polka dots or drizzles of lemon icing. A simple recipe: 1¼ cups powdered sugar, 5 teaspoons lemon juice and 1 drop yellow food coloring, if desired.

Prep Time: 1 hour 10 minutes (Ready in 2 hours 10 minutes)

½ cup sugar
¾ cup firmly packed brown sugar
1 cup margarine or butter, softened
1½ teaspoons vanilla
1 egg
1 egg, separated

3 cups all-purpose flour
1 tablespoon grated lemon peel
1½ teaspoons baking powder
¾ teaspoon salt
¾ cup finely chopped nuts
¼ cup sugar

1. In large bowl, combine ½ cup sugar, brown sugar, margarine, vanilla, egg and egg yolk; beat well. (Refrigerate remaining egg white.) Add flour, lemon peel, baking powder and salt; mix well. Divide dough into 3 equal parts on 3 sheets of waxed paper. Shape each into roll 1½ inches in diameter. Wrap; refrigerate 1 hour or until firm.

2. Heat oven to 400°F. Lightly grease cookie sheets. In small bowl, combine nuts and ¼ cup sugar. Slightly beat egg white. Brush chilled dough with egg white; roll in nut mixture, pressing nuts firmly into dough. Cut dough into ¼-inch slices. Place slices 1 inch apart on greased cookie sheets.

3. Bake at 400°F. for 5 to 7 minutes or until light golden brown. Immediately remove from cookie sheets.

Yield: 7 dozen cookies
High Altitude (Above 3,500 Feet): No change.

Tip: Cookie dough can be stored in refrigerator for up to 2 weeks or in freezer for up to 6 weeks. Slice and bake frozen dough as directed above.

Nutrition Information Per Serving
Serving Size: 1 Cookie. Calories 60 • Calories from Fat 25 • Total Fat 3 g
Saturated Fat 1 g • Cholesterol 5 mg • Sodium 55 mg • Dietary Fiber 0 g
Dietary Exchanges: ½ Starch, ½ Fat OR ½ Carbohydrate, ½ Fat

Nut-edged Lemon Cookie Slices

kid
pleaser

Slice 'n Bake Peanut Butter Cookies

About Wheat Germ

Wheat germ, the inner-most kernel of the grain, adds crunchy texture and nutty flavor to baked goods. Store it in the refrigerator, because its high oil content makes it prone to quicker spoilage at room temperature.

1$\frac{3}{4}$ cups firmly packed brown sugar
1 cup peanut butter
$\frac{3}{4}$ cup margarine or butter, softened
1 teaspoon vanilla
2 eggs

2 cups all-purpose flour
1 teaspoon baking powder
$\frac{1}{2}$ teaspoon baking soda
$\frac{1}{2}$ teaspoon salt
1 cup coconut
$\frac{3}{4}$ cup wheat germ
$\frac{1}{2}$ cup rolled oats

1. In large bowl, combine brown sugar, peanut butter and margarine; beat until light and fluffy. Add vanilla and eggs; blend well. Add flour, baking powder, baking soda and salt; mix well. Stir in coconut, wheat germ and oats. Divide dough in half. On waxed paper, shape each half into 2 × 1½-inch rectangular rolls. Wrap; freeze 8 hours or until firm.
2. Heat oven to 375°F. Cut dough into ¼-inch slices. Place slices 1 inch apart on ungreased cookie sheets.
3. Bake at 375°F. for 8 to 10 minutes or until edges are light golden brown. Cool 1 minute; remove from cookie sheets.

Yield: 5 dozen cookies
High Altitude (Above 3,500 Feet): No change.

Tip: Cookie dough can be stored in refrigerator for up to 2 weeks or in freezer for up to 6 weeks. Slice and bake frozen dough as directed above.

Nutrition Information Per Serving
Serving Size: 1 Cookie. Calories 90 • Calories from Fat 45 • Total Fat 5 g
Saturated Fat 1 g • Cholesterol 5 mg • Sodium 100 mg • Dietary Fiber 1 g
Dietary Exchanges: ½ Starch, 1 Fat OR ½ Carbohydrate, 1 Fat

Spiced Whole Wheat Refrigerator Cookies

Prep Time: 45 minutes (Ready in 2 hours 45 minutes)

½ cup sugar
½ cup firmly packed brown sugar
½ cup margarine or butter, softened
2 tablespoons water
2 teaspoons vanilla
1 egg

1¾ cups whole wheat flour
1 teaspoon baking powder
1 teaspoon cinnamon
½ teaspoon baking soda
¼ teaspoon salt
¼ teaspoon cloves
½ cup finely chopped pecans or walnuts

1. In large bowl, combine sugar, brown sugar and margarine; beat until light and fluffy. Add water, vanilla and egg; blend well. Add flour, baking powder, cinnamon, baking soda, salt and cloves; mix well. Stir in pecans. Shape dough into two 6-inch rolls. Wrap each roll in plastic wrap; refrigerate 2 hours or until firm.

2. Heat oven to 375°F. Cut dough into ¼-inch slices. Place slices 2 inches apart on ungreased cookie sheets.

3. Bake at 375°F. for 6 to 8 minutes or until set. Cool 1 minute; remove from cookie sheets.

Yield: 3½ dozen cookies
High Altitude (Above 3,500 Feet): Decrease sugar and brown sugar to ⅓ cup each. Increase flour to 2 cups. Bake as directed above.

Nutrition Information Per Serving

Serving Size: 1 Cookie. Calories 70 • Calories from Fat 25 • Total Fat 3 g
Saturated Fat 1 g • Cholesterol 5 mg • Sodium 70 mg • Dietary Fiber 1 g
Dietary Exchanges: ½ Starch, ½ Fat OR ½ Carbohydrate, ½ Fat

Recipe Fact

Because of their firm, chewy texture, these traditional icebox cookies are ideal for mailing. Pack the cookies snugly in rows in a firm box or metal container. If necessary, cushion the cookies with crumpled waxed paper.

About Whole Wheat

Whole wheat flour is milled from the entire wheat kernel, so it has more fiber than all-purpose flour. The fiber interferes with the flour's gluten (the elastic substance that helps bread dough to stretch under the influence of yeast), which means that bread made entirely with whole wheat flour tends to be heavier and denser. For cookies, however, you can usually substitute whole wheat flour for all-purpose to good effect. The resulting cookies will be slightly heartier and more nutty-tasting.

Rum Cherry Slices

Prep Time: 1 hour (Ready in 9 hours)

1½ cups sugar
1 cup margarine or butter, softened
1 teaspoon vanilla
1 egg
2½ cups all-purpose flour
1½ teaspoons baking powder

½ teaspoon salt
½ cup finely chopped maraschino cherries, well drained
1 teaspoon rum extract
½ cup finely chopped raisins

1. Line 9 × 5-inch loaf pan with waxed paper. In large bowl, combine sugar and margarine; beat until light and fluffy. Add vanilla and egg; blend well. Add flour, baking powder and salt; mix well.

2. Place ⅓ of dough in medium bowl; stir in cherries. Set aside. Stir rum extract and raisins into remaining ⅔ of dough. Divide in half; spread half in bottom of paper-lined pan. Cover evenly with cherry dough; top with remaining rum-raisin dough. Cover with waxed paper or plastic wrap; refrigerate 8 hours or until firm.

3. Heat oven to 375°F. Remove dough from pan; cut into thirds lengthwise. Cut dough into ¼-inch slices. Place slices 1 inch apart on ungreased cookie sheets.

4. Bake at 375°F. for 4 to 6 minutes or until edges are light golden brown.

Yield: 9 dozen cookies
High Altitude (Above 3,500 Feet): Increase flour to 2½ cups plus 2 tablespoons. Bake as directed above.

Nutrition Information Per Serving
Serving Size: 1 Cookie. Calories 40 • Calories from Fat 20 • Total Fat 2 g
Saturated Fat 0 g • Cholesterol 0 mg • Sodium 35 mg • Dietary Fiber 0 g
Dietary Exchanges: ½ Starch OR ½ Carbohydrate

Rum Cherry Slices

R

olled Cookies

A whole host of delicious cookie recipes rely on doughs that are flattened with a rolling pin and cut into shapes. Textures vary from meltingly crisp to cookie jar chewy, and styles range from simple diamonds quickly scored with a knife to fancy forms made with special cutters.

Rolled Cookies

generally start with a dough that must be chilled first to make handling easier. Remove from the refrigerator only as much dough as can be rolled out, and keep the rest chilled until you're ready for it. Lightly flour the work surface, your hands and the rolling pin to prevent sticking. Use the flour sparingly. The idea is to prevent stickiness without incorporating too much extra flour into the dough, which might lead to tougher or drier cookies.

Cut shapes as closely together as possible to minimize scraps. Rechill scraps before rerolling, but try not to reroll more than once or twice or the cookies may become tough.

Metal cookie cutters with open centers generally work better than shallow plastic or metal cutters with solid centers. The metal edges are sharper and give a cleaner cut, and dough won't get stuck in the center. While some of the plastic cutters have embossed designs that in theory add a decorative touch to the cookie, the detailing is often lost as the dough puffs up during baking.

Many rolled cookies offer the baker the opportunity to personalize this basic dough with sugar, sprinkles, chips, nuts, icing, frosting and more. Be creative!

Previous page: Old-fashioned Sugar Cookies, page 115

Old-fashioned Sugar Cookies

Prep Time: 1 hour 15 minutes (Ready in 2 hours 15 minutes)

3 cups all-purpose flour	2 eggs
1 teaspoon baking powder	1½ cups sugar
1 teaspoon baking soda	1 teaspoon vanilla
⅛ teaspoon salt	½ teaspoon lemon extract
1 cup margarine or butter	

1. In large bowl, combine flour, baking powder, baking soda and salt; mix well. Using fork or pastry blender, cut in 1 cup margarine until mixture is crumbly. In small bowl, beat eggs. Gradually add sugar, 1 teaspoon vanilla and lemon extract, beating until light. Add to flour mixture in large bowl. Stir by hand until dough forms. (If necessary, knead dough with hands to mix in dry ingredients.) Cover with plastic wrap; refrigerate 1 hour for easier handling.

2. Heat oven to 375°F. On lightly floured surface, roll out ⅓ of dough at a time to ⅛-inch thickness. (Keep remaining dough refrigerated.) Cut with 2½- to 3-inch floured cookie cutters. Place 1 inch apart on ungreased cookie sheets. If desired, decorate with decorator sugar or multicolored candy sprinkles.

3. Bake at 375°F. for 6 to 11 minutes or until edges are light golden brown. Immediately remove from cookie sheets. Cool 15 minutes or until completely cooled.

Yield: 5 dozen cookies
High Altitude (Above 3,500 Feet): Increase flour to 3¼ cups; decrease granulated sugar to 1¼ cups. Bake as directed above.

Nutrition Information Per Serving

Serving Size: 1 Cookie. Calories 70 • Calories from Fat 25 • Total Fat 3 g
Saturated Fat 1 g • Cholesterol 5 mg • Sodium 70 mg • Dietary Fiber 0 g
Dietary Exchanges: ½ Starch, ½ Fat OR ½ Carbohydrate, ½ Fat

Make It Special

For a whimsical touch, trace children's hands onto paper and cut out the shapes. Then place the cutouts on the dough and cut around the shapes. Decorate baked cookies with frosting to look like rings, bracelets, watches or colored fingernails.

Autumn Leaf Cookies

Prep Time: 1 hour 45 minutes (Ready in 3 hours 45 minutes)

Kitchen Tip

For more vivid tints, use paste food color instead of liquid.

Storage Tip

Cover any unused icing tightly with plastic wrap and refrigerate it for up to two weeks.

Cookies

1 cup sugar
1 cup margarine or butter, softened
1 (3-oz.) pkg. cream cheese, softened
2 tablespoons grated orange peel
2 tablespoons orange juice
1 teaspoon vanilla
1 egg
3½ cups all-purpose flour
1 teaspoon baking soda
1 teaspoon cream of tartar
½ teaspoon salt

Frosting

½ cup butter, softened
¼ cup shortening
1 teaspoon vanilla
⅛ teaspoon salt
4 cups powdered sugar
2 to 4 tablespoons milk
⅓ cup semi-sweet chocolate chips, melted
8 drops red food color
8 drops yellow food color

1. In large bowl, combine sugar, 1 cup margarine and cream cheese; beat until light and fluffy. Add orange peel, orange juice, 1 teaspoon vanilla and egg; blend well. Add flour, baking soda, cream of tartar and ½ teaspoon salt. Cover with plastic wrap; refrigerate 2 hours or until firm.

2. Heat oven to 375°F. Using stockinette-covered rolling pin and floured pastry cloth, roll out ¼ of dough at a time to ⅛-inch thickness. (Keep remaining dough refrigerated.) Cut with floured leaf-shaped cookie cutter. Place 1 inch apart on ungreased cookie sheets.

3. Bake at 375°F. for 4 to 6 minutes or until edges are light golden brown. Immediately remove from cookie sheets; cool 15 minutes or until completely cooled.

4. In large bowl, combine butter and shortening; beat until light and fluffy. Add 1 teaspoon vanilla and ⅛ teaspoon salt. Beat in powdered sugar 1 cup at a time, scraping down sides of bowl. Add 2 tablespoons milk; beat at high speed until light and fluffy. Add enough additional milk for desired spreading consistency.

5. Divide frosting into 2 small bowls. To one bowl of frosting, add melted chocolate; beat until well blended. To other bowl of frosting, add red and yellow food color; blend well. Spread cooled cookies with one of the frostings; pipe veins on leaves with other frosting. Let stand until set.

Yield: 8 dozen cookies
High Altitude (Above 3,500 Feet): No change.

Nutrition Information Per Serving

Serving Size: 1 Cookie. Calories 80 • Calories from Fat 35 • Total Fat 4 g
Saturated Fat 1 g • Cholesterol 5 mg • Sodium 65 mg • Dietary Fiber 0 g
Dietary Exchanges: ½ Starch, 1 Fat OR ½ Carbohydrate, 1 Fat

Autumn Leaf Cookies

Coconut Diamond Gems

About Powdered Sugar

Most powdered sugar, also known as confectioners' sugar, is blended with a small amount of cornstarch to prevent major lumping. Even so, it's usually best to sift it prior to use.

Ingredient Substitution

For a more traditional macaroon flavor in the coconut topping, substitute almond extract for the vanilla in this recipe.

Prep Time: 1 hour (Ready in 2 hours)

Cookies
$3/4$ cup sugar
$3/4$ cup margarine or butter, softened
1 teaspoon vanilla
1 egg yolk
$1^{1}/_{2}$ cups all-purpose flour
$1/2$ teaspoon cinnamon
$1/4$ teaspoon salt

Topping
2 cups coconut
$1/2$ cup powdered sugar
1 egg white, slightly beaten
1 tablespoon water
$1/2$ teaspoon vanilla
$1/2$ cup chopped nuts

Glaze
3 oz. semi-sweet chocolate
1 teaspoon shortening

1. In large bowl, combine $3/4$ cup sugar, margarine and 1 teaspoon vanilla; beat until light and fluffy. Add egg yolk; blend well. Add flour, cinnamon and salt; mix well. Cover with plastic wrap; refrigerate 1 hour or until firm.

2. Heat oven to 375°F. Lightly dust large cookie sheets with flour. On cookie sheet, roll out half of dough at a time to $10^{1}/_{2} \times 8^{1}/_{2}$-inch rectangle. (Keep remaining dough refrigerated.) With tip of sharp knife, score dough crosswise into seven $1^{1}/_{2}$-inch-wide strips. Score 8 diagonal markings to form 32 diamond-shaped pieces. In small bowl, combine all topping ingredients; mix well. Spoon 1 level teaspoon topping onto center of each diamond.

3. Bake at 375°F. for 8 to 11 minutes or until light golden brown. Cut completely through score marks to make diamonds. Remove from cookie sheet; cool.

4. In small saucepan over very low heat, melt chocolate and shortening, stirring constantly. Drizzle over cookies.

Yield: 64 cookies
High Altitude (Above 3,500 Feet): No change.

Nutrition Information Per Serving
Serving Size: 1 Cookie. Calories 70 • Calories from Fat 35 • Total Fat 4 g
Saturated Fat 1 g • Cholesterol 3 mg • Sodium 40 mg • Dietary Fiber 0 g
Dietary Exchanges: $1/2$ Starch, $1/2$ Fat OR $1/2$ Carbohydrate, $1/2$ Fat

Chocolate Snowflake Cookies

Prep Time: 1 hour 30 minutes (Ready in 2 hours 30 minutes)

1 cup sugar
1 cup margarine or butter,
   softened
¼ cup milk
1 teaspoon vanilla
1 egg

2¾ cups all-purpose flour
½ cup unsweetened cocoa
¾ teaspoon baking powder
¼ teaspoon baking soda
Drinking straw
2 tablespoons powdered sugar

Kitchen Tip

To make snowflake holes with clean edges, hold the straw vertically and twist it slightly to make the openings.

1. In large bowl, combine sugar and margarine; beat until light and fluffy. Add milk, vanilla and egg; blend well. Add flour, cocoa, baking powder and baking soda; mix well. Cover with plastic wrap; refrigerate 1 hour for easier handling.

2. Heat oven to 350°F. On lightly floured surface, roll out ⅓ of dough at a time to ⅛-inch thickness. (Keep remaining dough refrigerated.) Cut with floured 2½-inch star-shaped cookie cutter. Using drinking straw, punch random holes in cutout stars. Place 2 inches apart on ungreased cookie sheets.

3. Bake at 350°F. for 8 to 11 minutes or until set. Immediately remove from cookie sheets. Cool 15 minutes or until completely cooled. Sprinkle with powdered sugar.

Yield: 8 dozen cookies
High Altitude (Above 3,500 Feet): Increase flour to 3 cups. Bake as directed above.

Nutrition Information Per Serving

Serving Size: 1 Cookie. Calories 40 • Calories from Fat 20 • Total Fat 2 g
Saturated Fat 0 g • Cholesterol 2 mg • Sodium 30 mg • Dietary Fiber 0 g
Dietary Exchanges: ½ Starch OR ½ Carbohydrate

Cream Cheese Cutout Cookies

Cream cheese, a mild, fresh, unripened cow's milk cheese, blends best if left to soften at room temperature for about an hour before mixing. If you're in a hurry, remove the foil wrapper and microwave the cheese for 30 seconds on MEDIUM or 50 percent power; check the softness and microwave longer, if necessary.

Prep Time: 1 hour 15 minutes (Ready in 2 hours 15 minutes)

1 cup sugar
1 cup margarine or butter, softened
1 (3-oz.) pkg. cream cheese, softened
1 teaspoon vanilla

1 egg
2½ cups all-purpose flour
¼ teaspoon salt
Colored decorator sugar, if desired

1. In large bowl, combine sugar, margarine and cream cheese; beat until light and fluffy. Add vanilla and egg; blend well. Add flour and salt; mix well. Cover with plastic wrap; refrigerate 1 to 2 hours for easier handling.

2. Heat oven to 375°F. On lightly floured surface, roll out half of dough at a time to ⅛-inch thickness. (Keep remaining dough refrigerated.) Cut into desired shapes with floured cookie cutters. Place 1 inch apart on ungreased cookie sheets. Leave cookies plain or sprinkle with colored sugar.

3. Bake at 375°F. for 7 to 10 minutes or until edges are light golden brown. Cool 1 minute; remove from cookie sheets. If desired, frost and decorate plain cookies.

Yield: 5 dozen cookies
High Altitude (Above 3,500 Feet): Increase flour to 2¾ cups. Bake as directed above.

Nutrition Information Per Serving
Serving Size: 1 Cookie. Calories 70 • Calories from Fat 35 • Total Fat 4 g
Saturated Fat 1 g • Cholesterol 5 mg • Sodium 50 mg • Dietary Fiber 0 g
Dietary Exchanges: ½ Starch, ½ Fat OR ½ Carbohydrate, ½ Fat

Variation

Tri-Cornered Cream Cheese Cookies: Prepare and roll out dough as directed in recipe. Cut with floured 2½-inch round cookie cutter. Place 1 inch apart on ungreased cookie sheets. Spoon 1 teaspoon jam on center of each round. To shape into triangles, fold 3 sides in without covering jam; pinch corners to seal. Bake as directed in recipe. Dust with powdered sugar.

Yield: 5 dozen cookies

Tri-Cornered Cream Cheese Cookies

Lemon Brown-eyed Susan Cookies

Prep Time: 1 hour (Ready in 2 hours)

1 cup sugar
1 cup margarine or butter, softened
3 tablespoons lemon juice
1 egg
3 cups all-purpose flour
1½ teaspoons baking powder
¼ teaspoon salt
1 egg yolk
1 teaspoon water
Few drops yellow food color
¾ cup semi-sweet chocolate chips

1. In large bowl, combine sugar and margarine; beat until light and fluffy. Add lemon juice and egg; blend well. Add flour, baking powder and salt; mix well. Cover with plastic wrap; refrigerate 1 hour for easier handling.

2. Heat oven to 400°F. On lightly floured surface, roll out half of dough at a time to ¼-inch thickness. Cut with floured 2- to 3-inch flower-shaped cookie cutter. Place 1 inch apart on ungreased cookie sheets. In small bowl, combine egg yolk and water; blend well. Stir in food color. Brush cookies with egg yolk mixture.

3. Bake at 400°F. for 5 to 7 minutes or until edges are light golden brown. Immediately place chocolate chip in center of each cookie. Remove from cookie sheets.

Yield: 5½ dozen cookies
High Altitude (Above 3,500 Feet): No change.

Kitchen Tip

For a more lemony flavor, add 2 teaspoons finely grated lemon peel to the dough.

Ingredient Substitution

Pipe a dot of chocolate frosting into the center of each flower after baking instead of using the chocolate chips.

Recipe Variation

To make Sunflower Cookies, use a larger flower cookie cutter and fill the center area with miniature chocolate chips. Increase the baking time slightly.

Nutrition Information Per Serving
Serving Size: 1 Cookie. Calories 80 • Calories from Fat 35 • Total Fat 4 g
Saturated Fat 1 g • Cholesterol 5 mg • Sodium 55 mg • Dietary Fiber 0 g
Dietary Exchanges: ½ Starch, 1 Fat OR ½ Carbohydrate, 1 Fat

Russian Sour Cream Tarts

Prep Time: 1 hour

Cookies
1¼ cups all-purpose flour
¼ cup sugar
¼ teaspoon salt
½ cup butter
1 egg yolk, slightly beaten

Filling
1¼ cups ground blanched
    almonds

2 tablespoons powdered sugar
3 tablespoons sour cream
2 tablespoons peach or apricot
    preserves
1 egg

Meringue
2 egg whites
¼ cup sugar

1. Heat oven to 350°F. In large bowl, combine flour, sugar and salt. Using pastry blender or fork, cut in butter until mixture resembles coarse crumbs. Add egg yolk; knead until smooth dough forms, adding a few drops of ice water if necessary.
2. On lightly floured surface, roll out dough to ¼-inch thickness. Cut with floured small scalloped cookie cutter. Place 1 inch apart on ungreased cookie sheets.
3. In small bowl, combine ground almonds and powdered sugar. Add sour cream, preserves and egg; mix well. Spoon 1 rounded teaspoon filling onto each cookie; carefully spread.
4. In small bowl, beat egg whites until soft peaks form. Gradually add sugar, beating until stiff peaks form. Top each cookie with 1 teaspoon meringue; swirl top.
5. Bake at 350°F. for 10 to 12 minutes or until meringue is light golden brown. Remove from cookie sheets; cool.

Yield: 3 dozen cookies
High Altitude (Above 3,500 Feet): Decrease sugar in meringue to 3 tablespoons.
Bake at 325°F. for 10 to 15 minutes.

Nutrition Information Per Serving
Serving Size: 1 Tart. Calories 90 • Calories from Fat 45 • Total Fat 5 g
Saturated Fat 2 g • Cholesterol 20 mg • Sodium 45 mg • Dietary Fiber 0 g
Dietary Exchanges: ½ Starch, 1 Fat OR ½ Carbohydrate, 1 Fat

Recipe Fact

In their native Russia, these cookies are called **smettanich**.

Kitchen Tip

When beating egg whites, make sure the bowl contains absolutely no grease residue (including traces of egg yolk), or the whites will not whip. Ceramic or metal bowls are better than plastic, which may retain traces of grease.

Kitchen Tip

To maintain tenderness in the pastrylike sugar cookie base, knead the dough as little as possible—just enough to allow it to stick together smoothly. Overkneading will develop the flour's gluten and make the cookies tough.

Grandma's Date-filled Cookies

Prep Time: 1 hour (Ready in 3 hours)

Cookies
1½ cups firmly packed brown sugar
1 cup margarine or butter, softened
1 teaspoon vanilla
3 eggs

3½ cups all-purpose flour
1 teaspoon baking soda

Filling
2 cups chopped dates
1 cup sugar
1 cup water

1. In large bowl, combine brown sugar and margarine; beat until light and fluffy. Add vanilla and eggs; beat well. Add flour and baking soda; mix well. Cover with plastic wrap; refrigerate at least 2 hours for easier handling.

2. Meanwhile, in medium saucepan, combine all filling ingredients. Bring to a boil. Reduce heat to low; simmer 10 minutes, stirring frequently. Refrigerate until ready to use. (Mixture will thicken as it cools.)

3. Heat oven to 375°F. On well-floured surface, roll out ⅓ of dough at a time to ⅛-inch thickness. (Keep remaining dough refrigerated.) Cut with floured 2½-inch round cookie cutter. In half of cookies, cut and remove 1-inch round or desired shape hole from center. Place whole cookies on ungreased cookie sheets. Spoon 1 teaspoon cooled filling onto center of each. Top each with dough ring. Using fingertips or fork, press edges of dough to seal. Return dough centers to remaining dough for rerolling.

4. Bake at 375°F. for 7 to 10 minutes or until light golden brown. Cool 1 minute; remove from cookie sheets.

Yield: 3½ dozen cookies
High Altitude (Above 3,500 Feet): No change.

Nutrition Information Per Serving

Serving Size: 1 Cookie. Calories 160 • Calories from Fat 45 • Total Fat 5 g
Saturated Fat 1 g • Cholesterol 15 mg • Sodium 90 mg • Dietary Fiber 1 g
Dietary Exchanges: 1 Starch, ½ Fruit, 1 Fat OR 1½ Carbohydrate, 1 Fat

Grandma's Date-filled Cookies

Mint-filled Chocolate Creams

Recipe Fact

Ice cream in the dough contributes to the tender texture of these cookies.

Recipe Variation

For Orange-filled Chocolate Creams, substitute orange extract for mint, and yellow and red food color for the green. For Peppermint-filled Chocolate Creams, substitute peppermint extract for the mint and tint it pink instead of green.

Prep Time: 1 hour 10 minutes (Ready in 2 hours 25 minutes)

Cookies
2 cups all-purpose flour
1 cup margarine or butter, softened
3/4 cup vanilla ice cream, softened
1/4 cup sugar

Filling
2 1/4 cups powdered sugar

1/4 cup margarine or butter, softened
1/8 teaspoon mint extract
1 to 2 drops green food color
2 to 3 tablespoons milk

Glaze
1 (6-oz.) pkg. (1 cup) semi-sweet chocolate chips
1 tablespoon shortening

1. In large bowl, combine flour, 1 cup margarine and ice cream; mix well. (Dough will be firm.) Cover with plastic wrap; refrigerate 1 hour for easier handling.

2. Heat oven to 375°F. On lightly floured surface, roll out half of dough at a time to 1/8-inch thickness. (Keep remaining dough refrigerated.) Cut with floured 2-inch round cookie cutter. Coat each side of cookie with sugar. Place on ungreased cookie sheets. Prick cookies several times with fork.

3. Bake at 375°F. for 8 to 10 minutes or until edges are light golden brown. (Cookies shrink slightly during baking.) Cool 1 minute; remove from cookie sheets. Cool 15 minutes or until completely cooled.

4. Meanwhile, in small bowl, combine all filling ingredients, adding enough milk for desired spreading consistency; blend well. To make sandwich cookies, spread filling between 2 cooled cookies, placing flat sides together.

5. In small saucepan over low heat, melt glaze ingredients, stirring constantly. Remove from heat. Place saucepan in pan of warm water to maintain dipping consistency. Line cookie sheet with waxed paper. Dip half of each sandwich cookie into chocolate (edge first). Shake off excess chocolate. Place cookies on waxed paper–lined cookie sheet, standing on edge. Refrigerate 15 to 20 minutes or until glaze is set.

Yield: 3 dozen sandwich cookies
High Altitude (Above 3,500 Feet): No change.

Nutrition Information Per Serving

Serving Size: 1 Sandwich Cookie. Calories 150 • Calories from Fat 80 • Total Fat 9 g • Saturated Fat 2 g • Cholesterol 1 mg • Sodium 80 mg • Dietary Fiber 0 g
Dietary Exchanges: 1 Fruit, 2 Fat OR 1 Carbohydrate, 2 Fat

Brown Sugar Cutouts

kid pleaser

Prep Time: 1 hour (Ready in 2 hours)

1 cup margarine or butter, softened
1 cup firmly packed brown sugar
1 teaspoon vanilla
1 egg
2½ cups all-purpose flour
½ teaspoon baking soda

1. In large bowl, combine margarine and brown sugar; beat until light and fluffy. Add vanilla and egg; blend well. Add flour and baking soda; mix well. Cover with plastic wrap; refrigerate 1 to 2 hours for easier handling.
2. Heat oven to 375°F. On floured surface, roll out ⅓ of dough at a time to ⅛-inch thickness. (Keep remaining dough refrigerated.) Cut with floured 1¾- to 2-inch cookie cutter. Place 1 inch apart on ungreased cookie sheets.
3. Bake at 375°F. for 5 to 8 minutes or until light golden brown. Immediately remove from cookie sheets.

Yield: 4 dozen cookies
High Altitude (Above 3,500 Feet): Increase flour to 3 cups. Bake as directed above.

Nutrition Information Per Serving

Serving Size: 1 Cookie. Calories 80 • Calories from Fat 35 • Total Fat 4 g
Saturated Fat 1 g • Cholesterol 4 mg • Sodium 60 mg • Dietary Fiber 0 g
Dietary Exchanges: ½ Starch, 1 Fat OR ½ Carbohydrate, 1 Fat

Kitchen Tip

Rechill dough scraps before rerolling.

Make It Special

For a holiday cookie tray, decorate the cookies with a simple vanilla icing.

Linzer Stars

Prep Time: 1 hour 15 minutes (Ready in 4 hours 15 minutes)

½ cup sugar	1 teaspoon cream of tartar
½ cup margarine or butter, softened	½ teaspoon baking soda
1 tablespoon milk	¼ teaspoon salt
1 teaspoon vanilla	½ cup cherry or red currant jelly
1 egg	2 teaspoons powdered sugar
1¼ cups all-purpose flour	

Recipe Fact

These stellar cookies are a variation of classic round Austrian **linzertorte**, a jam tart.

1. In large bowl, combine sugar and margarine; beat until light and fluffy. Add milk, vanilla and egg; blend well. Add flour, cream of tartar, baking soda and salt; mix well. Cover with plastic wrap; refrigerate 3 hours for easier handling.

2. Heat oven to 425°F. Using stockinette-covered rolling pin and well-floured pastry cloth, roll out ⅓ of dough at a time to ⅛-inch thickness. (Keep remaining dough refrigerated.) Cut with floured 3-inch star-shaped cookie cutter. Using 1-inch round cookie cutter, cut out center of half of dough stars to form cookie tops. Place 1 inch apart on ungreased cookie sheets. Return dough centers to remaining dough for rerolling.

3. Bake at 425°F. for 3 to 5 minutes or until edges are light golden brown. Cool 1 minute; remove from cookie sheets. Cool 15 minutes or until completely cooled.

4. To assemble cookies, spread ½ teaspoon jelly over bottom side of each whole cookie. Sprinkle powdered sugar over tops of cutout cookies; place over jelly.

Yield: 4 dozen sandwich cookies
High Altitude (Above 3,500 Feet): Increase flour to 1¼ cups plus 2 tablespoons. Bake as directed above.

Nutrition Information Per Serving
Serving Size: 1 Cookie. Calories 50 • Calories from Fat 20 • Total Fat 2 g
Saturated Fat 0 g • Cholesterol 4 mg • Sodium 50 mg • Dietary Fiber 0 g
Dietary Exchanges: ½ Fruit, ½ Fat OR ½ Carbohydrate, ½ Fat

Linzer Stars

Vanilla Sandwich Cookies

Prep Time: 1 hour 15 minutes (Ready in 4 hours 15 minutes)

About Cream of Tartar

Cream of tartar, a by-product of wine making, is a fine, powdery substance similar in appearance to baking powder. It's often used in combination with baking soda to provide leavening for baked goods. It also can help lend creaminess to candy and frosting mixtures.

About Coffee Liqueur

Coffee liqueur is a versatile flavoring that can be stirred into frosting, drizzled on ice cream or blended with a milkshake or cappuccino.

Cookies
½ cup sugar
½ cup butter, softened
1 tablespoon milk
1 teaspoon vanilla
1 egg
1¼ cups all-purpose flour
1 teaspoon cream of tartar
½ teaspoon baking soda
¼ teaspoon salt

2 tablespoons sugar

Filling
2 tablespoons butter
1⅓ cups powdered sugar
⅓ cup unsweetened cocoa
4 teaspoons hot water
2 to 3 tablespoons coffee-flavored liqueur or coffee

1. In large bowl, combine ½ cup sugar and ½ cup butter; beat until light and fluffy. Add milk, vanilla and egg; blend well. Add flour, cream of tartar, baking soda and salt; mix well. Cover with plastic wrap; refrigerate 3 hours or until firm.

2. Heat oven to 425°F. Using covered rolling pin and well-floured pastry cloth, roll out ⅓ of dough at a time to ⅛-inch thickness. (Refrigerate remaining dough.) Cut with floured 1½-inch round cookie cutter. Sprinkle tops with sugar. Place 1 inch apart on ungreased cookie sheets.

3. Bake at 425°F. for 3 to 5 minutes or until edges are light golden brown. Immediately remove from cookie sheets. Cool 15 minutes or until completely cooled.

4. Meanwhile, in small bowl, combine all filling ingredients, adding enough liqueur for desired spreading consistency. To make sandwich cookies, spread rounded ½ teaspoon filling between 2 cooled cookies, placing flat sides together.

Yield: 5 dozen sandwich cookies
High Altitude (Above 3,500 Feet): Increase flour to 1¼ cups plus 2 tablespoons.
Bake as directed above.

Nutrition Information Per Serving
Serving Size: 1 Cookie. Calories 45 • Calories from Fat 20 • Total Fat 2 g
Saturated Fat 1 g • Cholesterol 10 mg • Sodium 40 mg • Dietary Fiber 0 g
Dietary Exchanges: ½ Fruit, ½ Fat OR ½ Carbohydrate, ½ Fat

Chocolate Ginger Zebras

Prep Time: 45 minutes (Ready in 3 hours)

¼ cup sugar
⅓ cup shortening
¼ cup unsweetened cocoa
¼ cup dark corn syrup
2 tablespoons milk
1 egg
1½ cups all-purpose flour
½ teaspoon baking soda

½ teaspoon baking powder
½ teaspoon ginger
½ teaspoon cinnamon
⅛ teaspoon cloves
3 oz. vanilla-flavored candy coating
2 tablespoons shortening

1. In large bowl, combine sugar and ⅓ cup shortening; beat until light and fluffy. Add cocoa, corn syrup, milk and egg; blend well. Add flour, baking soda, baking powder, ginger, cinnamon and cloves; mix well. Cover with plastic wrap; refrigerate 1½ to 2 hours for easier handling.

2. Heat oven to 350°F. Lightly grease cookie sheets. On floured surface, roll out dough to ⅛-inch thickness. Cut with floured 2½- to 3-inch cookie cutter. Place 1 inch apart on greased cookie sheets.

3. Bake at 350°F. for 6 to 9 minutes or until set. Immediately remove from cookie sheets. Cool 15 minutes or until completely cooled.

4. In small saucepan, melt candy coating and 2 tablespoons shortening over low heat, stirring constantly. Drizzle over cooled cookies. Let stand until set.

Yield: 3 dozen cookies
High Altitude (Above 3,500 Feet): Increase flour to 1½ cups plus 1 tablespoon. Bake as directed above.

Nutrition Information Per Serving
Serving Size: 1 Cookie. Calories 80 • Calories from Fat 35 • Total Fat 4 g
Saturated Fat 1 g • Cholesterol 5 mg • Sodium 30 mg • Dietary Fiber 0 g
Dietary Exchanges: ½ Starch, 1 Fat OR ½ Carbohydrate, 1 Fat

About Corn Syrup

Corn syrup, a thick liquid that's a product of sweet corn, is widely used as a commercial sweetener. It's available in dark or light versions.

About Candy Coating

Vanilla-flavored candy coating, available in the grocery store baking aisle and specialty shops, comes in solid bars that you melt for dipping or otherwise covering candies or cookies.

Kitchen Tip

To prevent the corn syrup from clinging to the side of the measuring cup, lightly grease the cup first or spray it with nonstick cooking spray.

Bars

Bar cookies and brownies are made from dough that is spread and baked in a pan. Varieties range from simple, unembellished chocolate brownies to elegant layered creations. They're a special boon to the hurried baker because, once the dough is mixed, there's no fussing with sheet after sheet of individual cookies.

& Brownies

Bar Cookies and Brownies

Bar Cookies and Brownies are best when baked in the pan specified in the recipe. Cakelike brownies are done when they just begin to pull away from the sides of the pan, when a toothpick inserted into the center comes out clean or when they are set in the center. Fudgy brownies are trickier to test. Observe the listed range of baking times. The shorter time will usually produce moist, almost "wet" brownies, while the longer time will yield more set but still moist brownies. In any case, remove the pan from the oven after the maximum suggested baking time, even if the center still looks fairly moist. The brownies will continue to solidify and set after removal from the oven, and baking them beyond the recommended time can result in dry, hard brownies, especially around the pan edges.

Previous page: Chocolaty Caramel Pecan Bars, page 135; Almond Fudge Brownies, page 136

Chocolaty Caramel Pecan Bars

Prep Time: 30 minutes (Ready in 1 hour 30 minutes)

Base
½ cup powdered sugar
½ cup margarine or butter, softened
1 tablespoon whipping cream
1 cup all-purpose flour

Filling
24 caramels, unwrapped

⅓ cup whipping cream
2 cups pecan halves

Topping
1 teaspoon margarine or butter
½ cup milk chocolate chips
2 tablespoons whipping cream

1. Heat oven to 325°F. Grease 9-inch square pan. In medium bowl, combine powdered sugar, ½ cup margarine and 1 tablespoon whipping cream; blend well. Add flour; mix until crumbly. With floured hands, press evenly in greased pan.

2. Bake at 325°F. for 15 to 20 minutes or until firm to touch.

3. Meanwhile, in medium saucepan, combine caramels and ⅓ cup whipping cream. Cook over low heat, stirring frequently, until caramels are melted and mixture is smooth. Remove from heat. Add pecans; stir well to coat. Immediately spoon over baked base; spread carefully to cover.

4. In small saucepan over low heat, melt 1 teaspoon margarine and chocolate chips, stirring constantly. Stir in 2 tablespoons whipping cream. Drizzle over filling. Refrigerate 1 hour or until filling is firm. Cut into bars.

Yield: 24 bars
High Altitude (Above 3,500 Feet): No change.

Nutrition Information Per Serving
Serving Size: 1 Bar. Calories 190 • Calories from Fat 120 • Total Fat 13 g
Saturated Fat 4 g • Cholesterol 8 mg • Sodium 70 mg • Dietary Fiber 1 g
Dietary Exchanges: 1 Starch, 2½ Fat OR 1 Carbohydrate, 2½ Fat

Recipe Fact

These gooey, yummy bars borrow some of the best qualities of chocolate "turtle" candies.

Storage Tip

Keep chocolate chips and bars in a cool, dry place. In humid weather or when stored in the refrigerator, chocolate may develop a harmless grayish coating called "bloom," which is nothing more than some of the fat rising to the surface.

Almond Fudge Brownies

Recipe Fact

Almond paste contributes to the velvety texture of these elegant brownies.

Make It Special

To decorate the frosted brownies, cut a stencil from waxed paper. Plan a large design to cover the entire top if you will present the pan at the table uncut, or plot individual cutouts to correspond to the cut squares. Lay the stencil on top of the frosting after it sets and sift powdered sugar over the top. Lift the stencil off carefully.

Prep Time: 45 minutes (Ready in 1 hour 55 minutes)

Brownies
- 1 teaspoon instant coffee granules or crystals
- 2 tablespoons hot water
- 4 eggs, separated
- 1 cup sugar
- ½ cup margarine or butter, softened
- 3½ oz. purchased almond paste, crumbled into small pieces
- 1 cup all-purpose flour
- 1 (6-oz.) pkg. (1 cup) semi-sweet chocolate chips, melted
- 1 teaspoon vanilla
- ½ cup semi-sweet chocolate chips

Frosting
- ¼ cup sugar
- ¼ cup firmly packed brown sugar
- ⅛ teaspoon salt
- ¼ cup milk
- 2 tablespoons margarine or butter
- ½ cup semi-sweet chocolate chips
- 1 cup powdered sugar
- ½ teaspoon vanilla

1. Heat oven to 350°F. Grease and flour bottom only of 13 × 9-inch pan. In small bowl, dissolve instant coffee in hot water. In another small bowl, beat egg whites until stiff peaks form.

2. In large bowl, combine 1 cup sugar and ½ cup margarine; beat until light and fluffy. Stir in almond paste; blend well. Add flour, coffee, egg yolks, melted chocolate chips and 1 teaspoon vanilla; mix well. Fold in beaten egg whites. Gently fold in ½ cup chocolate chips. Spread in greased and floured pan.

3. Bake at 350°F. for 25 to 35 minutes or until set. DO NOT OVERBAKE. Cool 1 hour or until completely cooled.

4. In small saucepan, combine ¼ cup sugar, brown sugar, salt, milk, 2 tablespoons margarine and ½ cup chocolate chips. Bring to a boil over medium heat, stirring constantly. Reduce heat; simmer 3 minutes. Remove from heat. Stir in powdered sugar and ½ teaspoon vanilla; beat until smooth. Frost cooled brownies. Cut into bars. Store in refrigerator.

Yield: 36 brownies
High Altitude (Above 3,500 Feet): No change.

Nutrition Information Per Serving

Serving Size: 1 Brownie. Calories 160 • Calories from Fat 60 • Total Fat 7 g
Saturated Fat 3 g • Cholesterol 25 mg • Sodium 55 mg • Dietary Fiber 1 g
Dietary Exchanges: 1½ Fruit, 1½ Fat OR 1½ Carbohydrate, 1½ Fat

Chocolate Chunk Pecan Brownies

Prep Time: 15 minutes (Ready in 1 hour 55 minutes)

1 cup margarine or butter	½ cup unsweetened cocoa
2 cups sugar	½ teaspoon salt
2 teaspoons vanilla	8 oz. semi-sweet chocolate,
4 eggs, slightly beaten	coarsely chopped
1 cup all-purpose flour	1 cup chopped pecans

1. Heat oven to 350°F. Grease 13 × 9-inch pan. In medium saucepan over low heat, melt margarine. Add sugar, vanilla and eggs; blend well. Add flour, cocoa and salt; mix well. Stir in chocolate and pecans. Pour into greased pan.
2. Bake at 350°F. for 30 to 40 minutes or until set. Cool 1 hour or until completely cooled. Cut into bars.

Yield: 36 brownies
High Altitude (Above 3,500 Feet): No change.

Nutrition Information Per Serving

Serving Size: 1 Brownie. Calories 170 • Calories from Fat 90 • Total Fat 10 g
Saturated Fat 2 g • Cholesterol 25 mg • Sodium 95 mg • Dietary Fiber 1 g
Dietary Exchanges: 1 Starch, 2 Fat OR 1 Carbohydrate, 2 Fat

editor's favorite   chocoholic's choice

About Semi-Sweet Chocolate

Any semi-sweet chocolate bar will work well in this recipe, whether it's your favorite from the candy counter or the baking aisle. Or visit a gourmet shop and treat yourself to a hunk of specialty chocolate cut from an impressive bulk block.

Make It Special

Top this moist, intensely flavored brownie with a scoop of ice cream (chocolate for true chocoholics, vanilla for traditionalists) and a drizzle of hot fudge for a decadent brownie nut sundae.

Gourmet Mint Brownies

Kitchen Tip

To "marbleize" the chocolate and mint batters, drag a butter knife through both layers, swirling gently so as not to completely blend the two flavors.

Make It Special

Garnish each square with a fresh mint leaf and a raspberry or small strawberry dipped in chocolate.

Filling
1 (8-oz.) pkg. cream cheese, softened
¼ cup sugar
1 egg
1 teaspoon mint extract
4 drops green food color

Brownies
1 cup margarine or butter
4 oz. unsweetened chocolate, cut into pieces
2 cups sugar

2 teaspoons vanilla
4 eggs
1 cup all-purpose flour

Frosting
2 tablespoons margarine or butter
2 tablespoons corn syrup
2 tablespoons water
2 oz. unsweetened chocolate, cut into pieces
1 teaspoon vanilla
1 cup powdered sugar

1. Heat oven to 350°F. Grease and flour 13 × 9-inch pan. In small bowl, combine cream cheese and ¼ cup sugar; beat until smooth. Add 1 egg, mint extract and food color; mix well. Set aside.

2. In large saucepan, melt 1 cup margarine and 4 oz. chocolate over very low heat, stirring constantly. Remove from heat; cool 15 minutes or until slightly cooled. Stir in 2 cups sugar and 2 teaspoons vanilla. Add 4 eggs 1 at a time, beating well after each addition. Stir in flour; mix well. Spread in greased and floured pan. Carefully spoon filling over brownie mixture. Lightly swirl filling into brownie mixture.

3. Bake at 350°F. for 45 to 50 minutes or until set. Cool 1 hour or until completely cooled.

4. In medium saucepan, combine 2 tablespoons margarine, corn syrup and water; bring to a rolling boil. Remove from heat. Add 2 oz. chocolate; stir until melted. Stir in 1 teaspoon vanilla and powdered sugar; beat until smooth. Frost cooled brownies. Cut into bars. Store in refrigerator.

Yield: 36 brownies
High Altitude (Above 3,500 Feet): No change.

Nutrition Information Per Serving

Serving Size: 1 Brownie. Calories 190 • Calories from Fat 100 • Total Fat 11 g
Saturated Fat 4 g • Cholesterol 35 mg • Sodium 95 mg • Dietary Fiber 1 g
Dietary Exchanges: ½ Starch, 1 Fruit, 2 Fat OR 1½ Carbohydrate, 2 Fat

Gourmet Mint Brownies

Almond Brickle Blond Brownies

Prep Time: 30 minutes (Ready in 1 hour 35 minutes)

About Almond Brickle Chips

Look for bags of almond brickle chips in the supermarket baking aisle near the chocolate chips.

Ingredient Substitution

Use butterscotch chips and ½ cup almonds for the topping if you can't find almond brickle chips.

Brownies
1 cup sugar
½ cup firmly packed brown sugar
½ cup margarine or butter, softened
1 teaspoon vanilla
2 eggs
1¾ cups all-purpose flour
1 teaspoon baking powder
½ teaspoon salt
½ cup chopped almonds

Topping
¾ cup almond brickle baking chips
¼ cup chopped almonds

1. Heat oven to 350°F. Grease 13 × 9-inch pan. In large bowl, combine sugar, brown sugar and margarine; beat until light and fluffy. Add vanilla and eggs; blend well. Add flour, baking powder and salt; mix well. Stir in ½ cup almonds. Spread in greased pan.

2. Bake at 350°F. for 20 to 30 minutes or until golden brown and set. Remove from oven; sprinkle evenly with topping ingredients. Return to oven; bake an additional 2 minutes. Cool 1 hour or until completely cooled. Cut into bars.

Yield: 36 brownies
High Altitude (Above 3,500 Feet): Decrease sugar to ¾ cup; increase flour to 2 cups. Bake as directed above.

Nutrition Information Per Serving
Serving Size: 1 Brownie. Calories 120 • Calories from Fat 45 • Total Fat 5 g
Saturated Fat 1 g • Cholesterol 15 mg • Sodium 85 mg • Dietary Fiber 0 g
Dietary Exchanges: 1 Starch, 1 Fat OR 1 Carbohydrate, 1 Fat

Bourbon Brownies

Prep Time: 45 minutes (Ready in 2 hours 5 minutes)

Brownies
½ cup sugar
⅓ cup margarine or butter
2 tablespoons water
1 (6-oz.) pkg. (1 cup) semi-
    sweet chocolate chips
1 teaspoon vanilla
2 eggs
¾ cup all-purpose flour
¼ teaspoon baking powder
¼ teaspoon salt

½ cup chopped walnuts or
    pecans
3 to 4 tablespoons bourbon

Frosting
1½ cups powdered sugar
3 tablespoons margarine or
    butter, softened
¼ teaspoon vanilla
2 to 3 teaspoons milk
1 oz. semi-sweet chocolate,
    melted, cooled

1. Heat oven to 350°F. Grease 8- or 9-inch square pan. In medium saucepan, combine sugar, ⅓ cup margarine and water. Cook over medium heat until mixture comes to a boil, stirring constantly. Remove from heat, stir in chocolate chips and 1 teaspoon vanilla. Add eggs; beat well. Add flour, baking powder and salt; mix well. Stir in walnuts. Spread evenly in greased pan.

2. Bake at 350°F. for 20 to 30 minutes or until toothpick inserted in center comes out clean. DO NOT OVERBAKE. Drizzle bourbon evenly over top. Cool 1 hour or until completely cooled.

3. In small bowl, combine powdered sugar, 3 tablespoons margarine, ¼ teaspoon vanilla and enough milk for desired spreading consistency; beat until smooth. Frost cooled brownies. Drizzle melted chocolate over frosting. Let stand 15 minutes or until set. Cut into bars.

Yield: 24 brownies
High Altitude (Above 3,500 Feet): Increase flour to ¾ cup plus 2 tablespoons. Bake as directed above.

Nutrition Information Per Serving
Serving Size: 1 Brownie. Calories 170 • Calories from Fat 70 • Total Fat 8 g
Saturated Fat 2 g • Cholesterol 20 mg • Sodium 80 mg • Dietary Fiber 1 g
Dietary Exchanges: ½ Starch, 1 Fruit, 1½ Fat OR 1½ Carbohydrate, 1½ Fat

chocoholic's choice

Recipe Fact

Brownies come of age in this adults-only version drizzled with bourbon.

About Bourbon

Bourbon is American whiskey brewed from corn, malt and rye.

Kitchen Tip

Using a fork, poke holes into the top of the brownies at intervals before drizzling the bourbon to help the liquor soak in.

Fruitcake Fantasy Brownies

Prep Time: 15 minutes (Ready in 1 hour 45 minutes)

Recipe Fact

These fruit-studded bars are a takeoff on the classic holiday fruitcake, but since they are flavored with rum extract rather than doused with the alcohol itself, they lack fruitcake's legendary keeping power.

Make It Special

Top the brownies with a traditional hard sauce (purchased or home-made). Hard sauce is sweetened, flavored butter made by beating butter with sugar and flavoring until it's smooth and creamy. (A basic recipe: ½ cup butter, ½ cup granulated or powdered sugar and 2 to 3 tablespoons of brandy, Grand Marnier or another liqueur.)

½ cup margarine or butter
4 oz. semi-sweet chocolate
1 (14-oz.) can sweetened condensed milk (not evaporated)
½ teaspoon rum extract
2 eggs

1¼ cups all-purpose flour
¾ teaspoon baking powder
¼ teaspoon salt
2 cups diced mixed candied fruit
1 cup chopped pecans or walnuts

1. Heat oven to 350°F. Grease 13 × 9-inch pan. In large saucepan, melt margarine and chocolate over low heat, stirring constantly. Remove from heat. Add sweetened condensed milk and rum extract; blend well. Add eggs 1 at a time, beating well after each addition. Add flour, baking powder and salt; mix well. Stir in candied fruit and pecans. Spread in greased pan.

2. Bake at 350°F. for 28 to 36 minutes or until toothpick inserted in center comes out clean. Cool 1 hour or until completely cooled. Cut into bars.

Yield: 36 brownies
High Altitude (Above 3,500 Feet): Increase flour to 1½ cups. Bake as directed above.

Nutrition Information Per Serving

Serving Size: 1 Brownie. Calories 140 • Calories from Fat 60 • Total Fat 7 g
Saturated Fat 2 g • Cholesterol 16 mg • Sodium 75 mg • Dietary Fiber 1 g
Dietary Exchanges: ½ Starch, ½ Fruit, 1½ Fat OR 1 Carbohydrate, 1½ Fat

Fruitcake Fantasy Brownies; Date Pecan Blondies, page 145

Chocolate Almond Linzer Bars

Recipe Fact

These bars take their inspiration from Austrian **linzertorte**, a nutty tart filled with raspberry preserves. This recipe works well for a party, since it's both pretty and rich enough to cut into small portions—one batch yields four dozen squares.

About Almond Paste

Almond paste, available in cans or plastic tubes in grocery store baking aisles, is a pastelike mixture of ground almonds, sugar and glycerine, sometimes including egg white or other flavorings. Store unused almond paste in the refrigerator.

Recipe Variation

Make the bars with apricot preserves instead of raspberry.

Prep Time: 45 minutes (Ready in 2 hours 5 minutes)

3½ oz. purchased almond paste, softened	1 teaspoon almond extract
½ cup margarine or butter, softened	2 eggs
½ cup sugar	3 cups all-purpose flour
½ cup firmly packed brown sugar	1½ cups raspberry preserves
¼ teaspoon salt	½ cup sliced almonds
	½ cup miniature chocolate chips
	1 teaspoon powdered sugar

1. Heat oven to 350°F. Grease 15 × 10 × 1-inch baking pan. In large bowl, combine almond paste and margarine; blend until smooth. Add sugar, brown sugar, salt, almond extract and eggs; mix well. Add flour gradually, stirring to form a smooth dough.

2. Divide dough in half. Roll out half of dough between 2 sheets of waxed paper to form 15 × 10-inch rectangle. Remove top sheet of waxed paper. To prepare decorative top crust, using small heart-shaped canapé cutter, cut out 48 hearts (6 rows of 8 hearts each). Return dough cutouts to remaining half of dough. Set top crust aside.

3. With floured fingers, press remaining dough in bottom of greased pan. Bake at 350°F. for 10 minutes. Cool 5 minutes.

4. Spread evenly with raspberry preserves; sprinkle with almonds and chocolate chips. Lifting top crust with waxed paper, place dough side down over filling; carefully remove waxed paper. Trim edges if necessary.

5. Bake at 350°F. for an additional 20 to 25 minutes or until golden brown. Cool 1 hour or until completely cooled. Sprinkle with powdered sugar. Cut into 48 bars with heart cutout centered on each. Store in tightly covered container.

Yield: 48 bars
High Altitude (Above 3,500 Feet): No change.

Date Pecan Blondies

Prep Time: 15 minutes (Ready in 1 hour 35 minutes)

1½ cups firmly packed brown
  sugar
½ cup margarine or butter,
  softened
2 teaspoons vanilla
2 eggs
1½ cups all-purpose flour

1 teaspoon baking powder
½ teaspoon nutmeg
¼ teaspoon salt
1 cup chopped dates
½ cup chopped pecans
1 tablespoon powdered sugar

1. Heat oven to 350°F. Grease 13 × 9-inch pan. In large bowl, combine brown sugar and margarine; beat until light and fluffy. Add vanilla and eggs; blend well. Add flour, baking powder, nutmeg and salt; mix well. Stir in dates. Spread in greased pan. Sprinkle with pecans.

2. Bake at 350°F. for 18 to 28 minutes or until set and golden brown. Cool 1 hour or until completely cooled. Sprinkle with powdered sugar. Cut into bars.

Yield: 36 bars
High Altitude (Above 3,500 Feet): Increase flour to 1¾ cups. Bake as directed above.

Recipe Fact

The term "blondie" refers to a golden-tan "brownie" that contains no chocolate. It has the same texture as a traditional chocolate brownie but is made with brown sugar.

Make It Special

Instead of sprinkling the finished brownies with powdered sugar, top them with a glaze: 1 cup powdered sugar flavored with 3 to 5 teaspoons orange juice or orange liqueur and ½ teaspoon finely grated orange peel.

German Chocolate Saucepan Brownies

Prep Time: 25 minutes (Ready in 1 hour 45 minutes)

Brownies

½ cup margarine or butter
4 oz. sweet baking chocolate, chopped
½ cup sugar
1 teaspoon vanilla
2 eggs
1 cup all-purpose flour
½ teaspoon baking powder
¼ teaspoon salt

Topping

2 tablespoons margarine or butter, melted
½ cup firmly packed brown sugar
2 tablespoons corn syrup
2 tablespoons milk
1 cup coconut
½ cup finely chopped pecans or walnuts

1. Heat oven to 350°F. Grease bottom only of 8- or 9-inch square pan. In medium saucepan, melt ½ cup margarine and chocolate over low heat, stirring constantly. Cool 10 minutes or until slightly cooled.

2. Add sugar and vanilla; blend well. Add eggs; beat well. Add flour, baking powder and salt; mix well. Spread in greased pan.

3. Bake at 350°F. for 18 to 23 minutes or until toothpick inserted in center comes out clean. Remove brownies from oven. Set oven to broil.

4. In small bowl, combine 2 tablespoons margarine, brown sugar, corn syrup and milk; blend well. Stir in coconut and pecans. Drop mixture by teaspoonfuls evenly over warm brownies; spread gently. Broil 4 inches from heat for 1 to 1½ minutes or until bubbly. Cool 1 hour or until completely cooled. Cut into bars.

Yield: 20 brownies
High Altitude (Above 3,500 Feet): Increase flour to 1¼ cups. Bake as directed above.

German Chocolate Saucepan Brownies

Nutrition Information Per Serving
Serving Size: 1 Brownie. Calories 200 • Calories from Fat 100 • Total Fat 11 g
Saturated Fat 4 g • Cholesterol 20 mg • Sodium 130 mg • Dietary Fiber 1 g
Dietary Exchanges: 1 Starch, ½ Fruit, 2 Fat OR 1½ Carbohydrate, 2 Fat

Date Maple Cream Bars

About Sour Cream

The term "sour cream" is a misnomer in the sense that this dairy product is not at all spoiled. It is produced deliberately at the processing plant with the addition of an acidifier or lactic acid–producing bacteria to transform sweet cream into a tart, thick substance suitable for a wide range of sweet and savory dishes.

Kitchen Tip

Egg yolks and sour cream add richness and smoothness to the date filling, but both are delicate ingredients to use in a cooked sauce or filling. To prevent the mixture from curdling as it cooks, stir it constantly and make sure it doesn't come to a boil.

Prep Time: 45 minutes (Ready in 2 hours 5 minutes)

Filling
$3/4$ cup firmly packed brown sugar
1 tablespoon cornstarch
$1^1/2$ cups finely chopped dates
$1^1/2$ cups sour cream
1 teaspoon imitation maple extract
3 egg yolks

Base and Topping
$1^1/4$ cups all-purpose flour
2 cups quick-cooking rolled oats
$3/4$ cup firmly packed brown sugar
$1/2$ teaspoon baking soda
$3/4$ cup margarine or butter

1. Heat oven to 350°F. Grease 13 × 9-inch pan. In medium saucepan, combine all filling ingredients. Cook over medium heat until slightly thickened, stirring constantly. Cool slightly.

2. Meanwhile, in medium bowl, combine flour, oats, $3/4$ cup brown sugar and baking soda; mix well. With pastry blender or fork, cut in margarine until mixture is crumbly. Reserve $1^1/2$ cups oat mixture for topping. Press remaining oat mixture evenly in bottom of greased pan to form base.

3. Bake at 350°F. for 10 minutes. Spoon filling evenly over base. Sprinkle with reserved topping. Bake an additional 20 to 30 minutes or until light golden brown and set. Cool 1 hour or until completely cooled. Cut into bars.

Yield: 36 bars
High Altitude (Above 3,500 Feet): No change.

Nutrition Information Per Serving
Serving Size: 1 Bar. Calories 160 • Calories from Fat 60 • Total Fat 7 g
Saturated Fat 2 g • Cholesterol 25 mg • Sodium 70 mg • Dietary Fiber 1 g
Dietary Exchanges: $1^1/2$ Fruit, $1^1/2$ Fat OR $1^1/2$ Carbohydrate, $1^1/2$ Fat

Fudgy Brownies

Prep Time: 30 minutes (Ready in 2 hours)

Brownies
4 oz. unsweetened chocolate
½ cup margarine or butter
2 cups sugar
2 teaspoons vanilla
4 eggs
1 cup all-purpose flour

¼ teaspoon salt

Glaze
½ cup semi-sweet chocolate chips
1 tablespoon margarine or butter

1. Heat oven to 350°F. Grease 13 × 9-inch pan. In small saucepan over low heat, melt chocolate and ½ cup margarine, stirring constantly until smooth. Remove from heat; cool 10 minutes or until slightly cooled.

2. In medium bowl, combine sugar, vanilla and eggs; beat until light and fluffy. Add flour, salt and chocolate mixture; blend well. Spread in greased pan.

3. Bake at 350°F. for 30 to 38 minutes. DO NOT OVERBAKE. Cool 1 hour or until completely cooled.

4. In small saucepan, melt glaze ingredients over low heat, stirring constantly until smooth. Drizzle glaze over cooled brownies. Let stand until set. Cut into bars.

Yield: 24 brownies
High Altitude (Above 3,500 Feet): No change.

Nutrition Information Per Serving
Serving Size: 1 Brownie. Calories 120 • Calories from Fat 50 • Total Fat 6 g
Saturated Fat 2 g • Cholesterol 24 mg • Sodium 55 mg • Dietary Fiber 1 g
Dietary Exchanges: 1 Starch, 1 Fat OR 1 Carbohydrate, 1 Fat

Recipe Fact

This is the purist's back-to-basics brownie at its best—just smooth, rich chocolate with no nuts or other distractions. You can even skip the glaze, if you like.

Kitchen Tip

Remove brownies from the oven while they are still barely moist in the center. They will continue to firm up as they sit on the countertop.

Storage Tip

Brownies freeze very well. Wrap them individually in plastic wrap, then pop a bunch into a heavy-duty freezer bag. Defrost in the microwave for a quick cure when the next chocolate emergency strikes.

Fudgy Butterscotch Bars

Prep Time: 20 minutes (Ready in 1 hour 45 minutes)

1 (12-oz.) pkg. (2 cups) semi-
   sweet chocolate chips
2 tablespoons margarine or
   butter
1 (14-oz.) can sweetened
   condensed milk (not
   evaporated)
1 cup margarine or butter
2¼ cups firmly packed brown
   sugar

2 eggs
2 cups all-purpose flour
½ cup coconut
½ cup chopped pecans or
   walnuts
1 teaspoon salt
1 teaspoon vanilla

1. Heat oven to 350°F. Grease 15 × 10 × 1-inch baking pan. In medium saucepan, combine chocolate chips, 2 tablespoons margarine and sweetened condensed milk. Cook over low heat until chocolate is melted and mixture is smooth, stirring constantly. Set aside.

2. In large saucepan, melt 1 cup margarine over low heat. Remove from heat. Add brown sugar and eggs; blend well. Add all remaining ingredients; mix well. Spread half of batter in greased pan. Drop chocolate mixture by tablespoonfuls over batter; carefully spread to cover. Drop remaining batter by teaspoonfuls over chocolate mixture. With tip of knife, swirl slightly to marble mixture.

3. Bake at 350°F. for 25 to 35 minutes or until light golden brown and center is set. Cool 1 hour or until completely cooled. Cut into bars.

Yield: 48 bars
High Altitude (Above 3,500 Feet): Decrease brown sugar to 2 cups; increase flour to 2½ cups. Bake as directed above.

Nutrition Information Per Serving
Serving Size: 1 Bar. Calories 170 • Calories from Fat 70 • Total Fat 8 g
Saturated Fat 3 g • Cholesterol 12 mg • Sodium 115 mg • Dietary Fiber 1 g
Dietary Exchanges: ½ Starch, 1 Fruit, 1½ Fat OR 1½ Carbohydrate, 1½ Fat

About Canned Milk

Sweetened condensed milk and evaporated milk both come in cans, but they are not interchangeable. Evaporated milk, processed to reduce its water content, has the pouring consistency of cream and a slight off-white color. Sweetened condensed milk also has been processed to reduce moisture content, but added sugar gives it a very sweet flavor and more syrupy consistency. Refrigerate both after opening.

Kitchen Tip

Nuts contain essential oils, which can turn rancid at room temperature. For long-term keeping, store nuts in a tightly sealed bag or container in the freezer.

Fudgy Butterscotch Bars; White Chocolate Cranberry Bars, page 153

Glazed Cheesecake Brownies

Prep Time: 20 minutes (Ready in 6 hours)

Topping
1 (8-oz.) pkg. cream cheese, softened
2 tablespoons margarine, softened
½ cup sugar
1 teaspoon vanilla
2 eggs

Brownies
4 oz. semi-sweet chocolate

3 tablespoons margarine
½ cup sugar
1 teaspoon vanilla
2 eggs
½ cup all-purpose flour
½ teaspoon baking powder
¼ teaspoon salt

Glaze
1 oz. semi-sweet chocolate
2 teaspoons margarine

1. Heat oven to 350°F. Grease and flour 9-inch square pan. In small bowl, combine all topping ingredients; blend well. Set aside.

2. In medium saucepan, melt 4 oz. chocolate and 3 tablespoons margarine over low heat, stirring constantly until smooth. Remove from heat; cool 15 minutes. Add ½ cup sugar and vanilla; blend well. Beat in 2 eggs 1 at a time, blending well after each addition. Add flour, baking powder and salt; stir just until blended. Pour into greased and floured pan. Pour topping over batter.

3. Bake at 350°F. for 40 to 50 minutes or until toothpick inserted in center comes out clean. Cool completely.

4. In small saucepan, melt glaze ingredients until smooth, stirring constantly. Drizzle over brownies. Refrigerate at least 4 hours. Cut into bars. Store in refrigerator.

Yield: 24 brownies
High Altitude (Above 3,500 Feet): Increase flour to ½ cup plus 2 tablespoons. Bake as directed above.

Nutrition Information Per Serving
Serving Size: 1 Brownie. Calories 150 • Calories from Fat 80 • Total Fat 9 g
Saturated Fat 4 g • Cholesterol 45 mg • Sodium 105 mg • Dietary Fiber 0 g
Dietary Exchanges: 1 Fruit, 2 Fat OR 1 Carbohydrate, 2 Fat

White Chocolate Cranberry Bars

Prep Time: 15 minutes (Ready in 1 hour 45 minutes)

2¼ cups all-purpose flour
1 teaspoon baking powder
½ teaspoon baking soda
½ teaspoon salt
⅔ cup firmly packed brown sugar
½ cup sugar
½ cup unsalted or regular butter, softened

2 eggs
2 teaspoons vanilla
1 cup coarsely chopped fresh or frozen cranberries
1 cup chopped walnuts
1 (12-oz.) pkg. (2 cups) white vanilla chips
1 tablespoon shortening

Make It Special

Experiment with various ways to drizzle the icing onto the bars: make dots and squiggles, for example, cross-hatch designs or spirals.

1. Heat oven to 350°F. Grease 13 × 9-inch pan. In large bowl, combine flour, baking powder, baking soda and salt; mix well.

2. In another large bowl, combine brown sugar, sugar and butter; beat until light and fluffy. Add eggs 1 at a time, beating well after each addition. Add vanilla; blend well. Gradually add flour mixture; blend at low speed just until combined. Fold in cranberries, walnuts and 1½ cups of the vanilla chips. (Reserve remaining chips for topping.) Spread batter in greased pan.

3. Bake at 350°F. for 30 to 40 minutes or until golden brown.

4. In small saucepan over low heat, melt reserved ½ cup vanilla chips and shortening, stirring occasionally. Drizzle over warm bars. Cool 1 hour or until completely cooled. Cut into bars.

Yield: 36 bars
High Altitude (Above 3,500 Feet): No change.

Nutrition Information Per Serving
Serving Size: 1 Bar. Calories 160 • Calories from Fat 70 • Total Fat 8 g
Saturated Fat 4 g • Cholesterol 21 mg • Sodium 75 mg • Dietary Fiber 1 g
Dietary Exchanges: 1½ Fruit, 1½ Fat OR 1½ Carbohydrate, 1½ Fat

Caramel Apple Bars

Prep Time: 30 minutes (Ready in 1 hour 50 minutes)

About Apples

Of the many varieties of apple available on the market, good choices for this recipe include McIntosh, Cortland, Granny Smith and Greening.

Kitchen Tip

For easier cutting, refrigerate the bars long enough to firm them up.

Make It Special

Serve these rich-tasting bars with a scoop of ice cream or dollop of whipped cream.

Base and Topping
2 cups all-purpose flour
2 cups quick-cooking rolled oats
1½ cups firmly packed brown sugar
1 teaspoon baking soda
1¼ cups margarine or butter, melted

Filling
1½ cups caramel ice cream topping
½ cup all-purpose flour
2 cups coarsely chopped apples
½ cup chopped walnuts or pecans

1. Heat oven to 350°F. Grease 15 × 10 × 1-inch baking pan. In large bowl, combine all base and topping ingredients; mix at low speed until crumbly. Press half of mixture (about 2½ cups) in bottom of greased pan to form base. Reserve remaining mixture for topping. Bake at 350°F. for 8 minutes.

2. Meanwhile, in small saucepan over medium heat, combine caramel topping and ½ cup flour. Bring to a boil, stirring constantly. Boil 3 to 5 minutes or until mixture thickens slightly, stirring constantly. Sprinkle apples and nuts over warm base. Pour caramel mixture evenly over top. Sprinkle with reserved topping mixture.

3. Bake at 350°F. for an additional 20 to 25 minutes or until golden brown. Cool 30 minutes. Refrigerate 30 minutes or until set. Cut into bars. Store in tightly covered container.

Yield: 48 bars
High Altitude (Above 3,500 Feet): Bake at 375°F. as directed above.

Nutrition Information Per Serving
Serving Size: 1 Bar. Calories 150 • Calories from Fat 50 • Total Fat 6 g
Saturated Fat 1 g • Cholesterol 0 mg • Sodium 120 mg • Dietary Fiber 1 g
Dietary Exchanges: 1½ Fruit, 1 Fat OR 1½ Carbohydrate, 1 Fat

Cashew Caramel Brownies

editor's favorite

Prep Time: 20 minutes (Ready in 2 hours 10 minutes)

Brownies
1½ cups firmly packed brown
    sugar
¾ cup unsalted or regular
    butter, softened
3 eggs
3 oz. unsweetened chocolate,
    melted, cooled
1 tablespoon vanilla

1¼ cups all-purpose flour
¼ teaspoon salt
1½ cups semi-sweet chocolate
    chips
1 cup chopped cashews

Topping
16 caramels, unwrapped
3 tablespoons milk

1. Heat oven to 325°F. Line two 9-inch square pans with foil, extending foil over edges; lightly grease foil. In large bowl, combine brown sugar and butter; beat until light and fluffy. Add eggs 1 at a time, beating well after each addition. Add cooled unsweetened chocolate and vanilla; blend well. Add flour and salt; mix well. Fold in chocolate chips. Pour batter into greased foil-lined pans. Sprinkle cashews evenly over batter; press lightly.

2. Bake at 325°F. for 20 to 25 minutes or until firm to touch. Cool 30 minutes.

3. In small saucepan, combine topping ingredients; cook over low heat, stirring frequently, until caramels are melted and mixture is smooth. Drizzle evenly over brownies. Cool 1 hour or until completely cooled. Remove brownies from pan by lifting foil; remove foil. Cut into bars.

Yield: 48 brownies
High Altitude (Above 3,500 Feet): Increase flour to 1½ cups; decrease brown sugar to 1¼ cups. Bake as directed above.

Nutrition Information Per Serving
Serving Size: 1 Brownie. Calories 130 • Calories from Fat 60 • Total Fat 7 g
Saturated Fat 4 g • Cholesterol 21 mg • Sodium 30 mg • Dietary Fiber 1 g
Dietary Exchanges: 1 Fruit, 1½ Fat OR 1 Carbohydrate, 1½ Fat

Kitchen Tip

When melting chocolate on the stovetop, place it in a saucepan set over low heat and stir it frequently to prevent scorching. Or put the chocolate in the top of a double boiler set over barely simmering—not boiling—water, as pure chocolate will seize up and turn hard if a drop of water or even a blast of steam should interfere with the melting.

Ingredient Substitution

If you don't have cashews on hand, use walnuts or pecans in their place.

Peanut Brittle Bars

Prep Time: 25 minutes (Ready in 1 hour 25 minutes)

Base

1½ cups all-purpose flour
½ cup whole wheat flour
1 cup firmly packed brown
    sugar
1 teaspoon baking soda
¼ teaspoon salt
1 cup margarine or butter

Topping

2 cups salted peanuts
1 cup milk chocolate chips
1 (12.5-oz.) jar caramel ice
    cream topping
3 tablespoons all-purpose flour

1. Heat oven to 350°F. Grease 15 × 10 × 1-inch baking pan. In large bowl, combine all base ingredients except margarine; mix well. Using pastry blender or fork, cut in margarine until crumbly. Press evenly in bottom of greased pan. Bake at 350°F. for 8 to 14 minutes or until golden brown.

2. Sprinkle peanuts and chocolate chips over warm base. In small bowl, combine caramel topping and 3 tablespoons flour; blend well. Drizzle evenly over chocolate chips and peanuts.

3. Bake at 350°F. for an additional 12 to 18 minutes or until topping is set and golden brown. Cool 1 hour or until completely cooled. Cut into bars.

Yield: 48 bars
High Altitude (Above 3,500 Feet): No change.

Nutrition Information Per Serving

Serving Size: 1 Bar. Calories 150 • Calories from Fat 70 • Total Fat 8 g
Saturated Fat 2 g • Cholesterol 0 mg • Sodium 140 mg • Dietary Fiber 1 g
Dietary Exchanges: 1 Starch, 1½ Fat OR 1 Carbohydrate, 1½ Fat

---

Recipe Fact

These bars embellish the flavors of classic peanut brittle. At its simplest, peanut brittle is a confection of melted, caramelized sugar poured over nuts and allowed to harden into a shiny, crisp sheet.

About Peanuts

Peanuts are not a true nut, but rather a legume that grows under the ground. Most nuts are sold roasted—the raw nuts have a softer texture and blander flavor.

Peanut Brittle Bars

Cranberry Orange Bars

Prep Time: 15 minutes (Ready in 1 hour 40 minutes)

Base and Topping
2 cups all-purpose flour
1½ cups old-fashioned rolled oats
1 cup coconut
1 cup firmly packed brown sugar
1 teaspoon baking soda
1½ teaspoons cinnamon
1 cup margarine or butter, softened
1 cup chopped walnuts

Filling
1 cup orange marmalade
1 (16-oz.) can whole berry cranberry sauce

1. Heat oven to 350°F. In large bowl, combine flour, oats, coconut, brown sugar, baking soda and cinnamon; mix well. Add margarine; mix until crumbly. Press 3 cups of mixture in bottom of ungreased 15 × 10 × 1-inch baking pan to form base. Add walnuts to remaining mixture; reserve for topping.

2. In small bowl, combine marmalade and cranberry sauce. Spread evenly over base. Sprinkle reserved topping evenly over filling; press lightly.

3. Bake at 350°F. for 25 to 30 minutes or until deep golden brown. Cool 1 hour or until completely cooled. Cut into bars.

Yield: 48 bars
High Altitude (Above 3,500 Feet): No change.

Nutrition Information Per Serving
Serving Size: 1 Bar. Calories 130 • Calories from Fat 50 • Total Fat 6 g
Saturated Fat 1 g • Cholesterol 0 mg • Sodium 75 mg • Dietary Fiber 1 g
Dietary Exchanges: 1½ Fruit, 1 Fat OR 1½ Carbohydrate, 1 Fat

Chocolate Syrup Pecan Brownies

Prep Time: 30 minutes (Ready in 3 hours)

Brownies
1 cup sugar
½ cup margarine or butter, softened
1 tablespoon vanilla
3 eggs
1 (16-oz.) can chocolate-flavored syrup
1¼ cups all-purpose flour

½ cup finely chopped pecans

Frosting
¼ cup margarine or butter
¼ cup unsweetened cocoa
1½ cups powdered sugar
½ teaspoon vanilla
2 to 3 tablespoons milk
½ cup finely chopped pecans

1. Heat oven to 350°F. Grease 13 × 9-inch pan. In large bowl, combine sugar and ½ cup margarine; beat until light and fluffy. Add 1 tablespoon vanilla, eggs and chocolate syrup; blend well. Add flour; mix well. Stir in ½ cup pecans. Spread in greased pan.

2. Bake at 350°F. for 30 to 35 minutes or until toothpick inserted in center comes out clean. Cool 1 hour or until completely cooled.

3. Melt ¼ cup margarine in medium saucepan over medium heat. Stir in cocoa; heat until mixture just comes to a boil, stirring constantly. Cool 10 minutes or until slightly cooled. Stir in powdered sugar, ½ teaspoon vanilla and enough milk for desired spreading consistency; blend until smooth. Stir in ½ cup pecans. Spread carefully over cooled brownies. Cool 1 hour or until completely cooled. Cut into bars.

Yield: 36 brownies
High Altitude (Above 3,500 Feet): No change.

Nutrition Information Per Serving

Serving Size: 1 Brownie. Calories 160 • Calories from Fat 60 • Total Fat 7 g
Saturated Fat 1 g • Cholesterol 20 mg • Sodium 65 mg • Dietary Fiber 1 g
Dietary Exchanges: 1½ Fruit, 1½ Fat OR 1½ Carbohydrate, 1½ Fat

---

About Chocolate Syrup

Chocolate-flavored syrup typically consists of corn syrup, cocoa and other ingredients. It must be labeled "chocolate-flavored" rather than just simply "chocolate" because it contains no chocolate liquor, the product of the cacao tree that's the basis for true chocolate.

Ingredient Substitution

Chocolate-flavored syrup from a squeeze bottle will work as well as the canned version.

Pecan Blondies with Browned Butter Frosting

Prep Time: 30 minutes (Ready in 1 hour 55 minutes)

Bars

1 cup sugar
$\frac{1}{2}$ cup firmly packed brown sugar
$\frac{1}{2}$ cup butter, softened
1 teaspoon vanilla
2 eggs
$1\frac{1}{2}$ cups all-purpose flour
1 teaspoon baking powder
$\frac{1}{2}$ teaspoon salt
$\frac{1}{2}$ cup chopped pecans

Frosting

2 tablespoons butter (do not use margarine)
2 cups powdered sugar
$\frac{1}{4}$ teaspoon vanilla
2 to 4 tablespoons milk
36 pecan halves, if desired

1. Heat oven to 350°F. Grease 13 × 9-inch pan. In large bowl, combine sugar, brown sugar and $\frac{1}{2}$ cup butter; beat until light and fluffy. Add 1 teaspoon vanilla and eggs; blend well. Add flour, baking powder and salt; mix well. Stir in $\frac{1}{2}$ cup pecans. Spread in greased pan.

2. Bake at 350°F. for 23 to 33 minutes or until toothpick inserted in center comes out clean. Cool 1 hour or until completely cooled.

3. Heat 2 tablespoons butter in medium saucepan over medium heat until light golden brown. Remove from heat. Stir in powdered sugar, $\frac{1}{4}$ teaspoon vanilla and enough milk for desired spreading consistency; blend until smooth. Spread over cooled bars. Arrange pecan halves over frosting. Cut into bars.

Yield: 36 bars
High Altitude (Above 3,500 Feet): Increase flour to $1\frac{3}{4}$ cups; decrease granulated sugar to $\frac{1}{2}$ cup. Bake as directed above.

Nutrition Information Per Serving

Serving Size: 1 Bar. Calories 130 • Calories from Fat 45 • Total Fat 5 g
Saturated Fat 2 g • Cholesterol 20 mg • Sodium 80 mg • Dietary Fiber 0 g
Dietary Exchanges: $1\frac{1}{2}$ Fruit, 1 Fat OR $1\frac{1}{2}$ Carbohydrate, 1 Fat

Pecan Blondies with Browned Butter Frosting

Ingredient Substitution

Use semi-sweet chocolate chips and vanilla milk chips instead of the chunks.

Make It Special

Add ½ cup chopped macadamia nuts to the batter.

White Chocolate Chunk Brownie Wedges

Prep Time: 30 minutes (Ready in 55 minutes)

Brownies
½ cup margarine or butter
4 oz. white chocolate baking bar, cut into pieces
2 eggs
⅛ teaspoon salt
½ cup sugar
1½ teaspoons vanilla

1¼ cups all-purpose flour
2 oz. semi-sweet chocolate, cut into pieces

Glaze
1 oz. semi-sweet chocolate
2 teaspoons margarine or butter

1. Heat oven to 350°F. Grease and flour 9-inch round cake pan. In small saucepan, melt ½ cup margarine and 2 oz. of the white chocolate pieces over low heat, stirring constantly until melted. Remove from heat; set aside.
2. In small bowl, combine eggs and salt; beat until frothy. Add sugar and continue beating for about 3 minutes or until light in color and thickened. Add melted white chocolate mixture and vanilla; blend well. Add flour; mix well. Fold in remaining 2 oz. white chocolate pieces and 2 oz. semi-sweet chocolate pieces. Spread in greased and floured pan.
3. Bake at 350°F. for 23 to 28 minutes or until toothpick inserted in center comes out clean. Cool 1 hour or until completely cooled.
4. In small saucepan, melt glaze ingredients until smooth, stirring constantly. Drizzle glaze over brownies. Let stand until set. Cut into wedges.

Yield: 12 brownie wedges
High Altitude (Above 3,500 Feet): Increase flour to 1⅓ cups. Bake as directed above.

Nutrition Information Per Serving
Serving Size: 1 Wedge. Calories 250 • Calories from Fat 130 • Total Fat 14 g
Saturated Fat 5 g • Cholesterol 35 mg • Sodium 140 mg • Dietary Fiber 1 g
Dietary Exchanges: 2 Fruit, 2 Fat OR 2 Carbohydrate, 2 Fat

Peanut Butter Macaroon Brownies

Prep Time: 15 minutes (Ready in 1 hour 45 minutes)

Brownies

2 cups sugar

1 cup margarine or butter, softened

$1\frac{1}{4}$ teaspoons vanilla

4 eggs

$1\frac{1}{2}$ cups all-purpose flour

$\frac{2}{3}$ cup unsweetened cocoa

1 cup peanut butter chips

Topping

1 (14-oz.) can sweetened condensed milk (not evaporated)

1 (7-oz.) pkg. ($2\frac{2}{3}$ cups) coconut

1 (6-oz.) pkg. (1 cup) semi-sweet chocolate chips

1. Heat oven to 350°F. Grease 15 × 10 × 1-inch baking pan. In large bowl, combine sugar, margarine and vanilla; beat until light and fluffy. Add eggs 1 at a time, beating well after each addition. Add flour and cocoa; mix well. Stir in peanut butter chips. Spread in greased pan.
2. In small bowl, combine all topping ingredients. Spoon topping by teaspoonfuls over brownies; spread carefully.
3. Bake at 350°F. for 27 to 32 minutes or until topping is light golden brown. Cool 1 hour or until completely cooled. Cut into bars.

Yield: 36 brownies
High Altitude (Above 3,500 Feet): No change.

Nutrition Information Per Serving

Serving Size: 1 Brownie. Calories 240 • Calories from Fat 100 • Total Fat 11 g
Saturated Fat 5 g • Cholesterol 25 mg • Sodium 105 mg • Dietary Fiber 1 g
Dietary Exchanges: 1½ Starch, ½ Fruit, 2 Fat OR 2 Carbohydrate, 2 Fat

---

About Sweetened Condensed Milk

In some Spanish-speaking countries, sweetened condensed milk is a favorite lightener for **café cortado**—strong coffee "cut" with the addition of sweetened condensed milk.

Ingredient Substitution

For peanutty flavor with less sweetness, substitute 1 cup chopped roasted peanuts for the peanut butter chips.

Pineapple Nut Bars

Prep Time: 30 minutes (Ready in 2 hours 50 minutes)

Base
1 cup all-purpose flour
½ cup sugar
½ cup margarine or butter

Filling
1 (8-oz.) pkg. cream cheese, softened
2 tablespoons sugar
2 tablespoons milk
1 teaspoon vanilla
1 egg

1 (8-oz.) can crushed pineapple, well drained
1 cup coconut
½ cup chopped macadamia nuts or almonds
1 tablespoon margarine or butter, melted

Glaze
½ cup powdered sugar
¼ teaspoon rum extract
3 to 4 teaspoons milk

1. Heat oven to 350°F. In medium bowl, combine flour and ½ cup sugar. Using pastry blender or fork, cut in ½ cup margarine until mixture resembles coarse crumbs. Press in bottom of ungreased 9-inch square pan. Bake at 350°F. for 10 minutes.

2. Meanwhile, in small bowl, combine cream cheese, 2 tablespoons sugar, 2 tablespoons milk, vanilla and egg; beat until smooth. Stir in pineapple. Spread over partially baked base. In small bowl, combine coconut, nuts and 1 tablespoon margarine; sprinkle evenly over pineapple mixture.

3. Bake at 350°F. for an additional 18 to 20 minutes or until coconut is golden brown and filling appears set. Cool 1 hour or until completely cooled.

4. In small bowl, combine powdered sugar, rum extract and enough milk for desired drizzling consistency; blend until smooth. Drizzle over cooled bars. Refrigerate 1 hour or until set. Cut into bars. Store in refrigerator.

Yield: 36 bars
High Altitude (Above 3,500 Feet): No change.

Pineapple Nut Bars

Spicy Molasses Bars

Prep Time: 15 minutes (Ready in 1 hour 35 minutes)

About Molasses

Molasses is a by-product of the sugar-making process. Light molasses has a lighter color and flavor than the less sweet dark molasses. Dark molasses is typical in gingerbread and would be a fine choice for this bar.

Storage Tip

Keep these bars tightly covered to retain moistness.

½ cup sugar
½ cup oil
½ cup molasses
1 egg
1½ cups all-purpose flour
¾ teaspoon baking soda
½ teaspoon cinnamon
¼ teaspoon salt
¼ teaspoon nutmeg
¼ teaspoon cloves
¼ cup boiling water
½ cup granola
½ cup raisins
1 teaspoon powdered sugar, if desired

1. Heat oven to 350°F. Grease 13 × 9-inch pan. In large bowl, combine sugar, oil and molasses; blend well. Add egg; blend well. Add flour, baking soda, cinnamon, salt, nutmeg and cloves; mix well. Add boiling water; blend well. Stir in granola and raisins. Spread in greased pan.
2. Bake at 350°F. for 20 to 30 minutes or until toothpick inserted in center comes out clean. Cool 1 hour or until completely cooled. Sprinkle with powdered sugar. Cut into bars.

Yield: 36 bars
High Altitude (Above 3,500 Feet): Increase flour to 2 cups; increase boiling water to ½ cup. Bake as directed above.

Nutrition Information Per Serving

Serving Size: 1 Bar. Calories 90 • Calories from Fat 35 • Total Fat 4 g
Saturated Fat 1 g • Cholesterol 5 mg • Sodium 45 mg • Dietary Fiber 0 g
Dietary Exchanges: ½ Starch, 1 Fat OR ½ Carbohydrate, 1 Fat

Rainbow Cookie Brittle

Prep Time: 25 minutes (Ready in 1 hour 25 minutes)

1 cup sugar
3/4 cup margarine or butter, softened
1 teaspoon vanilla

1 1/2 cups all-purpose flour
1/2 cup miniature candy-coated chocolate baking bits or miniature chocolate chips

1. Heat oven to 375°F. In large bowl, combine sugar and margarine; beat until light and fluffy. Add vanilla; blend well. Add flour; mix well. Stir in baking bits. Press dough into ungreased 15 × 10 × 1-inch baking pan.
2. Bake at 375°F. for 10 to 15 minutes or until light golden brown. Cool 1 hour or until completely cooled. Break into irregular-shaped pieces.

Yield: 48 pieces
High Altitude (Above 3,500 Feet): No change.

Nutrition Information Per Serving

Serving Size: 1 Piece Calories 70 • Calories from Fat 25 • Total Fat 3 g
Saturated Fat 1 g • Cholesterol 0 mg • Sodium 35 mg • Dietary Fiber 0 g
Dietary Exchanges: 1/2 Starch, 1/2 Fat OR 1/2 Carbohydrate, 1/2 Fat

Kitchen Tip

After the cookie is baked, turn it upside down onto a clean, dry work surface and break it into irregularly sized pieces. Let the kids help!

Sunburst Lemon Bars

Prep Time: 15 minutes (Ready in 2 hours)

Kitchen Tip

Cool these bars completely and let the filling set before attempting to cut them.

Recipe Variation

To simplify the final touch for this rich dessert, sift powdered sugar over the top instead of icing.

Base

2 cups all-purpose flour
½ cup powdered sugar
1 cup margarine or butter, softened

Filling

4 eggs, slightly beaten

2 cups sugar
¼ cup all-purpose flour
1 teaspoon baking powder
¼ cup lemon juice

Frosting

1 cup powdered sugar
2 to 3 tablespoons lemon juice

1. Heat oven to 350°F. In large bowl, combine all base ingredients at low speed until crumbly. Press mixture evenly in bottom of ungreased 13 × 9-inch pan. Bake at 350°F. for 20 to 30 minutes or until light golden brown.
2. Meanwhile, in large bowl, combine all filling ingredients except lemon juice; blend well. Stir in ¼ cup lemon juice. Pour mixture over warm base.
3. Bake at 350°F. for an additional 25 to 30 minutes or until top is light golden brown. Cool 1 hour or until completely cooled.
4. In small bowl, combine 1 cup powdered sugar and enough lemon juice for desired spreading consistency; blend until smooth. Frost cooled bars. Cut into bars.

Yield: 36 bars
High Altitude (Above 3,500 Feet): No change.

Nutrition Information Per Serving
Serving Size: 1 Bar. Calories 140 • Calories from Fat 50 • Total Fat 6 g
Saturated Fat 1 g • Cholesterol 24 mg • Sodium 75 mg • Dietary Fiber 0 g
Dietary Exchanges: 1½ Fruit, 1 Fat OR 1½ Carbohydrate, 1 Fat

Sunburst Lemon Bars

Glazed Rhubarb Pastry Bars

About Rhubarb

Rhubarb, a perennial easy-grow garden favorite in temperate and cold climates, has fibrous greenish red stalks similar to those of celery and dark green leaves that are beautiful—and poisonous. Only rhubarb's stalks are edible. Sweet strawberries are a traditional and pleasing foil to the rhubarb's tartness.

Kitchen Tip

Exposed to warm water, yeast will begin to foam and expand with leavening power. Do not use boiling water; it will kill the yeast. You can add a bit of the recipe's sugar to the yeast as it dissolves to encourage foaming, but never add salt directly to yeast—it too will reduce the leavening ability.

Pastry
1 pkg. active dry yeast
1/4 cup warm water
4 cups all-purpose flour
1/4 cup sugar
1/4 teaspoon salt
1 cup margarine or butter
3/4 cup warm milk

Filling
4 cups finely chopped fresh or
    frozen rhubarb

3/4 cup sugar
1 (3-oz.) pkg. strawberry flavor
    gelatin

Glaze
1 cup powdered sugar
1 tablespoon margarine or
    butter, melted
1 to 2 tablespoons milk

1. Heat oven to 400°F. Grease 15 × 10 × 1-inch jelly roll pan. In small bowl, soften yeast in warm water (105 to 115°F.). In large bowl, combine flour, 1/4 cup sugar and salt. With pastry blender or fork, cut in 1 cup margarine until crumbly. Add yeast mixture and 3/4 cup warm milk (105 to 115°F.); mix well.

2. Divide pastry dough in half; shape into balls. Between sheets of waxed paper, roll out each ball of pastry to 17 × 12-inch rectangle. Remove top sheet of waxed paper from 1 rectangle. Place pastry rectangle in greased pan; remove remaining waxed paper. Press pastry over bottom and slightly up sides of pan.

3. In medium bowl, combine all filling ingredients. Spread evenly in pastry-lined pan. Remove top sheet of waxed paper from remaining pastry rectangle; place over filling. Remove remaining waxed paper. Seal edges securely. Prick top pastry with fork in several places.

4. Bake at 400°F. for 25 to 35 minutes or until light golden brown.

5. In small bowl, combine all glaze ingredients, adding

enough milk for desired glaze consistency; blend until smooth. Drizzle over warm bars. Cool 1 hour or until completely cooled. Cut into bars.

Yield: 48 bars
High Altitude (Above 3,500 Feet): No change.

Nutrition Information Per Serving

Serving Size: 1 Bar. Calories 110 • Calories from Fat 35 • Total Fat 4 g
Saturated Fat 1 g • Cholesterol 0 mg • Sodium 65 mg • Dietary Fiber 1 g
Dietary Exchanges: 1 Fruit, 1 Fat OR 1 Carbohydrate, 1 Fat

Jan Hagel Bars

Prep Time: 15 minutes (Ready in 1 hour 45 minutes)

½ cup sugar
1 cup margarine or butter,
    softened
¼ teaspoon almond extract
1 egg, separated

2 cups all-purpose flour
½ teaspoon cinnamon
1 tablespoon water
½ cup sliced almonds
¼ cup sugar

1. Heat oven to 350°F. Grease 15 × 10 × 1-inch baking pan. In large bowl, combine ½ cup sugar, margarine, almond extract and egg yolk; blend well. Add flour and cinnamon; mix well. Press evenly in greased pan.
2. In small bowl, combine water and egg white; beat until frothy. Brush over dough. Sprinkle evenly with almonds and ¼ cup sugar.
3. Bake at 350°F. for 17 to 22 minutes or until light golden brown. Immediately cut into 3 × 1-inch bars. Cool in pan 1 hour or until completely cooled.

Yield: 50 bars
High Altitude (Above 3,500 Feet): No change.

Nutrition Information Per Serving

Serving Size: 1 Bar. Calories 70 • Calories from Fat 35 • Total Fat 4 g
Saturated Fat 1 g • Cholesterol 4 mg • Sodium 45 mg • Dietary Fiber 0 g
Dietary Exchanges: ½ Fruit, 1 Fat OR ½ Carbohydrate, 1 Fat

Recipe Fact

Jan Hagel Bars are a traditional Dutch cookie or small cake flavored with cinnamon and topped with almonds and sugar.

Kitchen Tip

Press the dough in an even layer in the pan to ensure uniform browning.

Ingredient Substitution

Sliced almonds are in keeping with the thin, crisp texture of the bars underneath, but you can substitute chopped almonds without sacrificing flavor.

Homemade Chewy Granola Bars

Prep Time: 15 minutes (Ready in 1 hour 30 minutes)

About Sesame Seeds

Small white sesame seeds add nutty flavor to recipes. To bring out the flavor, toast the seeds in a dry frying pan for a minute or two, just until they become fragrant and begin to brown. Watch them carefully, or they will also start to pop out of the pan! Sesame seeds have a high oil content, so buy them in small quantities and use them up before they develop an "off" flavor. Asian markets carry the black sesame seeds sometimes specified in Chinese recipes.

Ingredient Substitution

Granola by its very nature is a mix-and-match proposition, so if you find you lack some of the crunchy or chewy add-ins listed here, substitute more of another from the list or try something else such as chopped dried apricots or similar dried fruit, cashew nuts, etc.

1 cup firmly packed brown sugar
$^2/_3$ cup peanut butter
$^1/_2$ cup light corn syrup
$^1/_2$ cup margarine or butter, melted
2 teaspoons vanilla
3 cups quick-cooking rolled oats
$^1/_2$ cup coconut
$^1/_2$ cup shelled sunflower seeds
$^1/_2$ cup raisins
$^1/_3$ cup wheat germ
2 tablespoons sesame seed
1 (6-oz.) pkg. (1 cup) semi-sweet chocolate chips or carob chips, if desired

1. Heat oven to 350°F. Grease 13 × 9-inch pan. In large bowl, combine brown sugar, peanut butter, corn syrup, margarine and vanilla; blend well. Add all remaining ingredients; mix well. Press evenly in greased pan.
2. Bake at 350°F. for 15 to 20 minutes or until light golden brown. Cool 1 hour or until completely cooled. Cut into bars.

Yield: 24 bars
High Altitude (Above 3,500 Feet): No change.

Nutrition Information Per Serving

Serving Size: 1 Bar. Calories 270 • Calories from Fat 120 • Total Fat 13 g
Saturated Fat 3 g • Cholesterol 0 mg • Sodium 95 mg • Dietary Fiber 3 g
Dietary Exchanges: 2 Starch, 2$^1/_2$ Fat OR 2 Carbohydrate, 2$^1/_2$ Fat

Rum Raisin Custard Bars

Prep Time: 30 minutes (Ready in 2 hours)

1 cup raisins
½ cup water
1 cup firmly packed brown
   sugar
¾ cup margarine or butter,
   softened
1¼ cups all-purpose flour
2 cups quick-cooking rolled
   oats

½ teaspoon baking soda
½ cup sugar
½ cup firmly packed brown
   sugar
2½ teaspoons cornstarch
1½ cups sour cream
3 egg yolks
½ teaspoon vanilla
½ teaspoon rum extract

1. Heat oven to 350°F. Grease 13 × 9-inch pan. In small saucepan, combine raisins and water; bring to a boil. Drain; set aside.

2. In large bowl, combine 1 cup brown sugar and margarine; beat until light and fluffy. Add flour, oats and baking soda; mix at low speed until crumbly. Press half of mixture in bottom of greased pan to form base. Bake at 350°F. for 8 minutes.

3. In medium saucepan, combine sugar, ½ cup brown sugar and cornstarch. Stir in sour cream and egg yolks. Cook over medium heat until mixture thickens, stirring constantly. DO NOT BOIL. Stir in raisins, vanilla and rum extract. Pour evenly over base. Sprinkle remaining crumb mixture over filling.

4. Bake at 350°F. for an additional 30 to 40 minutes or until light golden brown. Cool 1 hour or until completely cooled. Cut into bars. Store in refrigerator.

Yield: 36 bars
High Altitude (Above 3,500 Feet): No change.

Nutrition Information Per Serving
Serving Size: 1 Bar. Calories 160 • Calories from Fat 60 • Total Fat 7 g
Saturated Fat 2 g • Cholesterol 20 mg • Sodium 75 mg • Dietary Fiber 1 g
Dietary Exchanges: 1½ Fruit, 1½ Fat OR 1½ Carbohydrate, 1½ Fat

Recipe Fact

Custard, a mixture of milk and egg cooked on the stovetop or in the oven until thickened, turns up in a number of ways. Thin, sweet saucepan versions, such as **crème anglaise**, are used for dessert sauces, while savory baked blends flecked with corn and bacon bits make a fine side dish for a hearty supper. Here, brown sugar and sour cream enrich a stovetop custard, which then bakes into a delightful filling for a crunchy crust.

About Raisins

Dark and golden raisins may be used interchangeably in recipes, though their flavors are not exactly the same. Dark raisins are sun-dried, while golden raisins are dried with artificial heat, making them somewhat plumper and moister.

Kitchen Tip

To prevent the custard mixture from curdling, stir it constantly and do not allow it to come to a boil.

Hol

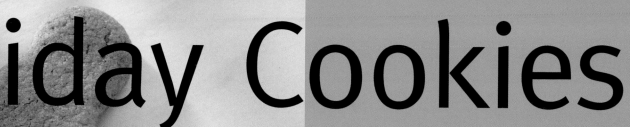

iday Cookies

As the spicy fragrance of cinnamon and ginger wafts through the house, can the holidays be far away? Cookie baking is an activity that young and old can enjoy together—both the mixing and the "quality control testing." Wrap cookies as presents, hang them as decorations, send them to friends, enjoy them yourself!

Holiday Cookies

Holiday Cookies make an appropriate and much-appreciated gift when an expensive purchase is inappropriate or out of the budget. To make the present special, wrap it with colorful holiday ribbons or pack the cookies in a special container.

To streamline holiday baking marathons, make cookie doughs well in advance and freeze or refrigerate them. For further ease of baking, plan to fill out a cookie tray of intricate, time-consuming cutouts with quicker-fix bars or sliced cookies. When giving a gift of several kinds of cookies, wrap each type separately to prevent flavors and textures from becoming muddled.

Previous page: Whole Wheat Gingerbread Cutouts, page 178

Cranberry Orange Meltaways

Prep Time: 1 hour

½ cup sugar
½ cup powdered sugar
½ cup margarine or butter,
   softened
½ cup oil
2 teaspoons grated orange
   peel
1 teaspoon vanilla

1 egg
2 cups all-purpose flour
½ teaspoon baking soda
½ teaspoon cream of tartar
¼ teaspoon salt
½ cup chopped fresh or frozen
   cranberries
Powdered sugar, if desired

1. Heat oven to 350°F. In large bowl, combine sugar, powdered sugar, margarine and oil; blend well. Add orange peel, vanilla and egg; blend well. Add flour, baking soda, cream of tartar and salt; mix well. Stir in cranberries. Drop dough by rounded teaspoonfuls 2 inches apart onto ungreased cookie sheets.

2. Bake at 350°F. for 10 to 15 minutes or until bottoms are light golden brown. Cool 1 minute; remove from cookie sheets. Cool 15 minutes or until completely cooled. Sprinkle with powdered sugar.

Yield: 3½ dozen cookies
High Altitude (Above 3,500 Feet): Increase flour to 2½ cups. Bake as directed above.

Nutrition Information Per Serving
Serving Size: 1 Cookie. Calories 80 • Calories from Fat 45 • Total Fat 5 g
Saturated Fat 1 g • Cholesterol 5 mg • Sodium 55 mg • Dietary Fiber 0 g
Dietary Exchanges: ½ Fruit, 1 Fat OR ½ Carbohydrate, 1 Fat

Holiday Note

To create a personalized plate for holiday gift giving, let children decorate sturdy paper plates with markers and stickers. Cover the plate with clear plastic wrap, taped underneath so it will stay secure, to keep the cookies clean and protect the artwork.

Kitchen Tip

For bigger bursts of cranberry flavor, use the berries whole instead of chopping them.

Kitchen Tip

A special tool called a zester makes short work of shredding citrus peel. It has a handle like a vegetable peeler topped with small metal head punched with several small, sharp holes. To use the tool, drag it firmly across the surface of the fruit to release shreds of the peel. The technique works best with fresh, firm fruit.

Whole Wheat Gingerbread Cutouts

Prep Time: 1 hour 40 minutes (Ready in 2 hours 10 minutes)

Cookies
1½ cups sugar
1 cup margarine or butter, softened
⅓ cup molasses
1 egg
2¼ cups all-purpose flour
1 cup whole wheat flour
2 teaspoons baking soda
2 teaspoons ginger
2 teaspoons cinnamon
½ teaspoon salt

Frosting
¼ cup butter, softened
2 tablespoons shortening
½ teaspoon vanilla
Dash salt
2 cups powdered sugar
1 to 2 tablespoons milk

1. In a large bowl, combine sugar and 1 cup margarine; beat until light and fluffy. Add molasses and egg; blend well. Add all remaining cookie ingredients; mix well. If necessary, cover with plastic wrap; refrigerate 1 hour for easier handling.

2. Heat oven to 350°F. On lightly floured surface, roll out ¼ of dough at a time to ⅛-inch thickness. (Keep remaining dough refrigerated.) Cut with floured 2½-inch round or desired shape cookie cutters. Place 1 inch apart on ungreased cookie sheets.

3. Bake at 350°F. for 6 to 9 minutes or until set. Cool 1 minute; remove from cookie sheets. Cool on wire racks 15 minutes or until completely cooled.

4. In a small bowl, combine ¼ cup butter and shortening; beat until light and fluffy. Add vanilla and dash salt. Gradually beat in powdered sugar until smooth. Add 1 tablespoon milk; beat at high speed until light and fluffy. Add enough additional milk for desired spreading or piping consistency. Frost or decorate cookies as desired. Let stand until frosting is set. Store in loosely covered container.

Yield: 8 dozen cookies
High Altitude (Above 3,500 Feet): Decrease sugar to 1 cup;
increase all-purpose flour to 2¾ cups. Bake as directed above.

Nutrition Information Per Serving
Serving Size: 1 Cookie. Calories 70 • Calories from Fat 25 • Total Fat 3 g
Saturated Fat 1 g • Cholesterol 2 mg • Sodium 70 mg • Dietary Fiber 0 g
Dietary Exchanges: ½ Starch, ½ Fat OR ½ Carbohydrate, ½ Fat

Cherry Chocolate Kisses

kid pleaser   chocoholic's choice

Prep Time: 1 hour

1 cup powdered sugar
1 cup butter, softened
2 teaspoons maraschino cherry
   liquid
½ teaspoon almond extract
3 to 4 drops red food color

2¼ cups all-purpose flour
½ teaspoon salt
½ cup maraschino cherries,
   drained, chopped
About 48 milk chocolate candy
   kisses, unwrapped

1. Heat oven to 350°F. In large bowl, combine powdered sugar, butter, cherry liquid, almond extract and food color; blend well. Add flour and salt; mix well. Stir in cherries. Shape dough into 1-inch balls. Place 2 inches apart on ungreased cookie sheets.

2. Bake at 350°F. for 8 to 10 minutes or until edges are light golden brown. Immediately top each cookie with candy kiss, pressing down firmly. Remove from cookie sheets.

Yield: 4 dozen cookies
High Altitude (Above 3,500 Feet): No change.

Nutrition Information Per Serving
Serving Size: 1 Cookie. Calories 90 • Calories from Fat 45 • Total Fat 5 g
Saturated Fat 3 g • Cholesterol 10 mg • Sodium 65 mg • Dietary Fiber 0 g
Dietary Exchanges: 1 Starch, 1 Fat OR 1 Carbohydrate, 1 Fat

Ingredient Substitution

Substitute 2 teaspoons of kirsch (cherry liqueur) for the maraschino cherry juice.

Make It Special

Roll each ball of cookie dough in red decorator sugar prior to baking.

Brown Sugar Shortbread Cookie Dough

Recipe Fact

Shortbread's origins are in Scotland, where it was originally served at the Christmas and New Year's holidays.

Kitchen Tip

Instead of dividing the dough for the three recipes, you can roll it out to a ⅛- to ¼-inch thickness. Cut the dough with cookie cutters, and bake it in a preheated 375°F. oven until golden brown, 5 to 7 minutes.

Brown Sugar Shortbread Cookie Dough with variations

Prep Time: 15 minutes

¾ cup sugar
¾ cup firmly packed brown sugar
1 cup butter, softened

1 teaspoon vanilla
1 egg
2½ cups all-purpose flour

1. In large bowl, combine sugar, brown sugar and butter; beat until light and fluffy. Add vanilla and egg; blend well. Add flour; mix well. Divide dough into thirds. Cover with plastic wrap; refrigerate until ready to use.

2. Use as directed to make Cherry Chocolate Brown Sugar Shortbread Bars (page 182), Jam-filled Brown Sugar Shortbread Cookies (page 181) and/or Maple Nut Brown Sugar Shortbread Cookies (page 183).

Yield: 6 dozen cookies
High Altitude (Above 3,500 Feet): Decrease sugar and brown sugar to ⅔ cup each; increase flour to 2¾ cups.

Nutrition Information Per Serving

Serving Size: 1 Cookie. Calories 60 • Calories from Fat 25 • Total Fat 3 g
Saturated Fat 2 g • Cholesterol 10 mg • Sodium 30 mg • Dietary Fiber 0 g
Dietary Exchanges: ½ Fruit, ½ Fat OR ½ Carbohydrate, ½ Fat

Jam-filled Brown Sugar Shortbread Cookies

Prep Time: 30 minutes

⅓ recipe Brown Sugar
   Shortbread Cookie Dough
   (page 180)

1 teaspoon grated orange peel
3 tablespoons raspberry or
   other jam

1. Heat oven to 375°F. In medium bowl, combine cookie dough and orange peel; blend well. On floured surface, roll out dough to ⅛-inch thickness. Cut with floured 2-inch round or scalloped cookie cutter.

2. In half of cookies, cut small decorative shape from centers. Place remaining half of cookies 2 inches apart on ungreased cookie sheets. Place about ½ teaspoon jam in center of each; top with cutout cookies. Return small shapes to dough for rerolling.

3. Bake at 375°F. for 7 to 10 minutes or until light golden brown. Cool 1 minute; remove from cookie sheets.

Yield: 18 cookies
High Altitude (Above 3,500 Feet): No change.

Nutrition Information Per Serving

Serving Size: 1 Cookie. Calories 80 • Calories from Fat 35 • Total Fat 4 g
Saturated Fat 2 g • Cholesterol 13 mg • Sodium 40 mg • Dietary Fiber 0 g
Dietary Exchanges: ½ Fruit, 1 Fat OR ½ Carbohydrate, 1 Fat

Holiday Note

Include a few cookie cutters on the plate or tied to the bow for a gift of Christmas sweets.

Make It Special

Choose a decorative small cookie cutter or use a sharp knife to cut a tree or star in the center of these filled cookies.

Cherry Chocolate Brown Sugar Shortbread Bars

Prep Time: 10 minutes (Ready in 1 hour)

Ingredient Substitution

Substitute dried cherries for maraschinos in the bars and kirsch (cherry liqueur) for the maraschino cherry liquid in the Cherry Glaze.

Bars
1/3 recipe Brown Sugar Shortbread Cookie Dough (page 180)
1/4 cup semi-sweet chocolate chips
1/4 cup chopped drained maraschino cherries

Cherry Glaze
1/4 cup powdered sugar
1 1/2 teaspoons maraschino cherry liquid

Chocolate Glaze
1/4 cup semi-sweet chocolate chips
1 teaspoon shortening

1. Heat oven to 350°F. Grease 8-inch square pan. In medium bowl, combine all bar ingredients; mix well. Press in bottom of greased pan.

2. Bake at 350°F. for 17 to 22 minutes or until set and light golden brown. Cool 15 minutes or until completely cooled.

3. Meanwhile, to make cherry glaze, combine powdered sugar and cherry liquid in small bowl; blend well. To make chocolate glaze, melt chocolate chips and shortening in small saucepan over low heat, stirring constantly. Drizzle glazes over bars; let stand until set. Cut into bars.

Yield: 24 bars
High Altitude (Above 3,500 Feet): No change.

Nutrition Information Per Serving
Serving Size: 1 Bar. Calories 80 • Calories from Fat 35 • Total Fat 4 g
Saturated Fat 2 g • Cholesterol 10 mg • Sodium 30 mg • Dietary Fiber 0 g
Dietary Exchanges: 1/2 Fruit, 1 Fat OR 1/2 Carbohydrate, 1 Fat

Maple Nut Brown Sugar Shortbread Cookies

Prep Time: 30 minutes

¹/₃ recipe Brown Sugar
   Shortbread Cookie Dough
   (page 180)

¼ cup chopped pecans
¼ teaspoon maple extract
Sugar

(page 180)

1. Heat oven to 375°F. In medium bowl, combine cookie dough, pecans and maple extract; blend well. Shape mixture into 1-inch balls; place 2 inches apart on ungreased cookie sheets. With glass dipped in sugar, flatten to about ¼-inch thickness.

2. Bake at 375°F. for 6 to 9 minutes or until light golden brown. Cool 1 minute; remove from cookie sheets.

Yield: 24 cookies
High Altitude (Above 3,500 Feet): No change.

Nutrition Information Per Serving

Serving Size: 1 Cookie. Calories 60 • Calories from Fat 25 • Total Fat 3 g
Saturated Fat 2 g • Cholesterol 10 mg • Sodium 30 mg • Dietary Fiber 0 g
Dietary Exchanges: ½ Starch, ½ Fat OR ½ Carbohydrate, ½ Fat

Chocolate-glazed Florentines

Prep Time: 1 hour

Recipe Fact

Although the name implies that this cookie originated in Florence, Italy, and the candied fruit and almonds are typical of Italian cooking, Austrian bakers also lay claim to its invention.

About Chocolate

Italy can indirectly take credit for popularizing chocolate, since it was Genoa's native son Christopher Columbus who introduced cocoa beans to Europe in 1502, when he returned to Spain after his fourth transatlantic round trip.

Cookies

⅓ cup margarine or butter
⅓ cup honey
¼ cup sugar
2 tablespoons milk
¼ cup all-purpose flour
⅓ cup finely chopped candied orange peel
⅓ cup chopped candied cherries
⅓ cup slivered almonds

Glaze

4 oz. semi-sweet chocolate
1 teaspoon shortening

1. Heat oven to 325°F. Generously grease and flour cookie sheets. Melt margarine in medium saucepan over medium heat; remove from heat. Stir in honey, sugar and milk; stir in flour. Cook over medium heat for 3 to 6 minutes or until slightly thickened, stirring constantly. Remove from heat; stir in candied peel, cherries and almonds. Drop mixture by teaspoonfuls 3 inches apart on greased and floured cookie sheets.

2. Bake at 325°F. for 8 to 13 minutes or until edges are light golden brown. (Edges will spread and centers will remain soft.) Cool 1 minute; carefully remove from cookie sheets. (If cookies harden on cookie sheet, return to oven for 30 to 60 seconds to warm.) Cool 15 minutes or until completely cooled.

3. Line large cookie sheet with waxed paper. Turn cookies upside down on lined cookie sheet. In small saucepan over low heat, melt glaze ingredients; stir to blend. Spread over flat surface of each cookie to within ¼ inch of edge. When set but not hard, use fork to make wavy lines in chocolate, if desired. Let stand until set. Store between sheets of waxed paper in tightly covered container in refrigerator.

Nutrition Information Per Serving

Serving Size: 1 Cookie. Calories 80 • Calories from Fat 35 • Total Fat 4 g
Saturated Fat 1 g • Cholesterol 0 mg • Sodium 30 mg • Dietary Fiber 0 g
Dietary Exchanges: ½ Fruit, 1 Fat OR ½ Carbohydrate, 1 Fat

Berlinerkranzer, page 186;
Chocolate-glazed Florentines;
Lebkuchen, page 188

Berlinerkranzer

Prep Time: 45 minutes (Ready in 2 hours 45 minutes)

Holiday Note

These tender, buttery cookies are a favorite for Norwegian Christmas celebrations.

Ingredient Substitution

Decorate the cookies with red and green sugar instead of the cherries.

2 hard-cooked egg yolks
2 uncooked egg yolks
³/₄ cup powdered sugar
1 cup butter, softened
1 teaspoon vanilla
2¹/₂ cups all-purpose flour

1 egg white, slightly beaten
8 red candied cherries, cut into 6 pieces
8 green candied cherries, cut into tiny pieces

1. In large bowl, mash hard-cooked egg yolks; combine with uncooked egg yolks and powdered sugar. Add butter and vanilla; blend well. Add flour; mix well. Cover with plastic wrap; refrigerate 2 to 3 hours for easier handling.

2. Heat oven to 350°F. On lightly floured surface, roll out ¹/₄ of dough at a time into 12-inch rope. Cut rope into 12 equal pieces. Roll each piece into 6-inch rope; shape each into wreath, overlapping ¹/₂ inch from ends. Place 1 inch apart on ungreased cookie sheets. Brush with egg white; decorate each wreath with 1 red cherry piece and 2 or 3 green cherry pieces.

3. Bake at 350°F. for 8 to 14 minutes or until edges are light golden brown. Remove from cookie sheets.

Yield: 4 dozen cookies
High Altitude (Above 3,500 Feet): No change.

Nutrition Information Per Serving

Serving Size: 1 Cookie. Calories 70 • Calories from Fat 35 • Total Fat 4 g
Saturated Fat 3 g • Cholesterol 30 mg • Sodium 50 mg • Dietary Fiber 0 g
Dietary Exchanges: ¹/₂ Fruit, 1 Fat OR ¹/₂ Carbohydrate, 1 Fat

---

Cardamom Krumkake

Prep Time: 2 hours

1 cup all-purpose flour
1 cup sugar
1 tablespoon freshly crushed
    cardamom

½ cup margarine or butter,
    melted
½ cup whipping cream
4 eggs

1. In medium bowl, combine all ingredients; mix well with wire whisk. Heat krumkake iron over medium-high heat on small surface unit of electric or gas range. Iron is ready when small drops of water sizzle and disappear almost immediately.

2. For each cookie, drop about ½ tablespoon of batter (for 6-inch iron) on ungreased iron; close gently. Bake 10 to 15 seconds on each side or until light golden brown. Immediately remove from iron with spatula; roll on cone or wooden roller. Cool slightly. Remove cookie from cone.

Yield: 6 dozen cookies
High Altitude (Above 3,500 Feet): No change.

Tips: Iron may need to be lightly greased before baking first few krumkake. If krumkake is not crisp, batter is too thick; stir in small amount of whipping cream.

Nutrition Information Per Serving

Serving Size: 1 Cookie. Calories 35 • Calories from Fat 20 • Total Fat 2 g
Saturated Fat 1 g • Cholesterol 15 mg • Sodium 20 mg • Dietary Fiber 0 g
Dietary Exchanges: ½ Starch OR ½ Carbohydrate

About Cardamom

Cardamom's peppercorn-sized seeds are bunched together and encased in small pods that may be green, white or brown. There are up to 20 seeds in each pod. Split open the pod, then crush the fragrant cardamom seeds with a mortar and pestle.

Kitchen Tip

Bake these crisp, cardamom-flavored cookies in a specially designed krumkake iron, a tool that's a cross between a small frying pan and a waffle iron. The tool is heated on the stovetop like a skillet, then closed like a waffle iron to cook the dough. Some irons come with a metal cone for shaping the warm cookies; otherwise, you can fashion a paper cone from a brown paper grocery bag.

Ingredient Substitution

Crushing cardamom seeds just before using gives you the best fragrance and flavor, but purchased ground cardamom also can be used.

Lebkuchen

Prep Time: 50 minutes (Ready in 1 hour 50 minutes)

Holiday Note

In Germany, as in many European countries, children celebrate St. Nicholas Day, December 6, by putting their shoes out for St. Nicholas to fill. Bakeries and home kitchens churn out all sorts of sweets such as these honey cookies. Lebkuchen are traditionally rolled-out cookies, but we've simplified the shaping.

About Candied Citron

When it comes to fruitcake, the world is firmly divided into those who love it and those who would just as soon use it as a **do**orstop. Candied citron, a quintessential ingredient in fruitcake and hot cross buns, incites reaction in both camps and is made from the peel of a fruit that resembles a quince. (Candied cherries can be substituted for the candied citron.)

Ingredient Substitution

Vary the icing by using orange or lemon extract in place of the almond.

Cookies

1 cup honey
3/4 cup firmly packed brown sugar
1 tablespoon grated lemon peel
1 egg, beaten
2 1/2 cups all-purpose flour
1/2 teaspoon baking soda
1/2 teaspoon salt
1 teaspoon cinnamon
1 teaspoon nutmeg
1 teaspoon ginger
1/2 to 1 teaspoon cloves
1/2 teaspoon allspice
1/4 cup chopped candied orange peel
1/4 cup chopped candied citron
1/3 cup chopped almonds
Sliced almonds

Glaze

1/2 cup powdered sugar
1/8 teaspoon almond extract
2 to 4 tablespoons water

1. Heat honey in medium saucepan over medium heat just until it begins to bubble. DO NOT BOIL. Remove from heat. Cool 15 minutes. Add brown sugar, lemon peel and egg; blend well.

2. In large bowl, combine all remaining cookie ingredients except sliced almonds. Add honey mixture; mix well. Cover with plastic wrap; refrigerate 1 to 2 hours for easier handling.

3. Heat oven to 400°F. Grease cookie sheets. In small bowl, combine glaze ingredients, adding enough water for desired glazing consistency; blend until smooth. Cover; set aside.

4. Shape dough into 1-inch balls. Place 2 inches apart on greased cookie sheets. With glass dipped in cool water, gently flatten balls to 1/4-inch thickness. Gently press 1 almond slice in center of each cookie.

5. Bake at 400°F. for 5 to 9 minutes or until set. Immediately remove from cookie sheets and immediately brush warm cookies with glaze. Cool 15 minutes or until completely cooled.

Yield: 5 dozen cookies
High Altitude (Above 3,500 Feet): Decrease brown sugar to ½ cup; increase flour to 2½ cups plus 2 tablespoons. Bake as directed above.

Nutrition Information Per Serving

Serving Size: 1 Cookie. Calories 70 • Calories from Fat 10 • Total Fat 1 g
Saturated Fat 0 g • Cholesterol 4 mg • Sodium 35 mg • Dietary Fiber 0 g
Dietary Exchanges: 1 Starch OR 1 Carbohydrate

Storage Tip

For softer cookies, store the Lebkuchen with a slice of apple in a tightly covered container.

Mexican Wedding Cakes

editor's favorite

Prep Time: 1 hour

½ cup powdered sugar
1 cup butter, softened
2 teaspoons vanilla
2 cups all-purpose flour

1 cup finely chopped or ground
   almonds or pecans
¼ teaspoon salt
½ cup powdered sugar

1. Heat oven to 325°F. In large bowl, combine ½ cup powdered sugar, butter and vanilla; beat until light and fluffy. Add flour, almonds and salt; mix until dough forms. Shape into 1-inch balls. Place 1 inch apart on ungreased cookie sheets.
2. Bake at 325°F. for 15 to 20 minutes or until set but not brown. Immediately remove from cookie sheets. Cool slightly; roll in ½ cup powdered sugar. Cool 15 minutes or until completely cooled. Reroll in powdered sugar.

Yield: 5 dozen cookies
High Altitude (Above 3,500 Feet): No change.

Nutrition Information Per Serving

Serving Size: 1 Cookie. Calories 60 • Calories from Fat 35 • Total Fat 4 g
Saturated Fat 2 g • Cholesterol 10 mg • Sodium 40 mg • Dietary Fiber 0 g
Dietary Exchanges: ½ Starch, ½ Fat OR ½ Carbohydrate, ½ Fat

Ingredient Substitution

Use walnuts in place of almonds or pecans.

Springerle

Prep Time: 1 hour 15 minutes (Ready in 10 hours 15 minutes)

4 eggs
2 cups sugar
½ to 1 teaspoon anise extract
  or 4 to 6 drops anise oil

3½ cups all-purpose flour
1 teaspoon baking powder
¼ teaspoon salt

1. Lightly grease cookie sheets. In large bowl, beat eggs at high speed for 3 to 4 minutes or until very thick. Gradually beat in sugar; beat an additional 15 minutes. Beat in anise extract. Add flour, baking powder and salt; mix well. Cover with plastic wrap; refrigerate 1 hour for easier handling.

2. On well-floured surface using regular rolling pin, roll dough into rectangle the same width as springerle rolling pin and ½ inch thick. Using springerle rolling pin, roll designs into dough.* Cut cookies along design lines; place on greased cookie sheets. Cover with cloth; let stand in cool place overnight.

3. Heat oven to 375°F. Place cookies in oven; immediately decrease temperature to 300°F. Bake 20 to 25 minutes or until set but not brown. Immediately remove from cookie sheets. Store in tightly covered container. Cookies can be served after 8 hours but are better if stored several weeks before serving.

Yield: 4 dozen cookies
High Altitude (Above 3,500 Feet): No change.

*Tip: If springerle mold is used, roll dough to ½-inch thickness. Press floured mold into dough; lift off and cut along design lines.

Nutrition Information Per Serving

Serving Size: 1 Cookie. Calories 70 • Calories from Fat 10 • Total Fat 1 g
Saturated Fat 0 g • Cholesterol 20 mg • Sodium 25 mg • Dietary Fiber 0 g
Dietary Exchanges: 1 Starch OR 1 Carbohydrate

Holiday Note

Springerle are among Germany's most famous Christmas cookies. These anise-flavored "pictures" are made by imprinting rolled-out dough with a special rolling pin or wooden mold. The recipe works best if the shaped and cut dough rests overnight.

Kitchen Tip

If you don't have the traditional carved rolling pin or wooden molds, improvise with a different textured item from the kitchen. Roll a cut-glass tumbler, for example, across the dough to create a pattern, or lightly stamp the surface with a potato masher, or press the top of a balloon whisk into dough just firmly enough to leave a flower-like impression.

Springerle

Fattimand

Prep Time: 2 hours (Ready in 10 hours)

These traditional Norwegian cookies contain relatively little sugar for the amount of flour in the dough. They gain richness from being deep fried and extra sweetness from a shake of spiced powdered sugar just before serving.

Kitchen Tip

Be patient and don't crowd the pan when deep frying these delicacies. The dough requires plenty of "elbow room" to achieve the desired golden brown exterior and properly cooked interior.

8 egg yolks
2 eggs
¾ cup sugar
3 tablespoons rum
1 cup whipping cream

5 cups all-purpose flour
1 teaspoon cardamom
Oil for deep frying
1 cup powdered sugar
½ teaspoon cinnamon

1. In large bowl, combine egg yolks, eggs, sugar and rum; beat 5 minutes or until thick and lemon colored. Add cream, blend well. With spoon, stir in flour and cardamom; mix well to form a soft dough. Wrap dough in plastic wrap; refrigerate 8 hours or overnight.

2. In deep fryer or heavy saucepan, heat 3 to 4 inches of oil to 365°F. On lightly floured surface, roll out ¼ of dough at a time to ¹⁄₁₆-inch thickness. (Keep remaining dough refrigerated.) Cut dough into diamond shapes about 5 × 2½ inches (see diagram). Make lengthwise slit in center of each diamond; pull 1 pointed end through slit.

3. Drop dough pieces 3 or 4 at a time into hot oil. Fry 1 to 1½ minutes or until puffed and deep golden brown. Drain on paper towels. Cool 15 minutes or until completely cooled. Repeat with remaining dough. Store in tightly covered container in cool dry place.

4. Just before serving, in small bowl, combine powdered sugar and cinnamon; mix well. Sprinkle lightly over cookies.

Yield: 8 dozen cookies
High Altitude (Above 3,500 Feet): No change.

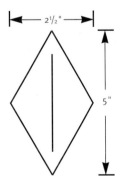

Diagram for Fattimand

Nutrition Information Per Serving
Serving Size: 1 Cookie. Calories 60 • Calories from Fat 25 • Total Fat 3 g
Saturated Fat 1 g • Cholesterol 25 mg • Sodium 0 mg • Dietary Fiber 0 g
Dietary Exchanges: ½ Starch, ½ Fat OR ½ Carbohydrate, ½ Fat

Frosted Pepparkakor

Prep Time: 2 hours (Ready in 5 hours)

Cookies

1½ cups sugar
1 cup butter, softened
3 tablespoons molasses
1 egg
2 tablespoons water or milk
3¼ cups all-purpose flour
2 teaspoons baking soda
½ teaspoon salt
2 teaspoons cinnamon
1½ teaspoons ginger
½ teaspoon cardamom
½ teaspoon cloves

Frosting

¾ cup water
1 envelope unflavored gelatin
¾ cup sugar
¾ cup powdered sugar
1 teaspoon baking powder
1 teaspoon vanilla

1. In large bowl, combine 1½ cups sugar, butter and molasses; beat until light and fluffy. Add egg and 2 tablespoons water; blend well. Add all remaining cookie ingredients; mix well to form a smooth dough. Cover with plastic wrap; refrigerate 1 hour for easier handling.

2. Heat oven to 350°F. On floured surface, roll out ⅓ of dough at a time to ⅛-inch thickness. (Keep remaining dough refrigerated.) Cut with floured 2½-inch cookie cutters. Place 1 inch apart on ungreased cookie sheets.

3. Bake at 350°F. for 9 to 11 minutes or until set. Immediately remove from cookie sheets. Cool completely.

4. In 2-quart saucepan, combine ¾ cup water and gelatin; let stand 5 minutes. Stir in ¾ cup sugar. Bring to a boil. Reduce heat; simmer 10 minutes. Stir in powdered sugar; beat until foamy. Stir in baking powder and vanilla; beat at high speed until thick, about 10 minutes. Frost cooled cookies or pipe frosting to outline cookies.

Yield: 10 dozen cookies
High Altitude (Above 3,500 Feet): No change.

Nutrition Information Per Serving

Serving Size: 1 Cookie. Calories 45 • Calories from Fat 20 • Total Fat 2 g
Saturated Fat 1 g • Cholesterol 5 mg • Sodium 50 mg • Dietary Fiber 0 g
Dietary Exchanges: ½ Fruit, ½ Fat OR ½ Carbohydrate, ½ Fat

Holiday Note

These crisp and fragrant Swedish ginger cookies are often hung on a tree made of wooden dowels, which is also decorated with apples and topped with a miniature sheaf of wheat. Traditional Swedish shapes for the cookies include pigs, horses, roosters, hearts and gingerbread boys.

Kitchen Tip

If the cookies will be hung, punch a hole at the top with a large drinking straw prior to baking; thread a shiny ribbon or a piece of bright yarn through the opening after the cookies have cooled.

Two-in-One Holiday Bars

Prep Time: 15 minutes (Ready in 1 hour 40 minutes)

Base
1 cup sugar
¾ cup margarine or butter, softened
1 teaspoon vanilla
1 egg
2 cups all-purpose flour
1 cup diced mixed candied fruit

½ cup semi-sweet chocolate chips
½ cup chopped pecans

Glaze
1 cup powdered sugar
1 to 2 tablespoons milk

1. Heat oven to 350°F. In large bowl, combine sugar and margarine; beat until light and fluffy. Add vanilla and egg; blend well. Add flour; mix well. Spread dough in ungreased 15 × 10 × 1-inch baking pan. Sprinkle half of dough with candied fruit; sprinkle other half with chocolate chips and pecans. Press lightly into dough.

2. Bake at 350°F. for 25 to 30 minutes or until edges are light golden brown. Cool 1 hour or until completely cooled.

3. In small bowl, combine powdered sugar and enough milk for desired drizzling consistency; blend until smooth. Drizzle over cooled bars. Let stand until set. Cut into bars.

Yield: 48 bars
High Altitude (Above 3,500 Feet): Increase flour to 2¼ cups. Bake as directed above.

Nutrition Information Per Serving
Serving Size: 1 Bar with Fruit. Calories 100 • Calories from Fat 35 • Total Fat 4 g
Saturated Fat 1 g • Cholesterol 4 mg • Sodium 55 mg • Dietary Fiber 0 g
Dietary Exchanges: 1 Fruit, 1 Fat OR 1 Carbohydrate, 1 Fat

Nutrition Information Per Serving
Serving Size: 1 Bar with Chips and Nuts. Calories 110 • Calories from Fat 50
Total Fat 6 g • Saturated Fat 1 g • Cholesterol 4 mg • Sodium 35 mg • Dietary
Fiber 1 g • Dietary Exchanges: 1 Fruit, 1 Fat OR 1 Carbohydrate, 1 Fat

Two-in-One Holiday Bars

Holiday Note

To decorate a dessert table featuring these stellar cookies, cut stars in varying sizes from silver foil or gold paper to scatter on the table and wind some sparkling metallic star garlands (available at discount stores and craft shops, especially around the holidays) around the serving plates. Or if the gathering doesn't include any kids of everything-goes-in-the-mouth age, sprinkle a trail of star-shaped sequins over the tablecloth.

About Cranberries

In the old days, cranberry merchants demonstrated the freshness of their wares by dropping berries on the floor: good-quality fresh cranberries bounce.

Glimmering Cranberry-filled Stars

Prep Time: 1 hour 15 minutes (Ready in 2 hours 15 minutes)

Filling
1 cup fresh or frozen
   cranberries
¼ cup sugar
1 (10-oz.) jar red currant jelly

Cookies
1 cup sugar
1 cup margarine or butter,
   softened

3 tablespoons milk
1 teaspoon vanilla
1 egg
3 cups all-purpose flour
2 tablespoons grated orange
   peel
1½ teaspoons baking powder
½ teaspoon salt
1 tablespoon coarse sugar or
   granulated sugar

1. In food processor bowl with metal blade or blender container, chop cranberries with ¼ cup sugar. In small saucepan, combine cranberry mixture and jelly. Bring to a boil, stirring occasionally. Reduce heat to low; simmer 5 minutes. Cover; refrigerate.

2. Meanwhile, in large bowl, combine 1 cup sugar, margarine, milk, vanilla and egg; blend well. Add flour, orange peel, baking powder and salt; mix well. Cover with plastic wrap; refrigerate 1 hour for easier handling.

3. Heat oven to 400°F. On well-floured surface, roll out half of dough at a time to ⅛-inch thickness. (Keep remaining dough refrigerated.) Cut with floured 2-inch star-shaped or round cookie cutter. Place half of cookies 1 inch apart on ungreased cookie sheets. Cut 1-inch star shapes from centers of remaining cookies. Place cookies and small star cutouts 1 inch apart on separate cookie sheets; sprinkle with coarse sugar.

4. Bake small star cutouts at 400°F. for 3 to 5 minutes and large cookies for 4 to 6 minutes or until edges are light golden brown. Immediately remove from cookie sheets. Cool 15 minutes or until completely cooled.

5. Spread bottom side of each whole cookie with about 1

teaspoon filling. Place cutout cookies over filling. Store between layers of waxed paper in tightly covered container. Reserve small star cookies for a later use, such as to top ice cream sundaes.

Yield: 60 sandwich cookies; 30 small star cookies
High Altitude (Above 3,500 Feet): Increase flour to 3 cups plus 2 tablespoons. Bake as directed above.

Nutrition Information Per Serving
Serving Size: 1 Sandwich Cookie. Calories 80 • Calories from Fat 25 • Total Fat 3 g
Saturated Fat 2 g • Cholesterol 10 mg • Sodium 60 mg • Dietary Fiber 0 g
Dietary Exchanges: 1 Fruit, ½ Fat OR 1 Carbohydrate, ½ Fat

Easy Cherry Rum Balls

editor's favorite

Prep Time: 20 minutes

**2 cups crushed vanilla wafers
    (40 to 45 wafers)**
1 cup powdered sugar
**½ cup finely chopped candied
    red and/or green cherries**
**½ cup finely chopped pecans
    or walnuts**

¼ cup rum
3 tablespoons corn syrup
2 tablespoons butter, melted
¼ cup powdered sugar

1. In medium bowl, combine vanilla wafers, 1 cup powdered sugar, cherries and pecans; mix well. Add rum, corn syrup and butter; mix well.
2. Shape mixture into 1-inch balls; roll in ¼ cup powdered sugar. Cover tightly. Let stand 24 hours to blend flavors.

Yield: 3 dozen cookies

Nutrition Information Per Serving
Serving Size: 1 Cookie. Calories 80 • Calories from Fat 25 • Total Fat 3 g
Saturated Fat 1 g • Cholesterol 2 mg • Sodium 25 mg • Dietary Fiber 0 g
Dietary Exchanges: 1 Fruit, ½ Fat OR 1 Carbohydrate, ½ Fat

Holiday Note
Pack these grown-up goodies in a decorative basket along with a bottle of the receiver's favorite liqueur.

Kitchen Tip
The rum flavor mellows as the cookies sit, so prepare them at least 24 hours before serving them.

Storage Tip
Store the rum balls tightly covered at room temperature.

Iced Chocolate Almond Rosettes

Recipe Fact

These crisp Scandinavian cookies are made with a rosette iron, a metal mold on a long handle. After heating the mold in hot oil, dip it into the batter; the hot rosette iron will begin to cook the batter immediately, even as it's being transferred back to the oil.

About Glitter

Edible glitter, available at kitchen specialty shops, adds wintry sparkle.

Kitchen Tip

If rosettes drop from the mold, the oil is too hot. If the rosettes are soft, increase the frying time slightly. If the rosettes have blisters, the eggs have been beaten too much. If the batter is too thick, stir in a small amount of milk.

Prep Time: 1 hour 30 minutes

Rosettes
Oil for deep frying
$\frac{1}{2}$ cup all-purpose flour
2 tablespoons sugar
2 tablespoons unsweetened cocoa
$\frac{1}{4}$ teaspoon salt
$\frac{1}{2}$ cup milk
1 tablespoon oil

$\frac{1}{4}$ teaspoon almond extract
1 egg

Icing
1 cup powdered sugar
$\frac{1}{2}$ teaspoon almond extract
3 to 4 tablespoons milk
2 tablespoons edible glitter or coarse sugar

1. In deep fryer or heavy saucepan, heat 2 to 3 inches of oil to 365°F. In small bowl, combine flour, sugar, cocoa and salt; mix well. Add all remaining rosette ingredients; beat with wire whisk or eggbeater until smooth.

2. Place rosette iron in hot oil for 30 to 60 seconds or until iron is hot. Drain excess oil from iron on paper towels. Gently dip hot iron into batter; DO NOT ALLOW BATTER TO RUN OVER TOP OF IRON. Return iron to hot oil, immersing completely for 25 to 30 seconds or until rosette is crisp. Remove from oil; allow oil to drip off. Gently slip rosette off iron onto paper towel, using fork if necessary. Cool 15 minutes or until completely cooled. Repeat with remaining batter, reheating iron and draining excess oil from iron on paper towels between rosettes.

3. In small bowl, combine powdered sugar, $\frac{1}{2}$ teaspoon almond extract and enough milk for desired dipping consistency; blend until smooth. (Mixture should be quite thin.) Gently dip top edges of each rosette (not rounded edges) into icing, then into edible glitter. Let stand until set, icing side up. Store in tightly covered container, making sure sides do not touch.

Yield: 22 cookies
High Altitude (Above 3,500 Feet): No change.

Kitchen Tip

While children will certainly enjoy eating the rosettes, this is not a good project to share with little helpers. Remember that oil hot enough for effective deep frying reaches 365°F., much hotter than boiling water. Watch out for splatters. If you do get hit, run the scalded area immediately under cold running water.

Iced Chocolate Almond Rosettes

Glazed Fruitcake Squares

editor's favorite

Prep Time: 30 minutes (Ready in 1 hour 30 minutes)

Ingredient Substitution

To substitute for the brandy called for in the bars, use ¼ cup water or orange juice and 1 teaspoon brandy extract. To replace the brandy in the glaze, combine 1 to 2 teaspoons water with ½ teaspoon brandy extract.

Bars

2 cups powdered sugar
½ cup margarine or butter, softened
¼ cup brandy
2 eggs
2 cups all-purpose flour
3 teaspoons baking powder
1 teaspoon salt
2 cups diced mixed candied fruit
1 cup coarsely chopped walnuts

Glaze

1 cup powdered sugar
1 tablespoon margarine or butter, softened
1 to 2 tablespoons brandy

1. Heat oven to 375°F. Grease 15 × 10 × 1-inch baking pan. In large bowl, combine 2 cups powdered sugar, ½ cup margarine, ¼ cup brandy and eggs; mix well. With spoon, stir in all remaining bar ingredients until well mixed. Press evenly in greased pan.

2. Bake at 375°F. for 15 to 25 minutes or until light golden brown. Cool 1 hour or until completely cooled.

3. In small bowl, combine all glaze ingredients, adding enough brandy for desired drizzling consistency; beat until smooth. Drizzle glaze over bars. Let stand until set. Cut into bars.

Yield: 48 bars
High Altitude (Above 3,500 Feet): No change.

Nutrition Information Per Serving

Serving Size: 1 Bar. Calories 120 • Calories from Fat 35 • Total Fat 4 g
Saturated Fat 1 g • Cholesterol 10 mg • Sodium 125 mg • Dietary Fiber 0 g
Dietary Exchanges: 1 Starch, 1 Fat OR 1 Carbohydrate, 1 Fat

Spritz Cookies

Prep Time: 1 hour

1 cup powdered sugar
1 cup butter, softened
½ teaspoon vanilla

1 egg
2⅓ cups all-purpose flour
¼ teaspoon salt

1. Heat oven to 400°F. In large bowl, combine powdered sugar, butter, vanilla and egg; beat until light and fluffy. Add flour and salt; mix well. Fit cookie press with desired template. Fill cookie press; press dough onto ungreased cookie sheets.

2. Bake at 400°F. for 5 to 7 minutes or until edges are firm but not brown. Immediately remove from cookie sheets. Cool 15 minutes or until completely cooled.

Yield: 5 dozen cookies
High Altitude (Above 3,500 Feet): No change.

Nutrition Information Per Serving
Serving Size: 1 Cookie. Calories 50 • Calories from Fat 25 • Total Fat 3 g
Saturated Fat 2 g • Cholesterol 12 mg • Sodium 40 mg • Dietary Fiber 0 g
Dietary Exchanges: ½ Fruit, ½ Fat OR ½ Carbohydrate, ½ Fat

Recipe Fact

Spritz is a generic term for cookies formed into fanciful shapes when the dough is forced through a cookie press. The name comes from the German verb **spritzen**, meaning "to squirt or to spray."

Variations

Chocolate Spritz Cookies: Prepare dough as directed in recipe, adding 2 oz. melted unsweetened chocolate to powdered sugar mixture.

Eggnog Spritz Cookies: Prepare dough as directed in recipe, substituting 1 teaspoon rum extract for vanilla and adding ¼ teaspoon nutmeg with dry ingredients.

Orange Spritz Cookies: Prepare dough as directed in recipe, adding 1 tablespoon grated orange peel with dry ingredients.

Orange Caramel Spritz

Prep Time: 30 minutes (Ready in 2 hours 30 minutes)

½ cup butter, softened
1 (3-oz.) pkg. cream cheese, softened
½ cup firmly packed brown sugar
2 teaspoons grated orange peel
1¼ cups all-purpose flour
¼ teaspoon salt
1 tablespoon colored decorator sugar

1. Heat oven to 375°F. In large bowl, combine butter and cream cheese; beat until creamy. Add brown sugar and orange peel; beat until light and fluffy. Add flour and salt; mix well. Cover with plastic wrap; refrigerate 2 hours for easier handling.

2. Fit cookie press with desired template. Fill cookie press; press dough onto ungreased cookie sheets. Sprinkle cookies with colored sugar.

3. Bake at 375°F. for 7 to 10 minutes or until bottoms are light golden brown. Cool 1 minute; remove from cookie sheets.

Yield: 3 dozen cookies
High Altitude (Above 3,500 Feet): Increase flour to 1½ cups. Bake as directed above.

Nutrition Information Per Serving

Serving Size: 1 Cookie. Calories 60 • Calories from Fat 25 • Total Fat 3 g
Saturated Fat 2 g • Cholesterol 10 mg • Sodium 50 mg • Dietary Fiber 0 g
Dietary Exchanges: ½ Starch, ½ Fat OR ½ Carbohydrate, ½ Fat

Ginger Heart Thins, page 204;
Orange Caramel Spritz

Ginger Heart Thins

Prep Time: 1 hour (Ready in 3 hours)

About Ginger

Powdered ginger, a key flavoring for gingerbread, spice cake and many other aromatic baked goods, is a dried version of the knobby root that's such an important fresh ingredient in the cuisines of Asia and India. The powdered version has a much gentler flavor than the spicy-hot fresh root. Look for good buys on powdered ginger in Indian grocery stores, and buy it in small quantities—there's a world of difference between really pungent ginger and the old can that's been on your pantry shelf since last Christmas.

Make It Special

For a coffee lover, wrap a few of these coffee-spice cookies in colored cellophane and tuck the packet into an oversized coffee mug. Tie a huge bow and one or two gourmet coffee sampler bags onto the handle.

$\frac{1}{2}$ cup molasses
$\frac{1}{4}$ cup strong coffee
$\frac{1}{2}$ cup firmly packed brown sugar
$\frac{1}{2}$ cup margarine or butter, softened
3 cups all-purpose flour
1 teaspoon baking soda

1 teaspoon ginger
$\frac{1}{2}$ teaspoon salt
$\frac{1}{2}$ teaspoon cinnamon
$\frac{1}{4}$ teaspoon cloves
3 tablespoons sugar

1. In medium saucepan, combine molasses and coffee. Bring to a boil. Add brown sugar and margarine; stir until margarine is melted. In large bowl, combine molasses mixture and all remaining ingredients except sugar; mix well. Cover with plastic wrap; refrigerate 2 hours or until firm.

2. Heat oven to 375°F. Lightly grease cookie sheets. On lightly floured surface, roll out half of dough at a time to $\frac{1}{8}$-inch thickness. Cut with floured $2\frac{1}{2}$-inch heart-shaped cookie cutter. Place 1 inch apart on greased cookie sheets. Sprinkle with sugar.

3. Bake at 375°F. for 5 to 8 minutes or until bottoms are light golden brown. Immediately remove from cookie sheets.

Yield: 5 dozen cookies
High Altitude (Above 3,500 Feet): No change.

Nutrition Information Per Serving
Serving Size: 1 Cookie. Calories 60 • Calories from Fat 20 • Total Fat 2 g
Saturated Fat 0 g • Cholesterol 0 mg • Sodium 60 mg • Dietary Fiber 0 g
Dietary Exchanges: $\frac{1}{2}$ Starch, $\frac{1}{2}$ Fat OR $\frac{1}{2}$ Carbohydrate, $\frac{1}{2}$ Fat

Almond Raspberry Hearts

Prep Time: 45 minutes (Ready in 1 hour 45 minutes)

1 cup all-purpose flour
½ cup sliced almonds,
   coarsely chopped
¼ cup sugar
¼ teaspoon almond extract

½ cup margarine or butter,
   softened
6 tablespoons raspberry
   preserves

1. In medium bowl, combine flour, almonds, sugar and almond extract; mix well. With pastry blender or fork, cut in margarine until mixture resembles fine crumbs. Shape dough into ball. If necessary, cover with plastic wrap; refrigerate 1 hour for easier handling.

2. Heat oven to 375°F. On well-floured surface, roll out half of dough at a time to ⅛-inch thickness. (Keep remaining dough refrigerated.) Cut with floured 2½-inch heart-shaped or round cookie cutter. Place half of cookies 1 inch apart on ungreased cookie sheets. Cut 1-inch heart shape from centers of remaining cookies. Place cookies and small heart cutouts on cookie sheets.

3. Bake at 375°F. for 5 to 8 minutes or until bottoms are light golden brown. Cool 1 minute; remove from cookie sheets. Cool 15 minutes or until completely cooled.

4. Spread bottom side of each whole cookie with about 1 teaspoon preserves. Place cutout cookies over preserves. Reserve small hearts for a later use, such as to top ice cream sundaes.

Yield: 16 sandwich cookies; 16 small heart cookies
High Altitude (Above 3,500 Feet): No change.

Nutrition Information Per Serving
Serving Size: 1 Sandwich Cookie. Calories 130 • Calories from Fat 70 • Total Fat 8 g • Saturated Fat 1 g • Cholesterol 0 mg • Sodium 70 mg • Dietary Fiber 1 g
Dietary Exchanges: 1 Fruit, 1½ Fat OR 1 Carbohydrate, 1½ Fat

Recipe Variation

To make Christmas wreath cookies, follow the directions, using round cookie cutters instead of heart-shaped ones. After the cookies are assembled, decorate the outer ring with green frosting and colored sprinkles.

Make It Special

Pipe chocolate in the shape of an arrow on top of each heart.

Chocolate Valentine Cookies

Prep Time: 1 hour 30 minutes

Cookies

1 cup sugar
1 cup margarine or butter, softened
¼ cup milk
1 teaspoon vanilla
1 egg
2¾ cups all-purpose flour
½ cup unsweetened cocoa
¾ teaspoon baking powder
¼ teaspoon baking soda

Frosting

2 cups powdered sugar
½ cup margarine or butter, softened
Red food color
2 to 3 tablespoons maraschino cherry liquid or milk

1. In large bowl, combine sugar and 1 cup margarine; beat until light and fluffy. Add milk, vanilla and egg; blend well. Add flour, cocoa, baking powder and baking soda; mix well. Cover with plastic wrap; refrigerate 1 hour for easier handling.

2. Heat oven to 350°F. On floured surface, roll out ⅓ of dough at a time to ⅛-inch thickness. (Keep remaining dough refrigerated.) Cut with floured 2½-inch heart-shaped cookie cutter. Place half of cookies 1 inch apart on ungreased cookie sheets. Cut 1-inch heart shape from centers of remaining cookies. Place cutout cookies on cookie sheets. Return small hearts to remaining dough for rerolling.

3. Bake at 350°F. for 9 to 11 minutes or until set. Immediately remove from cookie sheets. Cool 15 minutes or until completely cooled.

4. Meanwhile, in small bowl, combine all frosting ingredients, adding enough cherry liquid for desired spreading consistency; blend until smooth. Frost bottom side of each whole cooled cookie. Place cutout cookies over frosting.

Yield: 4 dozen sandwich cookies
High Altitude (Above 3,500 Feet): Decrease baking powder to ¼ teaspoon.
Bake as directed above.

Variation

Valentine Heart Bouquet: Prepare and bake cookies as directed in recipe. Frost bottom side of each whole cooled cookie. Press about 1½ inches of 12-inch wooden skewer into frosting on each whole cookie. If necessary, spread additional frosting to cover skewer. Place cutout cookies over frosting. Place on cookie sheets; refrigerate about 1 hour to set frosting. If desired, messages or designs can be added with decorator icing. Arrange bouquet in vase; add bows and baby's breath, if desired.

Chocolate Valentine Cookies

kid pleaser

Molasses Jack-o-lantern Cookies

Prep Time: 45 minutes (Ready in 1 hour 45 minutes)

Kitchen Tip

To make the faces with icing, spoon the icing into a small pastry tube, or improvise with a plastic bag or waxed paper cone and snip a hole in the corner. For easier piping, you may wish to add a little extra powdered sugar to make the icing a little stiffer.

Recipe Variation

To make whimsical cat cookies, frost circular cookies with chocolate or orange icing. Use candy corn for ears and pipe on a face and whiskers with icing.

Storage Tip

Make this icing up to 2 weeks in advance and refrigerate it in an air-tight container. Bring it to room temperature and rewhip it before using.

Cookies
1 cup sugar
½ cup margarine or butter, softened
⅓ cup molasses
1 egg
2 cups all-purpose flour
2 teaspoons grated orange peel
1½ teaspoons baking soda
1 teaspoon cinnamon
½ teaspoon ginger
¼ teaspoon salt
¼ teaspoon cloves

Frosting
½ cup butter, softened
¼ cup shortening
1 teaspoon vanilla
⅛ teaspoon salt
4 cups powdered sugar
2 to 4 tablespoons milk
3 drops red food color
6 drops yellow food color
4 drops green food color
½ cup candy corn
½ cup gumdrops
¼ cup miniature chocolate chips

1. In large bowl, combine sugar and margarine; beat until light and fluffy. Add molasses and egg; blend well. Add all remaining cookie ingredients; mix well. Cover with plastic wrap; refrigerate 1 to 3 hours for easier handling.

2. Heat oven to 350°F. On well-floured surface, roll half of dough at a time to ⅛-inch thickness. Cut with floured 3-inch pumpkin-shaped or round cookie cutter. Place 1 inch apart on ungreased cookie sheets.

3. Bake at 350°F. for 6 to 9 minutes or until set. Immediately remove from cookie sheets.

4. In large bowl, combine butter and shortening; beat until light and fluffy. Add vanilla and ⅛ teaspoon salt; mix well. Beat in powdered sugar 1 cup at a time, scraping down sides of bowl. Add 2 tablespoons milk; beat at high speed until light and fluffy. Add enough additional milk for desired spreading consistency.

5. In small bowl, combine half of frosting, 3 drops red food color and 3 drops of the yellow food color; blend well to make orange frosting. Divide remaining frosting mixture in half; place in 2 small bowls. Add 4 drops green food color to 1 bowl and remaining 3 drops yellow food color to second bowl; blend each well. To decorate cookies, frost each cookie with orange-colored frosting. Use green and yellow frostings, candy corn, gumdrops and chocolate chips to make faces on frosted cookies.

Yield: 24 cookies
High Altitude (Above 3,500 Feet): Decrease sugar to ²⁄₃ cup; increase flour to 2¹⁄₂ cups.
Bake as directed above.

Nutrition Information Per Serving

Serving Size: 1 Cookie. Calories 300 • Calories from Fat 100 • Total Fat 11 g
Saturated Fat 4 g • Cholesterol 20 mg • Sodium 210 mg • Dietary Fiber 1 g
Dietary Exchanges: 1 Starch, 2 Fruit, 2 Fat OR 3 Carbohydrate, 2 Fat

Molasses Jack-o-lantern Cookies

Shamrock Mint Cookies

Prep Time: 40 minutes (Ready in 1 hour 40 minutes)

³/₄ cup sugar
³/₄ cup firmly packed brown
   sugar
1 cup margarine or butter,
   softened
¹/₂ teaspoon mint extract
¹/₄ teaspoon green food color

2 eggs
3³/₄ cups all-purpose flour
1¹/₂ teaspoons baking powder
³/₄ teaspoon salt
3 tablespoons sugar
¹/₄ cup green-colored decorator
   sugar

Holiday Note

The shamrock is the national symbol of Ireland. According to legend, patron St. Patrick planted it in Ireland because its three small leaves represented the Holy Trinity.

Recipe Variation

Tint some of the dough yellow and sprinkle the cookies with golden-colored sugar to resemble the pot at the end of the rainbow.

Make It Special

Serve the cookies with glass mugs of Irish coffee (strong coffee, Irish whiskey and sugar, topped with a dollop of whipped cream and sprinkled with nutmeg).

1. In large bowl, combine ³/₄ cup sugar, brown sugar and margarine; beat until light and fluffy. Add mint extract, food color and eggs; beat well. Add flour, baking powder and salt; mix well. Cover with plastic wrap; refrigerate at least 2 hours for easier handling.

2. Heat oven to 375°F. Shape dough into 1-inch balls. For each cookie, place 3 balls, sides touching, in triangular shape on ungreased cookie sheet. Repeat with remaining dough, placing cookies 2 inches apart. With bottom of glass dipped in sugar, flatten each 3-leaved cookie. With sharp knife, score each leaf in half; do not cut through. Sprinkle cookies with green colored sugar.

3. Bake at 375°F. for 6 to 10 minutes or until light golden brown. Cool 1 minute; remove from cookie sheets.

Yield: 3 dozen cookies
High Altitude (Above 3,500 Feet): No change.

Nutrition Information Per Serving

Serving Size: 1 Cookie. Calories 140 • Calories from Fat 45 • Total Fat 5 g
Saturated Fat 1 g • Cholesterol 12 mg • Sodium 130 mg • Dietary Fiber 0 g
Dietary Exchanges: ¹/₂ Starch, 1 Fruit, 1 Fat OR 1¹/₂ Carbohydrate, 1 Fat

Rugalach

Prep Time: 1 hour (Ready in 2 hours)

Cookies

1 cup margarine or butter, softened
1 (8-oz.) pkg. cream cheese, softened
2 cups all-purpose flour

Filling

1¼ cups chopped almonds
½ cup firmly packed brown sugar

1 teaspoon cinnamon
⅔ cup apricot preserves
¼ cup margarine or butter, melted

Topping

2 tablespoons sugar
1 teaspoon cinnamon

1. In large bowl, combine 1 cup margarine and cream cheese; beat at medium speed until smooth. With spoon, gradually stir in flour until stiff dough forms. Knead in any remaining flour. If necessary, cover with plastic wrap; refrigerate 1 hour for easier handling.
2. Heat oven to 350°F. In small bowl, combine all filling ingredients except margarine; mix well. Set aside.
3. On lightly floured surface, roll out ¼ of dough at a time to 11-inch round. Brush each round with 1 tablespoon of the melted margarine. Cut each into 8 wedges. Spoon 2 teaspoons filling mixture onto center of each wedge. Roll up, starting at shortest side and rolling to opposite point. Place, point side down, 2 inches apart on ungreased cookie sheets; curve into crescent shape.
4. In small bowl, combine topping ingredients; sprinkle over cookies.
5. Bake at 350°F. for 15 to 20 minutes or until light golden brown. Immediately remove from cookie sheets.

Yield: 32 cookies
High Altitude (Above 3,500 Feet): No change.

Nutrition Information Per Serving

Serving Size: 1 Cookie. Calories 180 • Calories from Fat 110 • Total Fat 12 g
Saturated Fat 3 g • Cholesterol 8 mg • Sodium 110 mg • Dietary Fiber 1 g
Dietary Exchanges: 1 Starch, 2 Fat OR 1 Carbohydrate, 2 Fat

Holiday Note

These crescent-shaped cookies, made with a rich cream-cheese dough filled with a delectable apricot mixture, are a Hanukkah favorite.

Make It Special

For a Hanukkah hostess gift, decorate a plate of Rugalach with ribbons of silver and blue.

Bake-

Off® Favorites

Bake-Off® recipes have always reflected national trends in home cooking. Early Bake-Off® entries favored rich, elaborate desserts. As women entered the workforce in the 1960s, time-saving recipes emerged, and the 1970s saw a growing interest in nutrition and natural foods. Recent years have seen a merging of all those trends.

Since the first **Bake-Off® Contest** in 1949, some 3,700 recipes have been chosen out of the thousands upon thousands submitted in the five decades of Pillsbury Bake-Off® competitions.

The contest has created enduring recipe classics, celebrating the best of American home cooking—memory-evoking foods inseparable from the comforts and joys of a loving home. In this chapter, we present 37 of the greatest cookies from Bake-Off® competitions, dating right back to the first competition in 1949. On the following pages, you'll find Candy Bar Cookies, Peanut Blossoms, Starlight Mint Surprise Cookies and Snappy Turtle Cookies—just some of the Bake-Off® cookies that have become national classics.

Previous page: Salted Peanut Chews, page 216; Fudgy Bonbons, page 215

Fudgy Bonbons

Prep Time: 1 hour 10 minutes

1 (12-oz.) pkg. (2 cups) semi-
   sweet chocolate chips
¼ cup margarine or butter
1 (14-oz.) can sweetened
   condensed milk (not
   evaporated)
2 cups all-purpose flour
½ cup finely chopped nuts, if
   desired

1 teaspoon vanilla
60 milk chocolate candy kisses
   or white-and-chocolate-
   striped candy kisses,
   unwrapped
2 oz. white chocolate baking
   bar or vanilla-flavored
   candy coating
1 teaspoon shortening or oil

1. Heat oven to 350°F. In medium saucepan, combine chocolate chips and margarine; cook and stir over very low heat until chips are melted and smooth. (Mixture will be stiff.) Add sweetened condensed milk; mix well.

2. In large bowl, combine flour, nuts, chocolate mixture and vanilla; mix well. Shape 1 tablespoon dough (use measuring spoon) around each candy kiss, covering completely. Place 1 inch apart on ungreased cookie sheets.

3. Bake at 350°F. for 6 to 8 minutes. DO NOT OVER-BAKE. Cookies will be soft and appear shiny but will become firm as they cool. Remove from cookie sheets. Cool 15 minutes or until completely cooled.

4. In small saucepan, combine baking bar and shortening; cook and stir over low heat until melted and smooth. Drizzle over cooled cookies. Let stand until set. Store in tightly covered container.

Yield: 5 dozen cookies
High Altitude (Above 3,500 Feet): Increase flour to 2¼ cups. Bake as directed above.

Nutrition Information Per Serving

Serving Size: 1 Cookie. Calories 110 • Calories from Fat 45 • Total Fat 5 g
Saturated Fat 3 g • Cholesterol 5 mg • Sodium 20 mg • Dietary Fiber 1 g
Dietary Exchanges: 1 Fruit, 1 Fat OR 1 Carbohydrate, 1 Fat

Bake-Off® Trivia

When Mary Anne Tyndall was selected to compete in the 36th Bake-Off® Contest in 1994, she told us she loved creating new chocolate recipes. "Chocolate is my passion." A chocolate candy kiss is the special surprise hiding inside each of her Fudgy Bonbons, which were awarded the Grand Prize that year by host Alex Trebek.

Make It Special

Serve these rich cookies in miniature paper cups for a dazzling presentation.

Salted Peanut Chews

Prep Time: 35 minutes (Ready in 1 hour 35 minutes)

Bake-Off® Trivia

Bake-Off® contestants prepare their recipe at least twice for the competition—once for the judges and once for photography and display. Sufficient groceries are provided at each mini-kitchen to allow the recipe to be made three times, so entrants can choose their best effort for judging. Gertrude M. Schweterhof of Cupertino, California, baked these Salted Peanut Chews at the 29th contest, held in 1980 in Miami.

Base
1½ cups all-purpose flour
⅔ cup firmly packed brown sugar
½ teaspoon baking powder
½ teaspoon salt
¼ teaspoon baking soda
½ cup margarine or butter, softened
1 teaspoon vanilla
2 egg yolks

3 cups miniature marshmallows

Topping
⅔ cup corn syrup
¼ cup margarine or butter
2 teaspoons vanilla
1 (10-oz.) pkg. peanut butter chips
2 cups crisp rice cereal
2 cups salted peanuts

1. Heat oven to 350°F. In large bowl, combine all base ingredients except marshmallows at low speed until crumbly. Press firmly in bottom of ungreased 13 × 9-inch pan.

2. Bake at 350°F. for 12 to 15 minutes or until light golden brown. Remove from oven; immediately sprinkle with marshmallows. Return to oven; bake an additional 1 to 2 minutes or until marshmallows just begin to puff. Cool while preparing topping.

3. In large saucepan, combine all topping ingredients except cereal and peanuts. Heat just until chips are melted and mixture is smooth, stirring constantly. Remove from heat; stir in cereal and peanuts. Immediately spoon warm topping over marshmallows; spread to cover. Refrigerate 45 minutes or until firm. Cut into bars.

Yield: 36 bars

Microwave Directions: 1. Use half the amount of all ingredients. In large bowl, combine all base ingredients except marshmallows at low speed until crumbly. Press firmly in bottom of ungreased 8-inch square (1½-quart) microwave-safe dish. 2. Microwave on HIGH for 3½ to 4½ minutes or until base looks dry, rotating dish ½ turn halfway through cooking. Immediately sprinkle with marshmallows. Microwave on HIGH for 1 to 1½ minutes

or until marshmallows just begin to puff. Cool while preparing topping. 3. In 4-cup microwave-safe measuring cup, combine all topping ingredients except cereal and peanuts. Microwave on HIGH for 1 to 2 minutes or until chips are melted, stirring once halfway through cooking. Stir until smooth. Continue as directed above.

Yield: 18 bars
High Altitude (Above 3,500 Feet): No change.

Nutrition Information Per Serving

Serving Size: 1 Bar. Calories 200 • Calories from Fat 90 • Total Fat 10 g
Saturated Fat 2 g • Cholesterol 10 mg • Sodium 170 mg • Dietary Fiber 1 g
Dietary Exchanges: 1½ Starch, 2 Fat OR 1½ Carbohydrate, 2 Fat

Salted Peanut Chews

Chewy Date Drops

Prep Time: 1 hour (Ready in 1 hour 30 minutes)

Bake-Off® Trivia

Some of the early Bake-Off® competitions included a special category for brides. In 1957, Cynthia C. Anderson of Contoocook, New Hampshire, won that division with this recipe, a favorite treat for her husband's lunchbox.

About Dates

Store dates tightly wrapped at room temperature or in the refrigerator to keep them moist. If they do dry out, use them in a recipe that combines them with liquid before using, as this one does.

Make It Special

Decorate each cookie with a walnut half or quarter before baking.

2 cups chopped pitted dates
½ cup sugar
½ cup water
1 cup firmly packed brown sugar
½ cup sugar
1 cup margarine or butter, softened
1 teaspoon vanilla
3 eggs
4 cups all-purpose flour
1 teaspoon baking soda
1 teaspoon salt
1 cup chopped walnuts or pecans

1. In medium saucepan, combine dates, ½ cup sugar and water. Cook over medium heat until thickened, stirring occasionally. Cool 30 minutes.

2. Heat oven to 375°F. Grease cookie sheets. In large bowl, combine brown sugar, ½ cup sugar and margarine; beat until light and fluffy. Add vanilla and eggs; blend well. Add flour, baking soda and salt; mix well. Stir in date mixture and walnuts. Drop dough by rounded teaspoonfuls 2 inches apart onto greased cookie sheets.

3. Bake at 375°F. for 8 to 10 minutes or until light golden brown. Immediately remove from cookie sheets.

Yield: 6 dozen cookies
High Altitude (Above 3,500 Feet): Decrease granulated sugar beaten with margarine to ¼ cup. Bake as directed above.

Nutrition Information Per Serving

Serving Size: 1 Cookie. Calories 100 • Calories from Fat 35 • Total Fat 4 g
Saturated Fat 1 g • Cholesterol 10 mg • Sodium 75 mg • Dietary Fiber 1 g
Dietary Exchanges: 1 Fruit, 1 Fat OR 1 Carbohydrate, 1 Fat

Chocolate Pixies

Prep Time: 1 hour 15 minutes (Ready in 2 hours 15 minutes)

1/4 cup margarine or butter
4 oz. unsweetened chocolate
2 cups all-purpose flour
2 cups sugar
1/2 cup chopped walnuts or
    pecans

2 teaspoons baking powder
1/2 teaspoon salt
4 eggs
Powdered sugar

1. In large saucepan over low heat, melt margarine and chocolate, stirring constantly until smooth. Remove from heat; cool slightly. Add flour, sugar, walnuts, baking powder, salt and eggs; mix well. Cover with plastic wrap; refrigerate at least 1 hour for easier handling.

2. Heat oven to 300°F. Shape dough into 1-inch balls; roll in powdered sugar, coating heavily. Place 2 inches apart on ungreased cookie sheets.

3. Bake at 300°F. for 13 to 18 minutes or until set. Immediately remove from cookie sheets. Cool 15 minutes or until completely cooled. Store in tightly covered container.

Yield: 4 dozen cookies
High Altitude (Above 3,500 Feet): Increase flour to 2 1/4 cups. Bake as directed above.

Nutrition Information Per Serving
Serving Size: 1 Cookie. Calories 90 • Calories from Fat 25 • Total Fat 3 g
Saturated Fat 1 g • Cholesterol 20 mg • Sodium 60 mg • Dietary Fiber 1 g
Dietary Exchanges: 1 Fruit, 1/2 Fat OR 1 Carbohydrate, 1/2 Fat

Bake-Off® Trivia

Mrs. John L. Parisot of Marseilles, Illinois, won a prize in the 5th competition in 1953 with these cookies, which taste like black walnut brownies and look like old-fashioned molasses cookies with cracked tops. The cookie was a Christmas tradition with her family.

Kitchen Tip

If you wish to melt the chocolate and butter in the microwave, keep in mind that butter will melt much faster than chocolate, and that chocolate melted in the microwave deceptively keeps its shape even after it has begun to melt. The best strategy is to partially melt the chocolate in a microwave-safe mixing bowl on LOW power. Stir, add the butter and continue heating until all is melted.

Caramel Cream Sandwich Cookies

Helen Beckman of Mt. Vernon, Iowa, began cooking at the age of six and adapted this prize-winning recipe from one found in her mother's recipe box. The caramel-flavored cookies earned the 15-year-old $2,000 in the junior division at the 6th Bake-Off® event in 1954. That year, the contest took place at New York City's Waldorf-Astoria Hotel, which has hosted ten Bake-Off® competitions, including the first eight.

Prep Time: 1 hour 15 minutes

Cookies
¾ cup firmly packed brown sugar
1 cup butter, softened
1 egg yolk
2 cups all-purpose flour

Frosting
2 tablespoons butter (do not use margarine)
1¼ cups powdered sugar
½ teaspoon vanilla
4 to 5 teaspoons milk

1. In large bowl, combine brown sugar and 1 cup butter; beat until light and fluffy. Add egg yolk; blend well. Add flour; mix well. If necessary, cover with plastic wrap; refrigerate 15 minutes for easier handling.

2. Heat oven to 325°F. Shape dough into 1-inch balls. Place 2 inches apart on ungreased cookie sheets. With fork dipped in flour, flatten each to 1½-inch round.

3. Bake at 325°F. for 10 to 14 minutes or until light golden brown. Cool 1 minute; remove from cookie sheets. Cool 15 minutes or until completely cooled.

4. Meanwhile, in medium saucepan, heat 2 tablespoons butter over medium heat until light golden brown, stirring constantly. Remove from heat. Stir in remaining frosting ingredients, adding enough milk for desired spreading consistency; blend until smooth. Spread scant 1 teaspoon frosting between 2 cooled cookies. Repeat with remaining frosting and cookies.

Yield: 30 sandwich cookies
High Altitude (Above 3,500 Feet): No change.

Nutrition Information Per Serving
Serving Size: 1 Sandwich Cookie. Calories 140 • Calories from Fat 60 • Total Fat 7 g • Saturated Fat 4 g • Cholesterol 25 mg • Sodium 75 mg • Dietary Fiber 0 g Dietary Exchanges: 1 Starch, 1½ Fat OR 1 Carbohydrate, 1½ Fat

Caramel Cream Sandwich Cookies

Java Crunch Cookies

½ cup sugar
¼ cup firmly packed brown sugar
¾ cup shortening
1 tablespoon instant coffee granules or crystals

2 tablespoons hot water
1 egg
1½ cups all-purpose flour
1 teaspoon baking powder
½ teaspoon salt
1½ cups coconut

1. Heat oven to 350°F. In large bowl, combine sugar, brown sugar and shortening; beat until light and fluffy. In small bowl or cup, dissolve coffee in hot water. Add dissolved coffee and egg to sugar mixture; blend well. Add flour, baking powder and salt; mix well. Stir in coconut. Drop dough by rounded teaspoonfuls onto ungreased cookie sheets.

2. Bake at 350°F. for 11 to 15 minutes or until edges are golden brown. Cool 2 minutes; remove from cookie sheets.

Yield: 3 dozen cookies
High Altitude (Above 3,500 Feet): No change.

Nutrition Information Per Serving

Serving Size: 1 Cookie. Calories 90 • Calories from Fat 45 • Total Fat 5 g
Saturated Fat 2 g • Cholesterol 5 mg • Sodium 55 mg • Dietary Fiber 0 g
Dietary Exchanges: ½ Starch, 1 Fat OR ½ Carbohydrate, 1 Fat

Oatmeal Carmelitas

Prep Time: 30 minutes (Ready in 2 hours 55 minutes)

Base
2 cups all-purpose flour
2 cups quick-cooking rolled oats
1½ cups firmly packed brown sugar
1 teaspoon baking soda
½ teaspoon salt
1¼ cups margarine or butter, softened

Filling
1 (12.5-oz.) jar (1 cup) caramel ice cream topping
3 tablespoons all-purpose flour
1 (6-oz.) pkg. (1 cup) semi-sweet chocolate chips
½ cup chopped nuts

1. Heat oven to 350°F. Grease 13 × 9-inch pan. In large bowl, combine all base ingredients; mix at low speed until crumbly. Reserve half of crumb mixture (about 3 cups) for topping. Press remaining crumb mixture in bottom of greased pan. Bake at 350°F. for 10 minutes.

2. Meanwhile, in small bowl, combine caramel topping and 3 tablespoons flour. Remove partially baked base from oven; sprinkle with chocolate chips and nuts. Drizzle evenly with caramel mixture; sprinkle with reserved crumb mixture.

3. Bake at 350°F. for an additional 18 to 22 minutes or until golden brown. Cool 1 hour or until completely cooled. Refrigerate 1 to 2 hours or until filling is set. Cut into bars.

Yield: 36 bars
High Altitude (Above 3,500 Feet): No change.

Nutrition Information Per Serving
Serving Size: 1 Bar. Calories 200 • Calories from Fat 80 • Total Fat 9 g
Saturated Fat 2 g • Cholesterol 0 mg • Sodium 180 mg • Dietary Fiber 1 g
Dietary Exchanges: 1 Starch, 1 Fruit, 1½ Fat OR 2 Carbohydrate, 1½ Fat

Bake-Off® Trivia

On the day before entries were due for the 18th Bake-Off® Contest, Erlyce Larson of Kennedy, Minnesota, entered these chewy oatmeal bars. Her efforts paid off—she won a trip to compete, and her bars have become one of Pillsbury's most-requested recipes. In recognition of the continuing trend toward convenience foods, that year's contest theme was "Pillsbury Busy Lady Bake-Off."

Storage Tip

These bars stay soft and delicious when stored tightly covered in the baking pan.

Cherry Winks

Prep Time: 1 hour 20 minutes

1 cup sugar
³/₄ cup shortening
2 tablespoons milk
1 teaspoon vanilla
2 eggs
2¹/₄ cups all-purpose flour
1 teaspoon baking powder
¹/₂ teaspoon baking soda
¹/₂ teaspoon salt

1 cup chopped pecans
1 cup chopped dates
¹/₃ cup chopped maraschino
   cherries, well drained
1¹/₂ cups coarsely crushed corn
   flakes cereal
15 maraschino cherries,
   quartered

1. In large bowl, combine sugar, shortening, milk, vanilla and eggs; beat well. Add flour, baking powder, baking soda and salt; mix well. Stir in pecans, dates and ¹/₃ cup chopped cherries. If necessary, cover with plastic wrap; refrigerate 15 minutes for easier handling.
2. Heat oven to 375°F. Grease cookie sheets. Drop dough by rounded teaspoonfuls into cereal; thoroughly coat. Shape into balls. Place 2 inches apart on greased cookie sheets. Lightly press maraschino cherry quarter into top of each ball.
3. Bake at 375°F. for 10 to 15 minutes or until light golden brown. Remove from cookie sheets.

Yield: **5 dozen cookies**
High Altitude (Above 3,500 Feet): No change.

Nutrition Information Per Serving

Serving Size: 1 Cookie. Calories 90 • Calories from Fat 35 • Total Fat 4 g
Saturated Fat 1 g • Cholesterol 5 mg • Sodium 70 mg • Dietary Fiber 1 g
Dietary Exchanges: ¹/₂ Starch, 1 Fat OR ¹/₂ Carbohydrate, 1 Fat

---

Bake-Off® Trivia

Ruth Derousseau was a young Wisconsin mother of two back in 1950 when she won the Junior Division First Prize of $5,000 for Cherry Winks. The cookie was based on a recipe from her grandmother, who taught her to cook. Ruth and her husband went on to raise a grand total of sixteen children—nine girls and seven boys.

Kitchen Tip

For easier handling, cover the dough with plastic wrap and refrigerate it until firm.

Ingredient Substitution

Candied cherries can be used instead of maraschinos.

Cherry Winks; Peanut Blossoms, page 227

Raspberry-filled White Chocolate Bars

Prep Time: 25 minutes (Ready in 2 hours 20 minutes)

Bake-Off® Trivia

When Mark Bocianski of Wheaton, Illinois, prepared these striking red and white bars at the 34th Bake-Off® competition, he was one of twelve male finalists, the most men to ever compete in the contest.

Kitchen Tip

To toast almonds, spread them on a cookie sheet; bake at 325°F. for 6 to 10 minutes or until light golden brown, stirring occasionally. Or spread them in a thin layer in a microwave-safe pie pan. Microwave on HIGH for 3 to 4 minutes or until light golden brown, stirring frequently.

Make It Special

Garnish the plate with fresh raspberries and a sprig of fresh mint.

½ cup margarine or butter	1 cup all-purpose flour
1 (12-oz.) pkg. (2 cups) white vanilla chips or 12 oz. white chocolate baking bars, chopped	½ teaspoon salt
	1 teaspoon amaretto or almond extract
2 eggs	½ cup raspberry spreadable fruit or jam
½ cup sugar	¼ cup sliced almonds, toasted

1. Heat oven to 325°F. Grease and flour 9-inch square pan or 8-inch square (1½-quart) baking dish. Melt margarine in small saucepan over low heat. Remove from heat. Add 1 cup of the vanilla chips (or 6 oz. chopped baking bar). LET STAND; DO NOT STIR.

2. In large bowl, beat eggs until frothy. Gradually add sugar, beating at high speed until lemon colored. Stir in vanilla chip mixture. Add flour, salt and amaretto; mix at low speed just until combined. Spread half of batter (about 1 cup) in greased and floured pan. Set remaining batter aside.

3. Bake at 325°F. for 15 to 20 minutes or until light golden brown.

4. Stir remaining 1 cup vanilla chips (or 6 oz. chopped baking bar) into remaining half of batter; set aside. Melt spreadable fruit in small saucepan over low heat. Spread evenly over warm, partially baked crust. Gently spoon teaspoonfuls of remaining batter over spreadable fruit. (Some fruit may show through batter.) Sprinkle with almonds.

5. Bake at 325°F. for an additional 25 to 35 minutes or until toothpick inserted in center comes out clean. Cool 1 hour or until completely cooled. Cut into bars.

Peanut Blossoms

kid pleaser • chocoholic's choice •

Prep Time: 1 hour

1¾ cups all-purpose flour
½ cup sugar
½ cup firmly packed brown
   sugar
1 teaspoon baking soda
½ teaspoon salt
½ cup shortening

½ cup peanut butter
2 tablespoons milk
1 teaspoon vanilla
1 egg
Sugar
48 milk chocolate candy
   kisses, unwrapped

1. Heat oven to 375°F. In large bowl, combine flour, ½ cup sugar, brown sugar, baking soda, salt, shortening, peanut butter, milk, vanilla and egg; mix at low speed until stiff dough forms. Shape dough into 1-inch balls; roll in sugar. Place 2 inches apart on ungreased cookie sheets.

2. Bake at 375°F. for 10 to 12 minutes or until golden brown. Immediately top each cookie with 1 candy kiss, pressing down firmly so cookie cracks around edge. Remove from cookie sheets.

Yield: 4 dozen cookies
High Altitude (Above 3,500 Feet): No change.

Nutrition Information Per Serving

Serving Size: 1 Cookie. Calories 100 • Calories from Fat 45 • Total Fat 5 g
Saturated Fat 2 g • Cholesterol 5 mg • Sodium 70 mg • Dietary Fiber 0 g
Dietary Exchanges: 1 Fruit, 1 Fat OR 1 Carbohydrate, 1 Fat

Bake-Off® Trivia

The 100 contestants who ultimately prepare their recipes at the Bake-Off® competition reflect a cross section of Americans, and winning a prize in the contest has catapulted many excellent home cooks into the limelight. The late Freda Smith of Gibsonburg, Ohio, called the contest "the most wonderful experience of my life" and basked in the glow of local publicity and hundreds of fan letters from other avid bakers all over the country. Her Peanut Blossoms, a prize winner at the 9th contest in 1957, have become a cookie standard.

Lemon Kiss Cookies

Prep Time: 1 hour 20 minutes (Ready in 2 hours 20 minutes)

³/₄ cup sugar
1½ cups margarine or butter, softened
1 tablespoon lemon extract
2³/₄ cups all-purpose flour
1½ cups finely chopped almonds

1 (13-oz.) pkg. milk chocolate candy kisses, unwrapped
Powdered sugar
½ cup semi-sweet chocolate chips
1 tablespoon shortening

1. In large bowl, combine sugar, margarine and lemon extract; beat until light and fluffy. Add flour and almonds; beat at low speed until well blended. Cover with plastic wrap; refrigerate at least 1 hour for easier handling.

2. Heat oven to 375°F. Shape scant 1 tablespoon dough around each candy kiss, covering completely. Roll in hands to form ball; place on ungreased cookie sheets.

3. Bake at 375°F. for 8 to 12 minutes or until cookies are set and bottom edges are light golden brown. Cool 1 minute; remove from cookie sheets. Cool 5 minutes or until completely cooled.

4. Lightly sprinkle cooled cookies with powdered sugar. In small saucepan, combine chocolate chips and shortening; cook and stir over low heat until melted and smooth. Drizzle over cooled cookies. Let stand until set. Store in tightly covered container.

Yield: 6 dozen cookies
High Altitude (Above 3,500 Feet): Decrease margarine to 1¼ cups. Bake as directed above.

Nutrition Information Per Serving

Serving Size: 1 Cookie. Calories 110 • Calories from Fat 60 • Total Fat 7 g
Saturated Fat 4 g • Cholesterol 10 mg • Sodium 45 mg • Dietary Fiber 1 g
Dietary Exchanges: 1 Fruit, 1½ Fat OR 1 Carbohydrate, 1½ Fat

Lemon Kiss Cookies

Apricot Snowcaps

Prep Time: 1 hour

Bake-Off® Trivia

Virginia Johnson of Blanchardsville, Wisconsin, baked these thumbprint-style cookies for the 35th Bake-Off® Contest held in 1992 in Orlando, Florida. She got the idea for the cookie from a candy she had tasted and really enjoyed—dried apricots coated with white chocolate.

Ingredient Substitution

Use apricot preserves instead of the apricot filling.

Cookies
1/2 cup sugar
1/2 cup firmly packed brown sugar
1/4 cup margarine or butter, softened
1/4 cup shortening
1/2 teaspoon vanilla
1 egg
1 cup all-purpose flour
1/2 teaspoon baking powder
1/2 teaspoon baking soda
1/2 teaspoon salt
1 cup quick-cooking rolled oats
1/2 cup purchased apricot filling

Glaze
1 (6-oz.) white chocolate baking bar, chopped
2 tablespoons shortening

1. Heat oven to 350°F. In large bowl, combine sugar, brown sugar, margarine and 1/4 cup shortening; beat until light and fluffy. Add vanilla and egg; blend well. Add flour, baking powder, baking soda and salt; mix well. Stir in oats.

2. Shape dough into 1-inch balls. Place 2 inches apart on ungreased cookie sheets. With thumb or handle of wooden spoon, make small indentation in center of each cookie. Fill each with 1/2 teaspoon apricot filling.

3. Bake at 350°F. for 9 to 13 minutes or until light golden brown. Cool 1 minute; remove from cookie sheets.

4. Meanwhile, in small saucepan over very low heat, melt glaze ingredients. Spoon or drizzle over warm cookies. Let stand until set.

Yield: 3 dozen cookies
High Altitude (Above 3,500 Feet): Decrease sugar to 1/3 cup; increase flour to 1 1/3 cups. Bake as directed above.

Nutrition Information Per Serving
Serving Size: 1 Cookie. Calories 110 • Calories from Fat 45 • Total Fat 5 g
Saturated Fat 2 g • Cholesterol 5 mg • Sodium 75 mg • Dietary Fiber 0 g
Dietary Exchanges: 1 Fruit, 1 Fat OR 1 Carbohydrate, 1 Fat

Spicy Banana Bars

Prep Time: 15 minutes (Ready in 40 minutes)

Bars

¼ cup margarine or butter,
    softened, or shortening
⅓ cup mashed ripe banana
¼ cup milk
1 egg
1 cup all-purpose flour
¾ cup sugar
½ teaspoon baking powder
½ teaspoon salt
¼ teaspoon baking soda

¾ teaspoon cinnamon
¼ teaspoon cloves
¼ teaspoon allspice
⅓ cup chopped pecans

Frosting

2 tablespoons margarine or
    butter
1 cup powdered sugar
2 teaspoons lemon juice
2 to 4 teaspoons water

1. Heat oven to 350°F. Grease and flour 13 × 9-inch pan. In small bowl, combine ¼ cup margarine and banana; blend well. Add milk and egg beat well. Add all remaining bar ingredients; blend well. Spread in greased and floured pan.

2. Bake at 350°F. for 20 to 25 minutes or until light golden brown.

3. Meanwhile, melt 2 tablespoons margarine in small saucepan. Stir in powdered sugar, lemon juice and enough water for desired spreading consistency. Spread over warm bars. Cool completely. Cut into bars. Garnish as desired.

Yield: 36 bars
High Altitude (Above 3,500 Feet): Decrease sugar to ⅔ cup. Bake as directed above.

Nutrition Information Per Serving

Serving Size: 1 Bar. Calories 70 • Calories from Fat 25 • Total Fat 3 g • Saturated
Fat 0 g • Cholesterol 5 mg • Sodium 70 mg • Dietary Fiber 0 g
Dietary Exchanges: ½ Starch, ½ Fat OR ½ Carbohydrate, ½ Fat

Bake-Off® Trivia

Margaret Cummings of Enderlin, North Dakota, competed at the 6th Bake-Off® event, which took place at New York City's Waldorf Astoria Hotel in 1954. A tangy lemon frosting complements the moist, cakelike bars, which were a favorite with her children.

About Allspice

Despite its name, allspice is not a blend of ingredients but rather a single spice that contains flavor nuances similar to those of cinnamon, nutmeg and clove. Though American cooking treats it primarily as an ingredient in desserts, allspice plays a role in savory specialties from Greece, the Middle East and Africa.

Make It Special

For a party, cut the bars into narrow rectangles and garnish each with a pecan half.

Rocky Road Fudge Bars

Prep Time: 25 minutes (Ready in 2 hours 10 minutes)

Bake-Off® Trivia

Mary Wilson of Leesburg, Georgia, created this recipe specifically for the 23rd Bake-Off® Contest in 1972, serving it first to a group of men to see if they liked it. They did, and so did the judges, who awarded it the $5,000 first prize in the flour category. It's become one of Pillsbury's most-requested recipes.

Recipe Fact

The term "rocky road" refers to a chunky combination of nuts, chunks or chips of chocolate and marshmallow.

Base
1/2 cup margarine or butter
1 oz. unsweetened chocolate, cut into pieces
1 cup all-purpose flour
1 cup sugar
1 teaspoon baking powder
1 teaspoon vanilla
2 eggs
3/4 cup chopped nuts

Filling
6 oz. cream cheese (from 8-oz. pkg.), softened
1/4 cup margarine or butter, softened
1/2 cup sugar

2 tablespoons all-purpose flour
1/2 teaspoon vanilla
1 egg
1/4 cup chopped nuts
1 (6-oz.) pkg. (1 cup) semi-sweet chocolate chips
2 cups miniature marshmallows

Frosting
1/4 cup margarine or butter
1/4 cup milk
1 oz. unsweetened chocolate, cut into pieces
2 oz. cream cheese
3 cups powdered sugar
1 teaspoon vanilla

1. Heat oven to 350°F. Grease and flour 13 × 9-inch pan. In large saucepan, melt 1/2 cup margarine and 1 oz. unsweetened chocolate over low heat, stirring until smooth. Add all remaining base ingredients; mix well. Spread in greased and floured pan.

2. In small bowl, combine all filling ingredients except nuts, chocolate chips and marshmallows. Beat 1 minute at medium speed until smooth and fluffy. Stir in 1/4 cup nuts. Spread over chocolate mixture; sprinkle evenly with chocolate chips.

3. Bake at 350°F. for 25 to 35 minutes or until toothpick inserted in center comes out clean. Remove from oven; immediately sprinkle with marshmallows. Return to oven; bake an additional 2 minutes.

4. While marshmallows are baking, in large saucepan, combine all frosting ingredients except powdered sugar and vanilla. Cook over low heat, stirring until well blended. Remove from heat; stir in powdered sugar and 1 teaspoon vanilla until smooth. Immediately pour frosting over puffed marshmallows; lightly swirl with knife to marble. Refrigerate 1 hour or until firm. Cut into bars. Store in refrigerator.

Yield: 48 bars
High Altitude (Above 3,500 Feet): No change.

Nutrition Information Per Serving
Serving Size: 1 Bar. Calories 170 • Calories from Fat 80 • Total Fat 9 g
Saturated Fat 3 g • Cholesterol 20 mg • Sodium 75 mg • Dietary Fiber 1 g
Dietary Exchanges: 1½ Fruit, 2 Fat OR 1½ Carbohydrate, 2 Fat

Rocky Road Fudge Bars

Snappy Turtle Cookies

Prep Time: 1 hour 30 minutes (Ready in 2 hours 45 minutes)

Cookies
½ cup firmly packed brown sugar
½ cup margarine or butter, softened
¼ teaspoon vanilla
⅛ teaspoon imitation maple flavor, if desired
1 egg
1 egg, separated
1½ cups all-purpose flour
¼ teaspoon baking soda
¼ teaspoon salt
1 cup pecan halves, split lengthwise

Frosting
⅓ cup semi-sweet chocolate chips
3 tablespoons milk
1 tablespoon margarine or butter
1 cup powdered sugar

1. In large bowl, combine brown sugar and ½ cup margarine; beat until light and fluffy. Add vanilla, maple flavor, 1 whole egg and 1 egg yolk; beat well. Add flour, baking soda and salt; mix well. Cover with plastic wrap; refrigerate at least 1 hour for easier handling.

2. Heat oven to 350°F. Grease cookie sheets. Arrange pecan pieces in groups of 5 on greased cookie sheets to resemble head and legs of turtle. In small bowl, beat egg white. Shape dough into 1-inch balls. Dip bottoms in beaten egg white; press lightly onto pecans. (Tips of pecans should show.)

3. Bake at 350°F. for 10 to 12 minutes or until edges are light golden brown. Immediately remove from cookie sheets. Cool 15 minutes or until completely cooled.

4. Meanwhile, in small saucepan, combine chocolate chips, milk and 1 tablespoon margarine; cook over low heat, stirring constantly, until melted and smooth. Remove from heat; stir in powdered sugar. If necessary, add additional powdered sugar for desired spreading consistency. Frost cooled cookies. Let stand until set. Store in tightly covered container.

Yield: 3½ dozen cookies
High Altitude (Above 3,500 Feet): No change.

Nutrition Information Per Serving

Serving Size: 1 Cookie. Calories 90 • Calories from Fat 45 • Total Fat 5 g
Saturated Fat 1 g • Cholesterol 10 mg • Sodium 55 mg • Dietary Fiber 0 g
Dietary Exchanges: ½ Starch, 1 Fat OR ½ Carbohydrate, 1 Fat

Snappy Turtle Cookies

Peekaberry Boos

Prep Time: 1 hour

1 cup firmly packed brown
   sugar
³/₄ cup sugar
1 cup margarine or butter,
   softened
¹/₂ cup water
1 teaspoon almond extract
2 eggs

3 cups all-purpose flour
2 cups quick-cooking rolled
   oats
1 teaspoon baking soda
¹/₂ teaspoon salt
¹/₂ teaspoon cinnamon
²/₃ cup raspberry preserves

1. Heat oven to 400°F. In large bowl, combine brown sugar, sugar and margarine; beat until light and fluffy. Add water, almond extract and eggs; blend well. (Mixture will look curdled.) Add flour, oats, baking soda, salt and cinnamon; mix well. Drop dough by rounded teaspoonfuls 2 inches apart onto ungreased cookie sheets. With spoon, make imprint in center of each cookie. Fill each imprint with ¹/₂ teaspoon preserves. Drop scant teaspoon dough over preserves on each cookie.

2. Bake at 400°F. for 6 to 9 minutes or until light golden brown. Immediately remove from cookie sheets.

Yield: 5 dozen cookies
High Altitude (Above 3,500 Feet): Decrease sugar to ¹/₂ cup. Bake as directed above.

Nutrition Information Per Serving
Serving Size: 1 Cookie. Calories 90 • Calories from Fat 25 • Total Fat 3 g
Saturated Fat 1 g • Cholesterol 5 mg • Sodium 80 mg • Dietary Fiber 1 g
Dietary Exchanges: 1 Fruit, ¹/₂ Fat OR 1 Carbohydrate, ¹/₂ Fat

---

Bake-Off® Trivia

In 1958, Mrs. Robert Gregg of Spokane, Washington, won the Brides category with her raspberry-filled Peekaberry Boos. One of her fellow finalists never made it to the competition that year. The unoccupied range was decorated with an oversized bow—the contestant stayed home to have a baby.

About Eggs

To minimize the risk of purchasing eggs contaminated with salmonella bacteria, always open the egg carton before you buy and make sure there are no cracked or broken eggs. At home, store eggs in the refrigerator and avoid recipes in which the finished dish contains raw eggs. Unfortunately, this means it is also advisable to discontinue the much-loved custom of licking the spoon after mixing cookie dough, cake batter or other sweets that contain raw eggs.

Praline Cookies

Prep Time: 1 hour

Cookies

1½ cups firmly packed brown
    sugar
½ cup margarine or butter,
    softened
1 teaspoon vanilla
1 egg
1½ cups all-purpose flour
1½ teaspoons baking powder
½ teaspoon salt

Frosting

½ cup firmly packed brown
    sugar
¼ cup half-and-half
1 cup powdered sugar
½ cup coarsely chopped
    pecans

1. Heat oven to 350°F. Grease cookie sheets. In large bowl, combine 1½ cups brown sugar and margarine; beat until light and fluffy. Add vanilla and egg; blend well. Add flour, baking powder and salt; mix well. Drop dough by rounded teaspoonfuls 2 inches apart onto greased cookie sheets.

2. Bake at 350°F. for 10 to 12 minutes or until light golden brown. Cool 1 minute; remove from cookie sheets.

3. In small saucepan, combine ½ cup brown sugar and half-and-half. Bring to a boil over medium heat; boil 2 minutes, stirring constantly. Remove from heat. Stir in powdered sugar; beat until smooth. Place about ½ teaspoon pecans on each cookie. Drizzle with frosting, covering pecans.

Yield: 3 dozen cookies
High Altitude (Above 3,500 Feet): No change.

Nutrition Information Per Serving

Serving Size: 1 Cookie. Calories 120 • Calories from Fat 35 • Total Fat 4 g
Saturated Fat 1 g • Cholesterol 7 mg • Sodium 80 mg • Dietary Fiber 0 g
Dietary Exchanges: 1 Starch, 1 Fat OR 1 Carbohydrate, 1 Fat

Bake-Off® Trivia

Cheryl Matthews of Charlotte, North Carolina, was just fourteen in 1959 when she won second prize in the 11th contest. She did her recipe testing on the range that her mother won as a finalist in the 4th Grand National Cooking Contest in 1952.

Recipe Fact

Traditional pralines, a New Orleans specialty, are a mixture of pecans and caramelized sugar.

About Pecans

Pecans, widely grown in the southern United States, have smooth, tan, oval shells. The nut inside is shaped like a somewhat flattened walnut but has a softer texture and sweeter flavor.

Split Seconds

Prep Time: 1 hour 15 minutes

Bake-Off® Trivia

Karin Fellows learned to cook in her native Sweden and brought the recipe for these jam-filled butter cookies with her when she moved to the United States. The recipe, originally from her mother's family, won her a $1,000 prize at the 1954 Bake-Off® Contest.

Ingredient Substitution

Use any flavor jam or jelly.

²/₃ cup sugar
³/₄ cup margarine or butter, softened
2 teaspoons vanilla

1 egg
2 cups all-purpose flour
¹/₂ teaspoon baking powder
¹/₂ cup red jelly or preserves

1. Heat oven to 350°F. In large bowl, combine sugar and margarine; beat until light and fluffy. Add vanilla and egg; blend well. Add flour and baking powder; mix well.

2. Divide dough into 4 equal parts. On lightly floured surface, shape each part into 12-inch roll; place on ungreased cookie sheets. Using handle of wooden spoon or finger, make depression about ¹/₂ inch wide and ¹/₄ inch deep lengthwise down center of each roll. Fill each roll with 2 tablespoons jelly.

3. Bake at 350°F. for 15 to 20 minutes or until light golden brown. Cool slightly. Cut each baked roll diagonally into 12 cookies. Cool on wire racks.

Yield: 4 dozen cookies
High Altitude (Above 3,500 Feet): No change.

Nutrition Information Per Serving

Serving Size: 1 Cookie. Calories 70 • Calories from Fat 25 • Total Fat 3 g
Saturated Fat 1 g • Cholesterol 4 mg • Sodium 40 mg • Dietary Fiber 0 g
Dietary Exchanges: ¹/₂ Starch, ¹/₂ Fat OR ¹/₂ Carbohydrate, ¹/₂ Fat

Split Seconds

So-Easy Sugar Cookies

Prep Time: 35 minutes

Bake-Off® Trivia

If necessity is the mother of invention, mothering itself often necessitates invention. Kathryn Blackburn, a baking aficionado from National Park, New Jersey, had three young children at home when she streamlined sugar cookie preparation to develop this easy bar version. She made it for the judges at the 30th contest in 1982.

Make It Special

Sprinkle the bars with colored sugar before baking.

³/₄ cup sugar
¹/₃ cup margarine or butter, softened, or shortening
¹/₃ cup oil
1 tablespoon milk
1 to 2 teaspoons almond extract

1 egg
1¹/₂ cups all-purpose flour
1¹/₂ teaspoons baking powder
¹/₄ teaspoon salt
1 tablespoon sugar

1. Heat oven to 375°F. In large bowl, combine ³/₄ cup sugar, margarine, oil, milk, almond extract and egg; beat until light and fluffy. Add flour, baking powder and salt; mix well. Spread evenly in ungreased 15 × 10 × 1-inch baking pan; sprinkle with 1 tablespoon sugar.

2. Bake at 375°F. for 10 to 12 minutes or until light golden brown. Cool 5 minutes. Cut into 48 cookies.

Yield: 4 dozen cookies
High Altitude (Above 3,500 Feet): Decrease baking powder to 1 teaspoon. Bake as directed above.

Food Processor Directions: In food processor bowl with metal blade, combine ³/₄ cup sugar, margarine, oil, milk, almond extract and egg. Cover; process until light and fluffy. Add flour, baking powder and salt. Cover; process using on/off turns just until flour is well blended. DO NOT OVERPROCESS OR COOKIES WILL BE TOUGH. Continue as directed above.

Nutrition Information Per Serving
Serving Size: 1 Cookie. Calories 50 • Calories from Fat 25 • Total Fat 3 g
Saturated Fat 0 g • Cholesterol 4 mg • Sodium 45 mg • Dietary Fiber 0 g
Dietary Exchanges: ¹/₂ Fruit, ¹/₂ Fat OR ¹/₂ Carbohydrate, ¹/₂ Fat

Texan-sized Almond Crunch Cookies

Prep Time: 55 minutes (Ready in 1 hour 55 minutes)

1 cup sugar
1 cup powdered sugar
1 cup margarine or butter, softened
1 cup oil
1 teaspoon almond extract
2 eggs
3½ cups all-purpose flour
1 cup whole wheat flour
1 teaspoon baking soda
1 teaspoon salt
1 teaspoon cream of tartar
2 cups coarsely chopped almonds
1 (7.5-oz.) pkg. almond brickle baking chips
Sugar

1. In large bowl, combine 1 cup sugar, powdered sugar, margarine and oil; beat until well blended. Add almond extract and eggs; mix well. Gradually add all-purpose flour, whole wheat flour, baking soda, salt and cream of tartar; beat at low speed until well blended. With spoon, stir in almonds and brickle chips. If necessary, cover with plastic wrap; refrigerate 1 hour for easier handling.

2. Heat oven to 350°F. Shape dough into 1¾-inch balls; roll in sugar. Place 5 inches apart on ungreased cookie sheets. With fork dipped in sugar, flatten in crisscross pattern.

3. Bake at 350°F. for 12 to 18 minutes or until edges are light golden brown. Cool 1 minute; remove from cookie sheets.

Yield: 4 dozen cookies
High Altitude (Above 3,500 Feet): No change.

Nutrition Information Per Serving
Serving Size: 1 Cookie. Calories 210 • Calories from Fat 120 • Total Fat 13 g
Saturated Fat 2 g • Cholesterol 10 mg • Sodium 140 mg • Dietary Fiber 1 g
Dietary Exchanges: ½ Starch, 1 Fruit, 2½ Fat OR 1½ Carbohydrate, 2½ Fat

Bake-Off® Trivia

Barbara Hodgson of Elkhart, Indiana, developed these oversized treats specifically for the 30th Bake-Off® event, held in San Antonio, Texas, in 1982. Her son told her the cookies were a prize winner—and he was right. Hodgson won $2,000, which she used to take her husband to Hawaii for their 25th wedding anniversary.

About Almonds

Almonds fall into two categories: bitter and sweet. Only sweet almonds are used for cooking and baking, though bitter almonds can be processed to use as a flavoring.

Starlight Mint Surprise Cookies

Prep Time: 1 hour (Ready in 3 hours)

1 cup sugar
½ cup firmly packed brown sugar
¾ cup margarine or butter, softened
2 tablespoons water
1 teaspoon vanilla

2 eggs
3 cups all-purpose flour
1 teaspoon baking soda
½ teaspoon salt
2 (6-oz.) pkg. solid chocolate mint candy wafers
60 walnut halves or pieces

1. In large bowl, combine sugar, brown sugar, margarine, water, vanilla and eggs; blend well. In medium bowl, combine flour, baking soda and salt; mix well. Add to sugar mixture; mix at low speed until well blended. Cover with plastic wrap; refrigerate at least 2 hours for easier handling.

2. Heat oven to 375° F. Using about 1 tablespoon dough, press dough around each candy wafer to cover completely. Place 2 inches apart on ungreased cookie sheets. Top each with walnut half.

3. Bake at 375° F. for 7 to 9 minutes or until light golden brown. Immediately remove from cookie sheets.

Yield: 5 dozen cookies
High Altitude (Above 3,500 Feet): No change.

Nutrition Information Per Serving
Serving Size: 1 Cookie. Calories 100 • Calories from Fat 45 • Total Fat 5 g
Saturated Fat 2 g • Cholesterol 5 mg • Sodium 70 mg • Dietary Fiber 1 g
Dietary Exchanges: 1 Fruit, 1 Fat OR 1 Carbohydrate, 1 Fat

Bake-Off® Trivia

Back in 1949, at the very first Bake-Off® Contest, Laura Rott of Naperville, Illinois, won the $10,000 second prize for these cookies with a surprise center. The gift of a package of chocolate mints inspired her to create the winning recipe.

Recipe Fact

These walnut-topped cookies conceal a mouth-watering surprise: a chocolate mint in the center.

Starlight Mint Surprise Cookies

Treasure Chest Bars

Prep Time: 30 minutes (Ready in 2 hours)

Bars

2 cups all-purpose flour
$\frac{1}{2}$ cup sugar
$\frac{1}{2}$ cup firmly packed brown sugar
$1\frac{1}{2}$ teaspoons baking powder
Dash salt
$\frac{1}{2}$ cup butter, softened
$\frac{3}{4}$ cup milk
1 teaspoon vanilla
2 eggs
3 (1.55-oz.) bars milk chocolate candy, cut into small pieces
1 cup maraschino cherries, drained, halved
1 cup coarsely chopped mixed nuts

Frosting

$\frac{1}{4}$ cup butter (do not use margarine)
2 cups powdered sugar
$\frac{1}{2}$ teaspoon vanilla
2 to 3 tablespoons milk

1. Heat oven to 350°F. Grease and flour $15 \times 10 \times 1$-inch baking pan. In large bowl, combine all bar ingredients except chocolate candy, cherries and nuts. Beat 2 minutes at medium speed or until smooth. With spoon, stir in chocolate candy, cherries and nuts. Spread in greased and floured pan.

2. Bake at 350°F. for 25 to 30 minutes or until light golden brown.

3. Meanwhile, in small saucepan, heat $\frac{1}{4}$ cup butter over medium heat until light golden brown, stirring constantly. Remove from heat; stir in powdered sugar and $\frac{1}{2}$ teaspoon vanilla. Add 2 to 3 tablespoons milk, blending until smooth and of desired spreading consistency. Quickly spread over warm bars. Cool 1 hour or until completely cooled. Cut into bars.

Yield: 48 bars
High Altitude (Above 3,500 Feet): No change.

Nutrition Information Per Serving
Serving Size: 1 Bar. Calories 130 • Calories from Fat 50 • Total Fat 6 g
Saturated Fat 2 g • Cholesterol 10 mg • Sodium 70 mg • Dietary Fiber 1 g
Dietary Exchanges: 1 Starch, 1 Fat OR 1 Carbohydrate, 1 Fat

Whole Wheat Sugar Cookies

Prep Time: 45 minutes (Ready in 1 hour 15 minutes)

1 cup sugar
½ cup margarine or butter,
  softened
2 tablespoons milk
1 teaspoon grated lemon peel
1 teaspoon vanilla
1 egg

1¾ cups whole wheat flour
1 teaspoon baking powder
½ teaspoon baking soda
½ teaspoon salt
½ teaspoon nutmeg
2 tablespoons sugar
½ teaspoon cinnamon

1. In large bowl, combine 1 cup sugar and margarine; beat until light and fluffy. Add milk, lemon peel, vanilla and egg; blend well. Add flour, baking powder, baking soda, salt and nutmeg; mix well. Cover with plastic wrap; refrigerate 30 minutes for easier handling.

2. Heat oven to 375°F. In small bowl, combine 2 tablespoons sugar and cinnamon. Shape dough into 1-inch balls; roll in sugar-cinnamon mixture. Place 2 inches apart on ungreased cookie sheets.

3. Bake at 375°F. for 7 to 10 minutes or until light golden brown. Cool 1 minute; remove from cookie sheets.

Yield: 3 dozen cookies
High Altitude (Above 3,500 Feet): Increase flour to 2 cups. Bake as directed above.

Nutrition Information Per Serving

Serving Size: 1 Cookie. Calories 80 • Calories from Fat 25 • Total Fat 3 g
Saturated Fat 1 g • Cholesterol 5 mg • Sodium 95 mg • Dietary Fiber 1 g
Dietary Exchanges: 1 Fruit, ½ Fat OR 1 Carbohydrate, ½ Fat

---

editor's favorite

Bake-Off® Trivia

Over the years, Bake-Off® recipes have mirrored trends in American cuisine. Amid growing national interest in nutrition and healthful ingredients, Jane Harris of Columbia, Maryland, baked her Whole Wheat Sugar Cookies for the judges in Boston in 1976, at the 27th contest. One of the two grand prize winners that year was another whole wheat–based recipe.

About Whole Wheat Flour

Unlike the more refined all-purpose flour, whole wheat flour is ground from the entire grain, yielding a coarser-textured brown flour that imparts a nutty flavor to breads and baked goods. Whole wheat flour is more perishable than white flour and is best stored in the refrigerator.

White Chocolate Chunk Cookies

Bake-Off® Trivia

Dottie Due's entry in the 33rd Bake-Off® in 1988 was the result of twelve rounds of recipe testing in an effort to duplicate cookies from a trendy cookie shop when white chocolate was a novelty.

Ingredient Substitution

Vanilla milk chips work fine in place of the white chocolate chunks in these cookies.

Recipe Variation

Make chocolate chunk cookies by using regular semi-sweet chocolate in place of the white chocolate.

Prep Time: 1 hour 15 minutes

3/4 cup sugar
3/4 cup firmly packed brown sugar
1 cup shortening
3 eggs
1 teaspoon vanilla
2 1/2 cups all-purpose flour
1 teaspoon baking powder

1 teaspoon baking soda
1/2 teaspoon salt
1 cup coconut
1/2 cup rolled oats
1/2 cup chopped walnuts
12 oz. white chocolate baking bars, cut into 1/4- to 1/2-inch chunks

1. Heat oven to 350°F. In large bowl, combine sugar, brown sugar and shortening; beat until light and fluffy. Add eggs 1 at a time, beating well after each addition. Add vanilla; blend well. Add flour, baking powder, baking soda and salt; mix well. Stir in all remaining ingredients. Drop dough by rounded tablespoonfuls 2 inches apart onto ungreased cookie sheets.

2. Bake at 350°F. for 10 to 15 minutes or until light golden brown. Cool 1 minute; remove from cookie sheets.

Yield: 5 dozen cookies
High Altitude (Above 3,500 Feet): Decrease baking powder and baking soda to 1/2 teaspoon each. Bake at 375°F. for 8 to 12 minutes.

Nutrition Information Per Serving
Serving Size: 1 Cookie. Calories 110 • Calories from Fat 50 • Total Fat 6 g
Saturated Fat 2 g • Cholesterol 10 mg • Sodium 60 mg • Dietary Fiber 0 g
Dietary Exchanges: 1 Fruit, 1 Fat OR 1 Carbohydrate, 1 Fat

White Chocolate Chunk Cookies

Candy Bar Cookies

Prep Time: 1 hour 15 minutes (Ready in 2 hours 15 minutes)

Base
3/4 cup powdered sugar
3/4 cup margarine or butter, softened
2 tablespoons whipping cream
1 teaspoon vanilla
2 cups all-purpose flour

Filling
28 caramels, unwrapped
1/4 cup whipping cream
1/4 cup margarine or butter
1 cup powdered sugar

1 cup chopped pecans

Glaze
1/2 cup semi-sweet chocolate chips
2 tablespoons whipping cream
1 tablespoon margarine or butter
1/4 cup powdered sugar
1 teaspoon vanilla
48 pecan halves (2/3 cup), if desired

1. In large bowl, combine all base ingredients except flour; blend well. Stir in flour; mix well. If necessary, cover with plastic wrap; refrigerate 1 hour for easier handling.

2. Heat oven to 325°F. Divide dough in half. On well-floured surface, roll each half of dough into 12 × 8-inch rectangle. With pastry wheel or knife, cut into 2-inch squares. Place 1/2 inch apart on ungreased cookie sheets.

3. Bake at 325°F. for 12 to 16 minutes or until set. Remove from cookie sheets; cool on wire racks.

4. In medium saucepan, combine caramels, 1/4 cup whipping cream and 1/4 cup margarine; cook over low heat, stirring frequently, until caramels are melted and mixture is smooth. Remove from heat; stir in 1 cup powdered sugar and chopped pecans. (Add additional whipping cream a few drops at a time, if needed for desired spreading consistency.) Spread 1 teaspoon warm filling on each cookie square.

5. In small saucepan, combine chocolate chips, 2 tablespoons whipping cream and 1 tablespoon margarine; cook over low heat, stirring frequently, until chocolate

chips are melted and mixture is smooth. Remove from heat; stir in ¼ cup powdered sugar and 1 teaspoon vanilla. Spread glaze evenly over caramel filling on each cookie. Top each with pecan half.

Yield: 4 dozen cookies
High Altitude (Above 3,500 Feet): No change.

Tip: To make bars, in large bowl, combine all base ingredients at low speed until crumbly. Press in bottom of ungreased 15 × 10 × 1-inch baking pan. Bake at 325°F. for 15 to 20 minutes or until light golden brown. Cool. Prepare filling as directed above; spread over base. Prepare glaze; drizzle over filling. Top bars with pecan halves, forming 8 rows of 6 pecans each. Let stand until set. Cut into bars.

Nutrition Information Per Serving

Serving Size: 1 Cookie. Calories 130 • Calories from Fat 70 • Total Fat 8 g
Saturated Fat 2 g • Cholesterol 4 mg • Sodium 60 mg • Dietary Fiber 1 g
Dietary Exchanges: 1 Fruit, 1½ Fat OR 1 Carbohydrate, 1½ Fat

Index

Conversion Chart
Equivalent Imperial and Metric Measurements

American cooks use standard containers, the 8-ounce cup and a tablespoon that takes exactly 16 level fillings to fill that cup level. Measuring by cup makes it very difficult to give weight equivalents, as a cup of densely packed butter will weigh considerably more than a cup of flour. The easiest way therefore to deal with cup measurements in recipes is to take the amount by volume rather than by weight. Thus the equation reads:

1 cup = 240 ml = 8 fl. oz.   ½ cup = 120 ml = 4 fl. oz.

It is possible to buy a set of American cup measures in major stores around the world.

In the States, butter is often measured in sticks. One stick is the equivalent of 8 tablespoons. One tablespoon of butter is therefore the equivalent to ½ ounce/15 grams.

Liquid Measures

Fluid Ounces	U.S.	Imperial	Milliliters
	1 teaspoon	1 teaspoon	5
¼	2 teaspoons	1 dessertspoon	10
½	1 tablespoon	1 tablespoon	14
1	2 tablespoons	2 tablespoons	28
2	¼ cup	4 tablespoons	56
4	½ cup		110
5		¼ pint or 1 gill	140
6	¾ cup		170
8	1 cup		225
9			250, ¼ liter
10	1¼ cups	½ pint	280
12	1½ cups		340
15		¾ pint	420
16	2 cups		450
18	2¼ cups		500, ½ liter
20	2½ cups	1 pint	560
24	3 cups		675
25		1¼ pints	700
27	3½ cups		750
30	3¾ cups	1½ pints	840
32	4 cups or 1 quart		900
35		1¾ pints	980
36	4½ cups		1000, 1 liter
40	5 cups	2 pints or 1 quart	1120

Solid Measures

U.S. and Imperial Measures		Metric Measures	
Ounces	Pounds	Grams	Kilos
1		28	
2		56	
3½		100	
4	¼	112	
5		140	
6		168	
8	½	225	
9		250	¼
12	¾	340	
16	1	450	
18		500	½
20	1¼	560	
24	1½	675	
27		750	¾
28	1¾	780	
32	2	900	
36	2¼	1000	1
40	2½	1100	
48	3	1350	
54		1500	1½

Oven Temperature Equivalents

Fahrenheit	Celsius	Gas Mark	Description
225	110	¼	Cool
250	130	½	
275	140	1	Very Slow
300	150	2	
325	170	3	Slow
350	180	4	Moderate
375	190	5	
400	200	6	Moderately Hot
425	220	7	Fairly Hot
450	230	8	Hot
475	240	9	Very Hot
500	250	10	Extremely Hot

Any broiling recipes can be used with the grill of the oven, but beware of high-temperature grills.

Equivalents for Ingredients

all-purpose flour—plain flour
coarse salt—kitchen salt
cornstarch—cornflour
eggplant—aubergine

half and half—12% fat milk
heavy cream—double cream
light cream—single cream
lima beans—broad beans

scallion—spring onion
unbleached flour—strong, white flour
zest—rind
zucchini—courgettes or marrow